Numbers

INTERPRETATION
A Bible Commentary for Teaching and Preaching

INTERPRETATION

A BIBLE COMMENTARY FOR TEACHING AND PREACHING

James Luther Mays, *Editor*
Patrick D. Miller, *Old Testament Editor*
Paul J. Achtemeier, *New Testament Editor*

DENNIS T. OLSON

Numbers

**A Bible Commentary
for Teaching and Preaching**

John Knox Press
LOUISVILLE

Scripture quotations from the New Revised Standard Version of the Bible are copyright © 1989 by the Division of Christian Education of the National Council of the Churches of Christ in the U.S.A. and are used by permission. Italic emphasis has been added in some quotations.

Grateful acknowledgment is made to Mrs. Howard Nemerov for permission to reproduce a portion from "Runes," from *New and Selected Poems,* © 1960 by Howard Nemerov. Published by the University of Chicago Press.

Library of Congress Cataloging-in-Publication Data

Olson, Dennis T.
    Numbers / Dennis T. Olson. — 1st ed.
        p.   cm. — (Interpretation, a Bible commentary for teaching and preaching)
    Includes bibliographical references.
    ISBN 0-8042-3104-4 (alk. paper)
    1. Bible. O.T. Numbers—Commentaries.   I. Title.
II. Series.
BS1265.3.O57   1996
222'.1407—dc20   96-275

© copyright John Knox Press 1996
This book is printed on acid-free paper that meets the American National Standards Institute Z39.48 standard. ∞
96 97 98 99 00 01 02 03 04 05—10 9 8 7 6 5 4 3 2 1
Printed in the United States of America
John Knox Press
Louisville, Kentucky

SERIES PREFACE

This series of commentaries offers an interpretation of the books of the Bible. It is designed to meet the need of students, teachers, ministers, and priests for a contemporary expository commentary. These volumes will not replace the historical critical commentary or homiletical aids to preaching. The purpose of this series is rather to provide a third kind of resource, a commentary which presents the integrated result of historical and theological work with the biblical text.

An interpretation in the full sense of the term involves a text, an interpreter, and someone for whom the interpretation is made. Here, the text is what stands written in the Bible in its full identity as literature from the time of "the prophets and apostles," the literature which is read to inform, inspire, and guide the life of faith. The interpreters are scholars who seek to create an interpretation which is both faithful to the text and useful to the church. The series is written for those who teach, preach, and study the Bible in the community of faith.

The comment generally takes the form of expository essays. It is planned and written in the light of the needs and questions which arise in the use of the Bible as Holy Scripture. The insights and results of contemporary scholarly research are used for the sake of the exposition. The commentators write as exegetes and theologians. The task which they undertake is both to deal with what the texts say and to discern their meaning for faith and life. The exposition is the unified work of one interpreter.

The text on which the comment is based is the Revised Standard Version of the Bible and, since its appearance, the New Revised Standard Version. The general availability of these translations makes the printing of a text in the commentary unnecessary. The commentators have also had other current versions in view as they worked and refer to their readings where it is helpful. The text is divided into sections appropriate to the particular book; comment deals with passages as a whole, rather than proceeding word by word, or verse by verse.

Writers have planned their volumes in light of the requirements set by the exposition of the book assigned to them. Biblical books differ in character, content, and arrangement. They also differ in the way they have been and are used in the liturgy, thought, and devotion of the church. The distinctiveness and use of particular books have been taken into account in decisions about the approach, emphasis, and use of space in the commentaries. The goal has been to allow writers to develop the format which provides for the best presentation of their interpretation.

The result, writers and editors hope, is a commentary which both explains and applies, an interpretation which deals with both the meaning and the significance of biblical texts. Each commentary reflects, of course, the writer's own approach and perception of the church and world. It could and should not be otherwise. Every interpretation of any kind is individual in that sense; it is one reading of the text. But all who work at the interpretation of Scripture in the church need the help and stimulation of a colleague's reading and understanding of the text. If these volumes serve and encourage interpretation in that way, their preparation and publication will realize their purpose.

The Editors

PREFACE

My own wilderness journey with the book of Numbers began in a 1982 graduate seminar on Numbers taught by Brevard Childs at Yale University. That seminar led eventually to a dissertation on the literary and theological structure of Numbers within the Pentateuch. I am indebted to Professor Childs for his early encouragement in working theologically with this sometimes neglected book of the Bible. I am also indebted to a large number of scholars and commentators on Numbers from whom I have learned much. Many of them are listed in the bibliography at the end of the commentary. As is true of the other commentaries in this series, this is predominantly a theological study of the book of Numbers. I have sought to interpret the literary and theological structures and movements of Numbers in the hope that they may inform and excite the theological imagination of preachers, teachers, and students of Scripture in the context of the contemporary church. A number of other fine commentaries available on the book of Numbers will provide more detail on matters of textual, historical, and critical issues.

I wish to express my deep gratitude to my colleague, friend, and Old Testament Editor of this series, Patrick D. Miller, and to the General Editor, James Luther Mays, for their encouragement and guidance in helping to see this project through to its final completion. Finally, I dedicate this book to my wife, Carol. Her generous love and deep friendship have been gifts that continually bring joy to my heart and fullness to my life.

CONTENTS

Introduction

Origen, the early-third-century church father, wrote a series of sermons on the book of Numbers. Even then this fourth book of the Old Testament was neglected in relation to other biblical books, as Origen acknowledged:

> When the Gospels or the Apostle or the Psalms are read, another person joyfully receives them, gladly embraces them. . . . But if the book of Numbers is read to him, and especially those passages we have now in hand, he will judge that there is nothing helpful, nothing as a remedy for his weakness or a benefit for the salvation of his soul. He will constantly spit them out as heavy and burdensome food. (Origen, p. 246)

In a long series of sermons on Numbers, Origen sought to show that this popular impression of Numbers was misguided and untrue. For Origen, the book of Numbers was filled with insight, wisdom, and spiritual sustenance for anyone with a hunger for God's guidance through the wilderness journey of life. Origen's third-century assessment of the relative neglect of this book of Scripture rings true for most of us situated at the beginning of the twenty-first century. Numbers is not a well-known biblical book within most congregations. But the thesis of this commentary is that Origen's strong conviction about the enduring value and theological wisdom of Numbers is as accurate as his assessment of the book's relative neglect among contemporary readers of Scripture.

Journey through the Wilderness:
A Contemporary Theme

The book of Numbers, the fourth book of the Old Testament, derives its name from the census lists of the number of people in each of the twelve tribes of Israel in Numbers 1 and 26. The Hebrew title for the book, "In the Wilderness," comes out of the first verse of the book and accurately describes its setting. Numbers is the story of the people of Israel in the wilderness as they travel from the slavery of Egypt toward the freedom of Canaan.

The image of "the wilderness" has been a powerful metaphor for describing the experience of many people and communities, both

1

ancient and modern. Second Isaiah used the image to describe the promise of Israel's return from its Babylonian exile. God promised to do a new thing: "I will make a way in the wilderness and rivers in the desert" (Isa. 43:19). In the New Testament, John the Baptist was "a voice crying in the wilderness" to prepare the way of the Lord. John spoke from the outer margins of the wilderness into a world where power was concentrated in the hands of the few (Luke 3:1–2). Jesus was tested and tempted in the wilderness by Satan for forty days, an echo of ancient Israel's sojourn and testing in the wilderness for forty years (Luke 4; Mauser). Christian monks and hermits have lived out in the wilderness alone or in small communities in order to be on the front lines of spiritual battle. Jews throughout the centuries have found a resonance with the theme of living in the wilderness in times of exile, persecution, and diaspora.

The wilderness theme has reemerged as a way of capturing the experience of many people in our world today. Scholars representing the perspective of women, Asian Americans, and African American women have all used the metaphor of "wilderness" to describe their experience of being outside or on the margins of their society or culture (Lee, Williams, Sakenfeld, "In the Wilderness, Awaiting the Land"). Gary Eberle's study *The Geography of Nowhere: Finding Oneself in the Postmodern World,* argues that many who live today in the so-called postmodern world have lost the sense of being rooted in a "spiritual geography" that helped previous generations to feel at home in the world. In previous ages, human beings were able to locate themselves in time and space through sacred histories and mythologies. Eberle maintains that although we may know more about the world's physical geography, we often feel lost in a spiritual wilderness without reliable points of reference in terms of God, community, or sense of self (Eberle). The image of traveling through the wilderness may become an important biblical image to recapture in our time. Among all the books of the Bible, the book of Numbers is a particularly helpful resource for recapturing this wilderness image and its many implications for a postmodern world.

How Was Numbers Formed?
Critical Issues in the Book of Numbers

One of the distinctive features of the book of Numbers is the great variety of literary forms and topics within the book. The reader will find stories and laws, travel itineraries and census lists, lists of personal names and lists of instructions for worship, reports of military battles and accounts of legal disputes. This variety of material has led scholars

2

to study the book from a wide array of disciplines and perspectives.

Numbers is one of the five books of the Pentateuch, which runs from Genesis through Deuteronomy. Scholars have sought to discern separate literary sources or layers that have been woven together to form the present book. These sources or traditions are usually termed J for the Yahwist, E for the Elohist, and P for the Priestly traditions. In broad strokes, the earlier J and E traditions (dating anywhere from the tenth to the eighth centuries B.C.E.) are thought to be earlier and concentrated in Numbers 11—25. While scattered throughout the book, the later Priestly material (dating roughly from the sixth or fifth centuries B.C.E.) is most in evidence in chapters 1—10 and chapters 26—36. Most scholars further agree that supplementary material was subsequently added to Numbers even after the inclusion of the Priestly tradition.

Some scholars have attempted to reconstruct the original oral forms and traditions that may have preceded the writing of the literary sources. Attention has been focused on the twelve-tribe system; the ordering of the camp of Israel in Numbers 2; the traditions about the Levites in chapters 3—4; the wilderness murmuring traditions in chapters 11, 12, 13, 14, 16, 17, 21, and 25; the Balaam cycle in chapters 22—24; and the allocation of the land in chapters 26 and 34. Scholars interested in historical issues in ancient Israel have studied the early conquest traditions in Numbers 13, 14, 21, and 32; the Levitical cities in chapter 35; the development of the Israelite priesthood in chapters 16—17; and the census lists in chapters 1 and 26. Numbers is also an important resource for understanding Old Testament law, particularly in regard to ritual, festival, and purity laws (chaps. 5—9, 19, 27, and 36).

The diverse materials in Numbers were shaped and developed throughout many different periods and social situations, ranging from the earliest to the latest times in Israel's history. But the definitive shaping of the book of Numbers in roughly its present form likely occurred sometime after the Babylonian exile (587—538 B.C.E.). The book of Numbers was the product of the Jewish community's struggle to understand the pain and punishment of exile and its implications for Israel's relationship to God, Israel's definition as a people, and Israel's posture toward the promised land, which had been lost but was now about to be regained.

What Is the Structure of Numbers?
The Overarching Framework for the Book of Numbers

3

One important obstacle in interpreting Numbers has been the failure to detect a meaningful structure for the book as a whole. Many interpreters have complained that Numbers lacks any coherent structure or outline. The alternation of laws and stories seems haphazard and incoherent. Some have referred to Numbers as "the junk room of the Bible," suggesting that the book's editors simply threw miscellaneous bits of tradition randomly into the text without much thought or meaning.

It is true that the structures or story lines of Genesis, Exodus, or even Leviticus may be somewhat more obvious than those in Numbers. Genesis moves from "the generations of the heavens and the earth" (Gen. 2:4) at creation through the generations of the ancestors of Israel. Exodus and Leviticus tell the story of the generation that experienced the exodus out of Egypt and the events and laws connected with Mount Sinai. If we skip over Numbers for a moment to the book of Deuteronomy which follows, we see that Deuteronomy consists of Moses' last words to a brand-new generation of Israelites who had not experienced the events of the exodus or of Sinai. But when did this new generation appear? Where was the transition made from the old generation of the exodus and Sinai to the new generation of God's people on the edge of the promised land in Deuteronomy?

This important generational transition is made in the book of Numbers. In fact, the transition from the old generation of the wilderness to the new generation of hope and promise on the edge of the promised land forms the primary structure and theme for the book of Numbers. This structure is marked by the two census lists of the twelve tribes of Israel in Numbers 1 and 26. The census lists divide the book into two halves.

The first census list in Numbers 1 introduces the first half of the book, chapters 1—25. This first half of Numbers recounts the eventual death of the old generation of God's people out of Egypt as they march in the wilderness toward the promised land. The death of this old generation who had experienced the exodus and Sinai events is brought on by the people's relentless rebellion against God. The climactic rebellion is the spy story in Numbers 13—14.

The second census list in Numbers 26 introduces the second half of the book, chapters 26—36. This second census has many of the same features as the census in Numbers 1. God's command to take the census is virtually identical (Num. 1:2–3 and 26:2). The list of the twelve Israelite tribes in chapter 26 is presented in exactly the same order as in Numbers 1 except for a minor reversal in the order of the two Joseph tribes, Manasseh and Ephraim. Numbers 3—4 includes a census of the Levites (a priestly tribal group without any land) following the census of the twelve other tribes in chapter 1. A similar sequence is followed in

4

Numbers 26 where a census of the Levites follows the other twelve-tribe census list. This second half of Numbers recounts the emergence of a new generation of God's people as they prepare to enter the promised land of Canaan. The theme of this part of Numbers is radically different from the earlier chapters. New life and hope, not rebellion and death, characterize this new generation's story.

Apart from the two census lists, a number of other parallels between the two halves of the book strengthen the argument for a cohesive editorial construction of the book into two major parts that both echo and contrast with each other. Numerous events or laws in Numbers 1—25 reappear in altered form in the second half in Numbers 26—36. The following list of echoes between the two halves of the book of Numbers makes the division of the book between chapters 1—25 and 26—36 even more striking:

Numbers 1—25	*Numbers 26—36*
The Old Generation of Rebellion	***The New Generation of Hope***
1—census of 12 tribes	26—census of 12 tribes
3—census of the Levites	26—census of the Levites
5—legal discourse involving women	27—legal discourse involving women
6—laws concerning vows	30—laws concerning vows
7, 15—lists and laws concerning offerings	28, 29—lists and laws concerning offerings
9—celebration of Passover	28:16–25—instructions for future celebrations of Passover
10:8–9—law concerning the priests blowing the trumpets to sound the alarm for holy war	31:6—priests blow the trumpets to sound the alarm for holy war against Midian
13—list of spies from each of the 12 tribes chosen to spy out the promised land	34—list of tribal leaders from each of the 12 tribes chosen to divide the promised land
13—14—the spy story and Israel's rebellion which led to the death of the old generation	32:6–15—the spy story of Num. 13—14 recalled as a lesson for the new generation
10—25—scattered geographical notations about places Israel journeyed in the wilderness	33—summary of places Israel journeyed in wilderness, including notations of Aaron's death at Mount Hor (chap. 20) and the defeat of King Arad (chap. 21)
18:21–32—provisions for the Levites	35—provisions for the Levitical cities
21:21–35—victory over Kings Sihon and Og and capture of the land east of the Jordan	32—assignment of the land captured from Sihon and Og east of the Jordan River to the three tribes of Reuben, Gad, and Manasseh

Numbers 1—25	**Numbers 26—36**
The Old Generation of Rebellion	*The New Generation of Hope*
25—the Midianites cause Israel to sin and God's command to Israel to punish the Midianites (vv. 17–18)	31—holy war against the Midianites to punish them for what they did in chap. 25

This overarching structure of the death of the old generation and the birth of a new generation of hope provides the interpretive framework for the other varied contents of the book of Numbers.

The internal cohesiveness in tone and theme within each half of the book of Numbers and the resulting contrasts when comparing the two halves of Numbers further support viewing the census lists in chapters 1 and 26 as the major framework for the book as a whole. The first half of Numbers (chaps. 1—25) begins with the census and organization of the people of God on the march in the wilderness in chapters 1—10. When the preparations are completed and the march begins, however, the people immediately fall into rebellion (chaps. 11—12), which climaxes in the spy episode (chaps. 13—14). The members of that first generation in Numbers are then condemned to die. Much of the rest of the section up through chapter 25 recounts further rebellions and plagues and deaths (chaps. 16, 17, 20, 21, and 25). Some glimmers of hope shine through along the way. God proclaims regulations for a future time when the people will properly enter the promised land (chap. 15). God gives military victories to Israel over the king of Arad and Sihon and Og (chap. 21). A final crescendo of hope and promise is sounded in the Balaam oracles (chaps. 22—24), which look forward to a more distant generation. The first generation ends with the final rebellion of the people and the death of the remainder of the first generation (chap. 25).

The second half of Numbers (chaps. 26—36) is likewise internally cohesive in structure, tone, and theme. Again, the census list begins the section (chap. 26). The new generation does not begin in Numbers in the midst of the wilderness as the first generation did (Num. 1:1—"in the wilderness of Sinai"). Instead, the new generation begins its life at the edge of the wilderness, the entry point into the promised land on the plains of Moab by the Jordan River (Num. 26:3). Following the census in Numbers 26, the second half is bracketed by an inclusio in chapters 27 and 36. Both of these chapters relate a legal dispute involving the daughters of Zelophehad and the inheritance of property and thereby frame the second half of Numbers. The legal issue involving land is resolved in both cases, setting a positive and hopeful tone for the entire second half of the book. In contrast to the deaths of a whole generation in a series of rebellions and judgments in the first half of Numbers, the second half does not record the death of any Israelite. The Israelites are victorious in their first military engagement against the Midianites (chap. 31). Potential crises do not turn into rebellions but are successfully negotiated and resolved (Num. 27:1–11; 31:14–15; 32:1–42). Numerous laws are given that look forward to future residence in the promised land (chaps. 27, 34—36). The second half of Numbers, therefore, is uniformly hopeful and positive in tone.

Why Read Numbers?
Ongoing Theological Importance

The later traditions of both Jewish and Christian communities have taken up the witness of Numbers in important ways. The apostle Paul in the New Testament letter of I Corinthians recalls the story of the wilderness generation in Numbers as an example for his contemporary readers: "These things happened to them to serve as an example, and they were written down to instruct us" (I Cor. 10:11). The Jewish community continued its interpretation of Numbers through the *Midrash Sipre* on Numbers and the Talmud, which concentrated its interpretive energy on the legal sections of Numbers. The Aaronic blessing or benediction ("The LORD bless you and keep you . . .") has formed an important part of both Jewish and Christian worship practices throughout the centuries; the blessing comes from Num. 6:22–27.

The central significance of the book remains with the ongoing interpretation of Numbers in all its parts as part of the Scripture of the church. The book wrestles with the transition from the old generation to the new generation. How is faith transferred from one generation to another? How does the story of the past become fresh and alive for a new generation?

The book of Numbers wrestles throughout its pages with struggles to discern boundaries and polarities of life and death that may be in dispute in the community of God's people. Numbers contains stories and laws about boundaries involved in a wide array of issues: boundaries between old and new generations, boundaries between Israel and other nations, boundaries between God's holy presence and a sinful Israel, boundaries of authority between leaders and followers, boundaries that divide tribal territories, boundaries between wilderness and promised land, boundaries in time and space related to worship and festivals, boundaries between clean and unclean, boundaries between blessings and curses, boundaries between intentional sin and accidental transgression, boundaries between God's judgment and God's

7

forgiveness. The conflicts and struggles over these boundaries create in the book of Numbers a kind of dialogical theology, an ongoing and unsettled dialogue of varied voices. The dialogue of voices reaches provisional positions on which the reader can set up camp temporarily, much as Israel set up camp in the desert for a time and then moved on. The dominant voice of Numbers 1—10 is obedience and order, but the underlying voice of danger and death lurks just under the surface. In Numbers 11—25, death, disorder, and rebellion suddenly overwhelm the pages of Numbers with dead bodies of a whole generation of Israelites strewn along the desert road of Israel's forty-year sojourn. But these same chapters are also mixed with whispers of hope for a new generation and its eventual arrival in the promised land of Canaan (Numbers 15; 21). Chapters 26—36 focus on the story of the members of this new generation of hope as they prepare to enter the promised land, much as their parents had done a generation earlier. The overall voice in these concluding chapters of Numbers is positive and hopeful. But the reader also hears lingering threats, warnings, and conflicts over boundaries that are negotiated and temporarily resolved. By the end of Numbers, the holy camp of God's people is set to continue its march toward the promised land with the warnings of the past and the promises of the future in a dynamic dialogue of warning and promise.

The experience of the Christian church today has many notable parallels to issues faced by the community portrayed in the book of Numbers. We may assume that much of the book of Numbers was written in light of the experience of exile from Babylon and perhaps was written early in the return to the promised land of Judah. If that is true, then the community was faced with many competing interests, groups, and issues associated with a tradition in some disarray struggling to define itself and its mission in the world. The church today faces a similar predicament in many contexts in the world. As has often been true throughout its history, the church struggles to discern its way forward in a cultural wilderness filled with competing temptations, conflicts over authority, and both the potential promise and problems involved in encountering the "other" in our society—people of other cultures, other faiths, and other concerns. Scripture provides an important source for the church's discernment of its mission and work in such a time of wilderness or exile. The book of Numbers may be an especially appropriate resource for guidance through the contemporary wilderness of pluralism, competing voices, and shifting foundations in the journey of God's people into the twenty-first century.

PART ONE

The Death of the Old Generation

Numbers 1—25

I. Obedient Beginnings: Preparation for the March of the Holy People of God in the Wilderness

NUMBERS 1—10

The first half of Numbers recounts the fate of the old generation of Israelites who had been eyewitnesses to the exodus out of Egypt and the covenant with God made on Mount Sinai. The birth of this first wilderness generation had been marked by a census list already back in the book of Exodus, chapter 1. There seventy people were counted among the twelve tribes of Israel who came down to Egypt (Exod. 1:5). The new census list of the twelve tribes of Israel that appears in Numbers 1 marks a major transition in the people's wandering. They have been liberated from the bondage of Egypt. They have received God's commandments and entered into a covenant with God at Sinai. Now with Numbers 1, this first wilderness generation is ready to organize and begin its march in earnest toward the promised land of Canaan.

This first section of Numbers in chapters 1—10 is dominated by a positive tone. The people of Israel obediently follow God's instructions to prepare for the march from Sinai to the promised land. The twelve tribes of Israel undergo a census in which all warriors are counted and then organized into a four-sided military camp with three tribes on each of the four sides. Laws are given that preserve the holiness of the camp. The people dutifully prepare for a holy war against the Canaanite inhabitants of the promised land. These preparations for the journey through the wilderness dominate Num. 1:1—10:10.

Numbers 10:11–36 continues in this section with the actual inauguration of Israel's march and the events of the first three days. The holy camp of God's people sets out for the first time from the Wilderness of Sinai to the Wilderness of Paran. The first three days of the journey go smoothly and without incident. All seems to be moving according to God's plan and desire. That favorable impression will linger only for a time, ending abruptly when we come to Numbers 11.

Numbers 1
Census of the Twelve Tribes: Grains of Sand, Stars of Heaven, and the Promises of God

The book of Numbers begins with the Israelites situated in the Wilderness of Sinai fourteen months after the exodus out of Egypt. God instructs Moses to carry out a census of the twelve tribes of Israel. Not all the people are to be counted in this census. The census is only for the males who are over twenty years of age who are able to go to war (1:2–3). One person from each tribe is selected to supervise the counting (1:4–16). The results of the census for each of the twelve tribes is reported in 1:20–46. The census records a grand total of 603,550 males over twenty years of age (1:46). The central concern of this first census in Numbers 1 is determining the number of fighting men who are available for battle. With the goal of entering the promised land looming on the horizon, the census here functions as a key preparatory step for the military conquest of Canaan.

The census in Numbers 1 is the first census of the people since leaving Egypt. The only previous full counting of Israel's twelve tribes occurred back in Genesis 46; there the total number of the twelve sons of Jacob and their offspring is reported as seventy people. The book of Exodus repeats this list of Jacob's sons and their families totaling seventy people in its opening verses. Exodus 1:6–7 then reports the death of Joseph and "all his brothers and all that generation" and the emergence of a new and greatly expanded generation. The census at the beginning of Exodus marks an entirely new generation as well as a major transition from a state of blessing and abundance to slavery and oppression (Exod. 1:11). These earlier census lists in Genesis and Exodus should alert us to the function of the census lists as markers of major turning points in the life of Israel as a people.

As we turn to the census in Numbers 1, we note that an important transition is being made from a band of freed but unorganized slaves into an organized and holy military camp preparing for battle and the conquest of the promised land. Order, leadership, assignment of duties, calculations of available resources, organization of the community, and future planning are all made possible by such a census taking. But there is much more at stake in this census than just community planning and development. In order to understand the full meaning of the census in Numbers, we need to return to the book of Genesis and to two critical issues involved in the study of the census of Numbers 1: (1) the lists of the names of the twelve tribes of Israel and (2) the high numbers reported in the census lists.

Continuity and Inclusiveness: The Lists of the Twelve Tribes of Israel

The earliest version of the names of the twelve tribes in Numbers occurs in Num. 1:5–15, in which leaders from each of the twelve tribes are chosen to supervise the counting. The names of the tribes are enumerated in a particular order as follows: Reuben (the oldest son and thus the first tribe listed), Simeon, Judah, Issachar, Zebulun, Ephraim, Manasseh, Benjamin, Dan, Asher, Gad, and Naphtali. Other lists of the twelve tribes in Numbers occur in 1:20–43; 2:3–31; 7:12–83; 10: 14–28; 13:4–15; and 26:5–51.

These tribal lists in Numbers apparently build upon earlier versions of the twelve-tribe list in the book of Genesis, most notably the narrative of the twelve sons of Jacob in Gen. 29:31—30:24. This genealogical story about the birth of the twelve tribe ancestors is probably rooted in a time early in Israel's history when the genealogy functioned to express unity and interconnection among a diverse tribal community without any central ruler or government. With the rise of kings in Israel in the tenth century B.C.E., the genealogical lists of the twelve tribes lost this sociopolitical function and were then taken into the emerging literary tradition of Israel in order to express the theological unity of the people of God. When Israel lost its kingship during and after the Babylonian exile, the genealogical lists of the twelve tribes

11

became even more important as an expression of Israel's identity and unity as a people of God in a variety of social and political contexts. The lengthy genealogy that takes up the first nine chapters of the postexilic book of I Chronicles is a witness to the powerful need for a sense of continuity with the past which such tribal enumeration fulfilled in postexilic Judaism.

Another function of these twelve-tribe lists throughout Numbers is the assurance that all Israelites from whatever tribe have a place at the table. Anthropologist Mary Douglas argues in her study of the book of Numbers that the book is aimed to be welcoming and inclusive of all Israelites in the context of a postexilic situation in which many of the community leaders resisted such welcoming of the Israelite "stranger" (Douglas, pp. 35–41). Douglas points to Ezra and Nehemiah as examples of one dominant view in postexilic Israel that bestowed privilege on returned exiles from southern Judah and excluded other tribes, especially the Samaritans who had roots in northern Israel among the Joseph tribes of Ephraim, Manasseh, and Benjamin. These Joseph or northern Israelite tribes had been conquered earlier by the Assyrian empire. People of other nations and religions had been imported by the Assyrians into the regions of northern Israel, which resulted in intermarriage and a form of Israelite religion somewhat distinctive from that of southern Judah. When the southern Judahites were themselves conquered and exiled to Babylon and then returned to Judah by the Persians, the question naturally arose: who is the true Israel? Those like Ezra and Nehemiah seemed to keep the definition quite narrow by excluding the Samaritans and others who had intermarried with other peoples. But the writers of Numbers, Douglas argues, sought to undercut this exclusionary policy by emphasizing the inclusion of all twelve tribes, including the northern Israelite tribes, in both the judgments and the promises that the book of Numbers extends to all Israel. We will see in more detail how the text balances the need for structure with the need for broad inclusion in Numbers 2, with its carefully structured arrangement of the tribes in the mobile military camp.

The High Numbers in the Census Lists of Numbers 1 and 26

Moses is commanded by God to take a census of the tribes of Israel at two separate occasions in Numbers 1 and 26. In both cases, all twelve tribes are listed along with a numerical total for each tribe. The order of the tribal names is identical in both chapters. A grand total for all twelve tribes is given at the end of each census list. The numbers for the tribes and the total from each census are as follows:

	Numbers 1	**Numbers 26**
Reuben	46,500	43,730
Simeon	59,300	22,200
Gad	45,650	40,500
Judah	74,600	76,500
Issachar	54,400	64,300
Zebulun	57,400	60,500
Ephraim	40,500	32,500
Manasseh	32,200	52,700
Benjamin	35,400	45,600
Dan	62,700	64,400
Asher	41,500	53,400
Naphtali	53,400	45,400
Totals	603,550	601,730

The enormous size of the numbers in the census lists in Numbers 1 and 26 has often struck commentators as amazing or impossible. How could the tiny clan that began in Exodus 1 with a census list of seventy persons swell to over 600,000 fighting men plus women, children, and the elderly in the short span of a few hundred years? The figure of over 600,000 warriors presupposes a total population of over two million people who lived for forty years in the Sinai desert. The early church father Jerome held the numbers to be mysterious. John Calvin noted the enormous size of the numbers but argued against any who would deny God's miraculous ability to increase God's people from one family to over 600,000 within a period of 250 years.

Many solutions have been suggested. Some have suggested a possible alternate meaning for the Hebrew word for "thousand" to be a "tent-group" or "clan." For example, the tribe of Reuben is counted in Num. 1:20–21 as forty-six "thousand," five hundred. The number could be translated in an alternate way as forty-six "tent-groups," with a total of five hundred people. This proposal would significantly decrease the numbers in each of the tribes. While this and other proposed explanations may be possible, it is clear that the present form of the text intends these figures to be taken as they stand—as "thousands," and not "tent-groups."

The round number 600,000 as the total number of Israelites coming out of Egypt is attested in texts that many scholars see as firmly fixed in some of the earliest literary traditions in the Pentateuch. Scholars cite Exod. 12:37 as an example: "The Israelites journeyed from Rameses to Succoth, about six hundred thousand men on foot,

13

besides children." Numbers 11:21 may also be cited in this regard. The stylized and symbolic quality of the number 600,000 may be evident from the fact that it is a multiple of twelve representing the twelve tribes of Israel (12 × 50,000). The numbers of the individual tribes in Numbers 1 and 26 do not usually stray very far from the range of forty to sixty thousand, or an average of 50,000. In both lists, six tribes are above 50,000 and six tribes are below 50,000.

In any case, the high numbers in the census lists are difficult to reconcile historically. Their present function in the book of Numbers, however, seems in part to serve a broader theological purpose. The numbers express the extent to which God has graciously blessed Israel in multiplying their descendants to such large numbers. God's promises in Genesis to Abraham and Sarah that they will have innumerable descendants are clearly in view. In these Genesis texts, God promises descendants as numerous as the stars of heaven (Gen. 15:5) and the grains of sand on the seashore (Gen. 22:17; cf. also Gen. 17:4–8). The sheer number of stars or grains of sand are impossible to count. In addition, the emergence of the new generation in Egypt that "increased greatly" and "grew exceedingly strong" (Exod. 1:5–7) is part of this same theological concern to underscore God's faithfulness to promises made to the ancestors. The remarkably high numbers in the census lists in Numbers 1 and 26 represent God's significant down payment on the promise of innumerable descendants. But the census totals also underscore the partial character of the fulfillment of the ancestral promises. God is not finished with Israel yet. The promised land still lies in the future.

The large number of fighting men counted in Numbers 1 also ought to provide grounds for great confidence for the Israelites as they approach the border of the promised land. A total of 600,000 warriors would be a large army even in modern terms, but in its ancient Near Eastern context such a size would be massive indeed. The spy story in Numbers 13—14 will show that in spite of the huge army, the Israelites will lack confidence in God's power and will not trust God to bring them into the land.

Finally, the variations in the census numbers for each of the twelve tribes hold some interpretive significance as well. We have already noted how the average for each tribe approximates 50,000, with six tribes in each list below and six tribes in each list above the 50,000 mark. But there are other variations with some meaning as well. The tribe of Judah, for example, has the largest number in both census lists, which corresponds to its preeminence as the leader of the camp of Israel on the march in the wilderness. Judah occupies the favored posi-

14

tion in Israel's camp, which is to the east, the direction that the opening of the tent of meeting faces and that parallels the favored position of the priesthood of Aaron in the inner circle of the camp. The book of Numbers begins in chapters 1 and 2 with Reuben, the first-born of Jacob, as the preeminent tribe in first position. Then the census takes place and Judah is given the most favored position at the head of the tribes, as we shall see in Numbers 2.

This change in status between Reuben and Judah is also apparent when the census numbers in chapter 1 are compared with those in chapter 26. Judah remains the most numerous tribe and increases from 74,600 in Numbers 1 to 76,500 in Numbers 26. Reuben, on the other hand, decreases in size from 46,500 to 43,730, which corresponds to that tribe's demotion in status relative to Judah. The narrative in Numbers 16 involving the rebellion of Dathan and Abiram, who were members of the tribe of Reuben, may also reflect on a literary level this lowering of status in relation to Judah.

The most dramatic decrease among all the tribes is that of Simeon, from 59,300 in Numbers 1 to 22,200 in Numbers 26. This "demotion" may reflect the narrative in Numbers 25, in which the head of a Simeonite clan committed a grave sin against God that caused a severe plague among the people. The special census for the Levites in Numbers 3 and 26 is another literary device signaling the special position of this tribe in relation to the other tribal groups. Although not all of the numbers can be shown to have a particular literary significance within the narratives of the book of Numbers, the presence of some correspondences between the census lists and other stories in Numbers should urge us to pay attention to the important role these census lists play within the whole structure of the book.

For modern readers, the first chapter of Numbers is almost mind-numbing, with its roll call of tribal leaders and the repetitive listing of the twelve tribes and their census numbers. We may find it hard to get hooked into a story that seems to have such a mechanical and numerical beginning. But for the ancient readers of the book, such lists and numbers bore crucial insights into the very soul of their identity, their unity, their relationship to God, and their place within the community of God's people. The lists of names and numbers are the material and tangible signs of God's blessing, God's faithfulness to past promises, and the surety of God's future promise keeping.

In fact, we moderns can readily find analogies to the passion for lists of names and numbers evident in the book of Numbers. Children run hurriedly to lists of posted names to see who made the cut for an athletic team or the school play. Parents peruse newspapers to see whose children made the honor roll this semester. Frightened loved ones rush to the first-aid shelter or call the Red Cross to hear lists of names of people who died in an earthquake or have been found under the rubble of a fallen building. Families wait with strained faces for lists of names of those who died in combat or at the hands of death squads in terror-ridden places around the world. If we capture just a glimpse of the life-and-death stakes involved in such lists of names, we may begin to sense something of the passion for careful enumeration and careful naming that lies behind what seem to be cold lists in the book of Numbers. Who am I? Do I belong? Is God faithful? Who are my sister and brother? What are my roots? Do I have a future in this community? Such are the existentially charged questions that breathe through the names and numbers of Numbers 1 and 26.

Many today are fascinated with their own brand of numbers, censuses, polls, market indicators, interest rates, stock market averages, statistics, and number-crunching machines called computers. Many define their identity and value and future by computing numbers that measure our human accomplishments, whether of political strength or material possessions or military hardware or number of square feet. But the census list in Numbers reminds us that identity and value and future hope lie in the tangible and concrete ways in which God is working and stirring among us in this world. What is God accomplishing in and through us? What are the beginnings of the real fulfillment of God's intentions for us and our community in this time and place? In what ways might we gain confidence to pursue our vocations as God's people by glimpsing God's real fulfillments of promises already partially fulfilled?

The promise first given to Abraham in Gen. 12:1–3 involved both the promise of land and the promise that God would make Abraham a great nation. In a sense, both promises come to partial and tangible fulfillment in the census list of Numbers 1. The vast numbers of Israelites in the census totals suggest that Israel is indeed moving toward becoming a "great nation." The purpose of the census—counting warriors to take part in the conquest of the land—points toward progress in fulfilling the promise of the land. These are signs that God's promise is in the process of coming true.

Even Abraham himself in Genesis 15 sought a tangible sign that God would be true to the promise of descendants. Abraham "believed the LORD; and the LORD reckoned it to him as righteousness" (Gen. 15:6). But in verse 8, Abraham requests a more visible sign, "O Lord GOD, how am I to know that I shall possess it?" In response, God's presence moves as a flaming torch between the split carcasses of animals in a ceremony whereby God pledges to fulfill the promise to Abraham or else be split in half like those animals (Gen. 15:7–21). The census lists are not nearly as dramatic a sign, but they are nonetheless real and concrete indications that God intends to make good on the promises given to Israel long ago.

Numbers 1 concludes with verses 47–54, a general note and explanation about why the tribe of Levi was not counted in the preceding census list. The Levites are a priestly tribe exempted from military service and assigned to care for the tabernacle of the covenant and all the equipment associated with it. The Levites have several tasks. They are to carry the equipment when Israel is on the march. They are to erect and dismantle the tabernacle when the Israelites set up or break down the camp. The Levites are to camp around the tabernacle, forming a protective buffer zone between the tabernacle and the rest of the Israelite tribes. Finally, they are to perform guard duty for the tabernacle. The text suggests that their most significant task is protection. The Levites protect the tabernacle from encroachment by non-Levitical Israelites; thus "any outsider who comes near shall be put to death" (1:51). But the Levites also protect the other Israelite tribes from the awesome holiness of God's presence which is present in and through the tabernacle. Thus, the Levites camp around the inner circle surrounding the tabernacle "that there may be no wrath on the congregation of the Israelites" (1:53). The tabernacle represents something holy, powerful, dangerous, and yet central and crucial to the life of the community. What is this tabernacle, and how are we to understand its significance?

The tabernacle of the covenant is presented in Exodus and Numbers as a portable sanctuary or temple that provided a place by which God could be present in the midst of the people. The tabernacle consisted of a rectangular tent with curtains supported on poles. The size of the tent was approximately 145 feet long, 72 feet wide, and 7 feet high (Exod. 27:18). Inside this tent was another curtained enclosure divided into two rooms by a veil, behind which was the Holy of Holies containing the ark. The room in front of the veil contained the altar of incense, the lampstand, and the table for the bread of the divine Presence (Exodus 25). An altar for burnt offerings and a bronze basin of water for ritual cleansing of the priests stood in the courtyard outside the front door of the tabernacle (Exod. 30:18). The elaborate furnishings of the tabernacle were made of costly and fine materials (Exod. 25:3–7). The tabernacle was erected in the middle of the camp of Israelites.

17

As we begin the book of Numbers, we need to be aware of the

theological dynamics surrounding the presence of the tabernacle in the midst of Israel's camp in order to appreciate its significance for the theology of Numbers. The directions for building the tabernacle are first given in Exodus 25—30, and the actual construction of the tabernacle is recounted in Exodus 35—40. What occurs between the directions for building and the actual construction of the tabernacle is the dramatic golden calf story. In this act of blatant idolatry, the covenant established at Mount Sinai is broken and the relationship between the holy God and the sinful people of Israel is severed. Moses smashes to the ground the stone tablets with the Ten Commandments, a gesture which signifies the breaking of the covenant (Exod. 32:19). God initially decides to abandon the people of Israel entirely, but Moses prays to God and changes God's mind in a bold act of intercession (Exod. 32:9–14). God instructs Moses to continue the journey to the promised land, but with Moses and not God in the lead. God tells Moses, "I will not go up among you, or I would consume you on the way, for you are a stiff-necked people" (Exod. 33:3). But Moses refuses to leave Sinai without God's presence in Israel's midst (Exod. 33:15–16). Finally, God gives in to Moses and reveals to him God's deeper, loving character that allows the holiness of God's presence to dwell among a sinful people: "The LORD, the LORD, a God merciful and gracious, slow to anger, and abounding in steadfast love and faithfulness, keeping steadfast love for the thousandth generation, forgiving iniquity and transgression and sin, yet by no means clearing the guilty. . . ." (Exod. 34:6–7; compare the first Sinai covenant at Exod. 20:5–6, in which the revelation of God's loving and forgiving character is secondary and much more muted). It is only through these dramatic events and Moses' intense wrestling with God that the covenant relationship between God and Israel is renewed (Exod. 34:10–28). New stone tablets are made (Exod. 34:1–4). The tabernacle is actually constructed (Exod. 35—40). Thus, the construction of the tabernacle represents a tangible sign of God's loving concession to be present in all of God's holiness in the middle of a community of sinful human beings. But Israel cannot presume upon God's presence and power. It remains dangerous, and the people must be protected from its power. The extensive laws of Leviticus involving purity and ethics and holiness may be seen as attempts to place protective boundaries and structures within the community so as to allow God's holy presence to continue to dwell among the sinful but beloved people of God. The Levites in Numbers 1 are an extension of this protective strategy of surrounding the tabernacle and God's sacred nearness with a shielding priestly buffer zone embodied by the Levitical priests.

18

The importance of the tabernacle's placement in the center of Israel's camp is underscored by the alternate tradition of the "tent of meeting" that was pitched outside and far away from the Israelite community (Exod. 33:7–11). Unlike the tabernacle, which stood in the midst of the camp, this earlier tent of meeting was a shrine for receiving oracles from God; it was not a place for sacrifices nor did it house the Ark. God's presence did not reside permanently in the tent of meeting but would appear in the pillar of cloud whenever Moses entered the tent in search of a word from God. When the tabernacle is finally constructed at the end of Exodus, this early tradition of the more modest tent of meeting appears to merge with the tabernacle tradition, so that the tent of meeting becomes an alternate name for the tabernacle in the midst of the camp (Num. 2:2).

Thus, Numbers 1 introduces us to several important material and tangible assurances of God's favor toward Israel as the community prepares obediently to set out on its march toward the promised land. The ongoing life of the twelve tribes of Israel and their military preparations for conquest of the land assure the reader of God's faithfulness to the promises of land and progeny made to the ancestors in the book of Genesis. The high numbers of the census in Numbers 1 declare the richness of God's blessing among the house and families of Israel. The tabernacle and the Levites that surround it are continual visible signs of God's presence and love, pulsating with dangerous power but also with forgiving compassion.

Numbers 2
The Ministry of Administration:
The Organization and Leadership
of God's People

Numbers 1 recounted the large number of people in the twelve tribes of Israel. Chapter 2 delineates the arrangement of the camp by which this large community of tribes is to travel through the wilderness. The layout of the camp forms a square with the tabernacle or tent of meeting in the middle, priests and Levites surrounding the tabernacle, and four groups of three tribes at each cardinal point—east, south, west, and north. The structure of the camp may be diagrammed as follows:

19

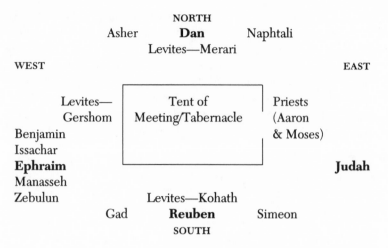

NORTH
Asher   **Dan**   Naphtali
Levites—Merari

WEST   EAST

Levites—	Tent of	Priests
Gershom	Meeting/Tabernacle	(Aaron
Benjamin		& Moses)
Issachar		
Ephraim		**Judah**
Manasseh		
Zebulun	Levites—Kohath	

Gad   **Reuben**   Simeon
SOUTH

The structure of the camp represents a geographical configuration which combines levels of relative holiness and prominence with ultimate inclusion of all the tribes within the camp. Everyone belongs somewhere, but some are more equal than others. This juggling between inclusiveness and hierarchy and the shifting positions of certain tribes probably reflect certain social realities within Israel's actual history. But they also reflect the literary destinies of individuals and tribes inscribed in the stories of Genesis and Exodus. As we will see in the stories of Numbers, these historical and literary realities of blessing and curse continue to echo throughout a number of the rebellion stories which follow.

The Levites are assigned a special role as guardians in the inner circle around the tent of meeting. This special function derives in part from the willingness of the Levites to stand with Moses against the other Israelites during the golden calf apostasy. For this they are blessed with ordination to special service in connection with the tabernacle (Exod. 32:25–29). But the Levites are also earlier cursed by their father Jacob along with Simeon because of their violence in Gen. 49:5–7 (cf. Gen. 34:25–31). Jacob condemns the Levites to be a tribe that is divided and scattered in Israel. This curse apparently came to be interpreted as a punishment whereby the Levites lost any claim to specific tribal land of their own. They would be scattered throughout Israel. Thus, the Levites are both blessed and cursed in their special service to God at the tabernacle in Numbers 2. Ordination for the Levites involved both a gift and a responsibility.

The relative statuses of Reuben, Simeon, Judah, and Ephraim in the camp arrangement in Numbers 2 reflect in part the birth stories of the twelve sons of Jacob to Leah and Rachel and their concubines in Gen. 29:31—30:24 and Gen. 35:22–36. The varied statuses also reflect Jacob's curses and blessings on his sons in Gen. 49:1–28. The shifts which take place in tribal ordering are evident when comparing the genealogy of the sons of Jacob in Gen. 35:22–26 with the three tribal lists in the first chapters of Numbers:

Gen. 35:22–26	*Num. 1:5–15*	*Num. 1:20–43*	*Num. 2:3–31*
(sons of Jacob)	*(tribal leaders)*	*(tribal census)*	*(12 tribes in 4 marching groups)*
LEAH'S SONS			
Reuben	Reuben	Reuben	Judah—leader
Simeon	Simeon	Simeon	Issachar (EAST)
Levi		Gad	Zebulun
Judah	Judah	Judah	Reuben—leader
Issachar	Issachar	Issachar	Simeon (SOUTH)
Zebulun	Zebulun	Zebulun	Gad
RACHEL'S SONS			
Joseph	Ephraim	Ephraim	Ephraim—leader
(later has two sons, Manasseh and Ephraim)	Manasseh	Manasseh	Manasseh (WEST)
Benjamin	Benjamin	Benjamin	Benjamin
SONS OF BILHAH, RACHEL'S MAID			
Dan	Dan	Dan	Dan—leader
Naphtali	Asher	Asher	Asher (NORTH)
SONS OF ZILPAH, LEAH'S MAID			
Gad	Gad		
Asher	Naphtali	Naphtali	Naphtali

As one moves from the tribal genealogy in Genesis 35 to the list of tribal leaders in Num. 1:5–15, the tribe of Levi drops out of the list of twelve tribes. In order to preserve the number twelve among the tribes, the Joseph tribe is replaced by Joseph's two sons, Manasseh and Ephraim. Birth order continues to place Reuben in the number one position. Being born of the maids of Leah and Rachel (the maids being of socially lower rank) places the tribes of Dan, Naphtali, Gad, and Asher in a lower position irrespective of their birth order.

Now as we move from the list of tribal leaders in Num. 1:5–15 to the tribal census list in 1:20–43, the only difference in tribal sequence

21

is that Gad has been moved up to replace the gap left by Levi after Reuben and Simeon. Gad was associated with Reuben as one of the tribes that settled on the east side of the Jordan River (Numbers 32).

Finally, we note the dramatic shift which occurs as we move from the tribal census in Num. 1:20–43 to the division of the twelve tribes into four marching groups gathered around the tabernacle in 2:3–31. The Judah-Issachar-Zebulun group takes over the most prominent position as leader of all the tribes, replacing Reuben the firstborn. The Judah group is now listed first in Numbers 2, and it is situated at the traditionally more sacred eastern side of the camp. East is the direction faced by the opening to the tabernacle, and it is on the eastern side that Moses, Aaron, and the other priests are stationed. But why has the tribal group led by Judah been promoted? Why has Reuben the first-born been demoted? And what is the significance of the other tribal configurations?

The prominence of Judah in this camp arrangement no doubt stems in part from the historical primacy that Judah possessed throughout much of Israel's history. The great King David was associated with the tribe of Judah. Judah was the dominant state after the northern kingdom of Ephraim fell to the Assyrians. In the postexilic period, Judah retained a claim to primacy with the building of the temple in Jerusalem, which was part of Judah. But this historical prominence of Judah is also reflected literarily in the Genesis blessing of Jacob. In Gen. 49:8–12, Judah receives the most lavish and extended blessing of all the twelve sons of Jacob. In contrast, Reuben the first-born receives a severe rebuke from Jacob for defiling his father's bed by sleeping with one of his concubines (Gen. 49:3–4; cf. Gen. 35:22). Like Judah, the Joseph tribe, which eventually splits into Ephraim and Manasseh, receives a generous blessing from Jacob (Gen. 49:22–26); earlier, Ephraim had been blessed as the dominant one over Manasseh (Gen. 48:8–20). The elevation of Ephraim as the leader of the Ephraim group and opposite Judah reflects the stories of Genesis, but it also reflects the history of Israel during the monarchy. Ephraim, or Israel, was the name of the northern kingdom after the split of north and south in 922 B.C.E. into the divided kingdom; Judah was the name of the southern kingdom. Thus, Judah and Ephraim emerged as the two leading tribes in Israel's story, a fact that is reflected in various ways in Genesis, Numbers, and Samuel-Kings.

The dialogical struggle continued on into the postexilic period, during which Judah and Samaria/Ephraim represented northern and southern communities with conflicting claims about the true identity of God's people. When we come to Numbers 13—14, we will see that the only two heroes to emerge out of the tragedy of the spy story are Caleb of the tribe of Judah and Joshua of the tribe of Ephraim. Through the arrangement of the camp in chapter 2, the writers of Numbers seek to affirm the inclusion of all twelve tribes as legitimate heirs to the promised land. Yet certain distinctions and prominence are given to some tribes over others as a consequence of history interpreted in light of traditional material in Genesis and Exodus.

Numbers 2 can remind us of certain truths we may be tempted to forget in our contemporary climate, in which much clamor is heard about tearing down hierarchies, getting rid of government and administration, undermining leaders and authority, and being suspect of anyone designated with official power or functions on behalf of the whole community.

1. Numbers 2 reminds us that order, structure, and clear lines of accountability may be helpful and important in moving a large community of God's people forward through a wilderness and toward a promised goal. Chaos, anarchy, and indecision are not necessarily virtues. Even communities that claim to be wholly egalitarian invariably develop pecking orders and subtle hierarchies. Human communities ranging from families to nations simply need some ordering, some distribution of functions, some decision makers, and some followers. It is better to be explicit about the shape and structure of such arrangements of leadership and power than to engage in the illusion of equal sharing of all functions and powers. The danger exists that some in the community may surreptitiously use or misuse power without the rest of the community being fully aware of how leadership and control are really being exercised within the community.

2. Numbers 2 reminds us that those with authority and in positions of prominence bear special responsibility for the whole community. The Levites were set aside not only to protect the tabernacle, but their special function included protecting the community from the power of the tabernacle. Their special position bore an extra measure of responsibility and the burden of self-giving as they gave up all claims to tribal land of their own.

3. Numbers 2 illustrates God's periodic tendency to reshuffle the deck of authority among God's people. The Reuben tribe enjoyed prominence as the firstborn of Jacob's sons. But that position was by no means guaranteed for all time. The restructuring of the Israelite camp that put Judah first among the tribes provides a warning to all who hold special position and power. Leaders and authority are always subject to critique and judgment if their power is misused. This was a lesson Israel learned through its experience with kingship, which led eventually

to the exile and a total upheaval of the bases of power and authority in Israelite society. This is a lesson that the old wilderness generation as a whole will learn as it forfeits its opportunity to be the first to step into the promised land. That opportunity and honor will be taken from the old generation who escaped from Egypt and offered to a new generation of "little ones" whom God will choose (Numbers 13—14).

4. The almost monotonous recitation of the tribal groups in the camp serves to create an atmosphere of careful and meticulous obedience to God's commands. There is no bickering among the tribes about relative positions of honor and leadership. The last verse of chapter 2 drives home the point: "The Israelites did just as the LORD had commanded Moses." The impression is given of an eager and obedient people, well organized and ready to join God's holy war as they enter into the promised land. The language of "regiments" and "companies" and "ensigns" suggests the military character of the Israelite camp that demands regimentation, order, and obedience. But this is not just a military camp dependent on its own human resources for battle. Indeed, all the tribes in their encampments are to face the center of the camp, the tabernacle that is a visible sign of God's presence in their midst. It is this near but elusive center, the God of power and the God of love, from which Israel derives any claim to power, greatness, and honor among all the other peoples of the world. As we exit Numbers 2, we are left with a high sense of readiness and rising expectation that the entry into the promised land is within the near grasp of the people as long as God is in their midst. This will be a lesson, however, all too soon forgotten.

Numbers 3—4
The Ministry of Priests and Levites:
The Interplay of Exclusion and Inclusion

Numbers 3 begins in v. 1 with a significant generational formula: "This is the lineage of Aaron and Moses" (NRSV) or more precisely, "These are the generations of Aaron and Moses" (author's translation). This precise generational formula occurs eleven times throughout the book of Genesis, beginning with 2:4: "These are the generations of the heavens and the earth." The recurring formula forms the backbone for the literary structure of the whole book of Genesis extending from the

24

creation story in Genesis 2 through the stories of Jacob and his sons in Gen. 37:2: "These are the generations of Jacob" (author's translation). A later editor has apparently taken this generational formula as it was used in Genesis and introduced it in this one occurrence in the book of Numbers (3:1). The use of the generational formula here in Numbers further reinforces the bond between Genesis and Numbers, which is evident already in the relationships of the tribal lists in Numbers and the tribal genealogies and lists in the book of Genesis.

In addition to their role as the key element in the structure of the book of Genesis, the generational formulas also have two other functions in Genesis. One function is an increasingly narrowing focus and exclusion of others. Some of the Genesis genealogies or family trees recount several generations of ancestors, but only one ancestor is named in each generation (e.g., Gen. 5:1–32, the generational line from Adam to Noah). These so-called vertical or linear genealogies narrow the focus of the line of promise down to a smaller and more restricted group. The progression begins with the expansive "generations of the heavens and the earth" (Gen. 2:4) and "the generations of Adam" (Gen. 5:1, au. trans.). But the generational formulas in Genesis progressively concentrate their focus to a smaller and smaller group or family until they reach Gen. 37:2 and "the generations of Jacob." By adding one more step in the generational formula, "These are the generations of Aaron and Moses," at the endpoint of this progression in Num. 3:1, the writer of Numbers has limited the focus even further to one group within the tribes of Jacob or Israel: the priests and Levites who are the generations of Aaron and Moses. The line of the promise is centered on an ever smaller group of people. The arrangement of the camp in Numbers 2 further highlights this narrowing of the focus as the priests and Levites reside at the center of the camp around the tent of meeting.

Although one function of the generational formulas is a narrowing and excluding, a second function is a broadening and opening wider the lens of the text's concern. Some of the generational formulas in Genesis introduce so-called horizontal or segmented genealogies or family trees. These genealogies usually have a depth of only two or three generations, but several members of each generation are named (e.g., the descendants of the three sons of Noah in Gen. 10:1–31 who represent the ancestors of various nations). These segmented genealogies keep the wider arena of the world and its many nations in view. Israel exists within a broader world and in the context of many peoples. The family of Jacob or Israel is not God's sole concern; this one family line lives and interacts within a wider world of people and exists for the

25

sake of the broader human community (Gen. 12:1–3). This motif of inclusivity is also carried into the book of Numbers. The census list of the twelve tribes and the numerous other lists of all Israelite tribes keep in view the fact that the priests and the Levites, "the generations of Aaron and Moses," do not live in isolation from but in service to the larger community of God's people. The relationship between clergy and laity is one of mutual interdependence and responsibility.

Thus, the two-pronged effect of a narrowing of focus coupled with a complementary broadening of perspective evident in Genesis has been enlarged beyond the boundaries of Genesis into the book of Numbers by a later editor. The more restricted focus on the priests and Levites (Num. 3:1) is counterbalanced by a concern to include *all* Israel within the purview of God's care in the census list of all twelve tribes (Numbers 1). The census list in Numbers continues the story of "the generations of Jacob" (Gen. 37:2, au. trans.). In contrast, the census list of the Levites in Numbers 3—4 narrows the focus begun in Genesis one more level to "the generations of Aaron and Moses" (au. trans.), whose members include Moses, Aaron, Aaron's sons, and the Levites (Num. 3:1).

Immediately following the generational formula in Num. 3:1 is a list of the names of Aaron's sons who were anointed to serve as priests: "Nadab the firstborn, and Abihu, Eleazar, and Ithamar" (3:2). The text continues with a cryptic note about the fate of the two first sons of Aaron: "Nadab and Abihu died before the LORD when they offered illicit fire before the LORD in the wilderness of Sinai, and they had no children" (3:4). The note is a brief reference back to an incident recounted in Lev. 10:1–3 when Aaron's two oldest sons offered strange or illicit fire in lighting the sanctuary's incense. The nature of the illicit fire is not clear from the story, whether it was fire not properly taken from the altar or fire in some way associated with a foreign god or cult. But the note in Num. 3:4 reinforces the warnings given already to the Levites in Num. 1:51, 53. Both alert the reader to the threat of danger and death associated with violating the holiness and purity of the tabernacle as the vehicle of God's presence in the midst of Israel. The warning is not without reason in Numbers. The story in Numbers 16 will recount the tale of rebels who die as Aaron's sons did, offering fire at the sanctuary. Numbers 3:10 contains yet another word of caution— only Aaron and his sons are to perform the duties of priesthood; all others (including the Levites) who inappropriately encroach upon the sacred space of the tabernacle will be put to death. In the midst of these opening chapters of Numbers that stress the compliance of Israel with all of God's commands, these scattered warnings of death remind the reader how precarious is Israel's journey with God in its midst. Nadab was the firstborn son of Aaron, the most prestigious rank among the priests, and yet his exclusive rank did not absolve him from responsibility for the obedient and careful execution of his office. This note about the death of Aaron's son hangs as another ominous cloud over what is otherwise a bright and optimistic picture of camp Israel in obedient and confident preparation for its march to the promised land.

As we turn to the two special census lists for the Levites in Numbers 3—4, the two concurrent themes of exclusion and inclusion that we noted in the Genesis genealogies again come into play. Two separate numberings of the Levites are actually performed in Numbers 3—4. One Levitical census in chapter 3 includes every male Levite over the age of one month (3:15). The literary context surrounding this first census of all male Levites stresses the Levites' role as substitutes for all firstborn males in Israel (3:40–51). An early tradition in Israel held that all the firstborn males, whether human or livestock, should be dedicated to God. In other ancient Near Eastern contexts, this may have meant the killing and sacrifice of firstborn male children and animals. But according to the present form of the tradition in the Old Testament, the firstborn children of the Israelites were redeemed by dedicating the whole tribe of Levi to God's service as a substitute for all the firstborn. According to Numbers, the tradition that all the firstborn belong to God derived from the last plague during the exodus out of Egypt. God declares, "For all the firstborn are mine; when I killed all the firstborn in the land of Egypt, I consecrated for my own all the firstborn in Israel, both human and animal; they shall be mine. I am the LORD" (Num. 3:11–13; cf. Exod. 13:2, 11–16).

Jon Levenson, in a study titled *The Death and Resurrection of the Beloved Son,* argues that the theme of the death of the firstborn or beloved son and his dedication to God has deep roots historically and theologically in both Jewish and Christian traditions (Levenson). As substitutes for the firstborn consecrated to God, the Levites in a sense experience the death of their existence as a normal landed tribe of Israel. Instead, the landless Levitical tribe exists on behalf of and for the sake of the larger community of the other twelve tribes of Israel. The Levites' substitution for the firstborn expresses the broader and inclusive character of the Levites' mission.

The purpose of the first Levitical census in Numbers 3 is thus to determine whether the number of Levites is sufficient to substitute on a one-for-one basis for all the firstborn children in the other tribes. The results of the Levites' census indicates they fall short of the total number of Israelite firstborn children. The numbers involved are some-

27

what problematic. A census is taken for each of the three groups of Levites headed by the three sons of Levi. The individual totals are Gershon—7,500, Kohath—8,600, and Merari—6,200 (Num. 3:22, 28, 34). The actual grand total of these three numbers is 22,300, but the total reported in Num. 3:39 is an even 22,000. This even number of 22,000 is the one used to compute the shortfall in the number of Levites compared to the number of Israelite firstborn, which is 22,273; the number of firstborn not covered by the number of Levites is stated as 273 (22,273 − 22,000 = 273; Num. 3:39, 43, 46). The discrepancy in the number of Levites may be due to an error in the transmission of the text. But the basic point is that if there are not enough Levites to equal all the Israelite firstborn, then these extra Israelites may be redeemed by another method: the payment of money (3:44–51).

At its most basic level, the tradition of dedicating the firstborn to God or some equivalent is a theological reminder that Israel owes its very life and freedom to God. The dedication of the firstborn is a tangible way of recalling Israel's history as a slave people redeemed by God. All that Israel has, including its very existence, is a gift from God. To return whatever first opens the womb to God is a tangible reminder that everything belongs to God and is available for our use only because God has given it as a gift.

The Sunday morning offering that Christians give in worship is not first of all for the sake of God or even for the operation of the church and its mission. The giving of the firstfruits of our labors in time, talents, and possessions is done first of all because we need to give. We need to give back to God in order to be reminded that all that we have belongs to God and is loaned to us for our careful stewardship. The sabbath and Jubilee laws in Leviticus 25 express a similar sentiment in regard to Israel's economic base of the land: God declares, "The land is mine; with me you are but aliens and tenants" (Lev. 25:23). The psalmist sings, "The earth is the LORD's and all that is in it, the world and those who live in it" (Ps. 24:1). Thus, behind the Levites' substitution for the firstborn is an important theology of stewardship that acknowledges the giftedness of all that we have and its ultimate ownership by God.

The second census of the Levites in Numbers 4 includes only those male Levites between the ages of thirty and fifty years old (4:2–3). This census numbers only the older adult Levites in preparation for their role in the service and maintenance of the tent of meeting. The Levites are to serve the sons of Aaron, who are the high priests in the worship life of the tabernacle (3:5–10). The census proceeds through the three households of Levites headed by the three sons of

28

Levi. The Kohathites are first for they are assigned to care for "the most holy things" in the tabernacle (4:4). The family members of Kohath are to work most closely with the sons of Aaron, who as the priests will be the ones who actually put up or take down and cover the tabernacle and its furnishings. After the holy things are properly covered, then the Kohathites may carry them. Again, a warning is given to Kohath: "They must not touch the holy things, or they will die" (Num. 4:5–15). An additional note of warning is added in Num. 4:17–20 that stresses the importance of the continuing existence of the Kohathite clan, ending with the another word of caution: "But the Kohathites must not go in to look on the holy things even for a moment; otherwise they will die" (4:20). The concern to preserve the Kohathite clan in their high-risk work with the holy things of the tabernacle will be threatened in the rebellion story of Numbers 16. Korah, son of Kohath, will die when he attempts to take over the priestly work of offering fire and incense at the tent of meeting. But the continuation of the Kohath clan is assured when the Kohathites are explicitly named in the Levitical census of the new generation in Num. 26:7.

The next group of Levites from thirty to fifty years old to be counted are the Gershonites, who are instructed to carry the curtains and outer coverings of the tent of meeting (4:21–28). The third group of Levites, the Merarites, are counted and charged to tend and carry the frames and bases of the tabernacle (4:29–33). The reader will discern a careful progression from the Kohathites, who deal with the most holy things inside the tabernacle, to the Gershonites and Merarites, who care for the progressively less holy and exterior parts of the tent of meeting. This is in line with the picture of concentric rings of holiness and danger that are part of the Israelite camp's arrangement. Just as there are concentric circles of holiness within the tabernacle itself (moving from interior to exterior), so there are circles of relative holiness within the whole camp. The tabernacle in the center is the most holy, the circle of Levites and Aaronic priests immediately surrounding the tabernacle are the next in order of holiness, and the twelve tribes are all equidistant in signifying the least holy part of the camp.

But the text nowhere suggests that these degrees of holiness correspond to levels of divine favor and value. Holiness has to do not so much with esteem or the deity's favor; rather, holiness has to do with danger. The one boundary which cannot be crossed is sinful human encroachment onto God's holy space and prerogative. All Israelite tribes—laity and clergy alike—are subject in the same way to the danger and death which occurs when humans seek to take the place of God. We have been reminded that even Aaron's firstborn sons were

29

subject to death by the fire of God. But the danger and threat of death associated with God's holy presence in the midst of Israel, we must remember, is the result of Moses' appeal to God's mercy and love. It is only with God's presence among them, as dangerous as that may be, that Israel has a future. Without God in their midst, God's people will be lost. That lesson will be learned more than once in the struggles of Israel's wilderness wandering.

In the meantime, Numbers 4 ends again with a sweeping note of reassurance. "According to the commandment of the LORD through Moses [the Levites] were appointed to their several tasks of serving or caring; thus they were enrolled by him, as the LORD commanded Moses" (4:49). The picture seems rosy indeed as the tabernacle and its personnel appear well instructed and in place.

Numbers 5:1—6:21

Preserving Boundaries of Holiness in the Camp—Impurity, Suspected Adultery, and Nazirite Vows

The preparations for beginning the march toward the promised land now move out from the tabernacle and its Levitical and priestly personnel at the center to issues of purity and holiness among all the people of Israel in the twelve tribes who are gathered around the center of the camp. The focus shifts from safeguarding holiness among the clergy to safeguarding holiness among the laity.

EXCURSUS:

Purity in the Bible

The concern for purity or cleanness is an important Old Testament concept that may be unfamiliar to many in our modern culture and time. Purity in ancient Israel meant being free from any physical, moral, or ritual contamination. Impurity came about through such things as contact with a corpse, the involuntary flow of fluids (e.g., blood or semen) from the human body, certain skin diseases (often translated incorrectly in English versions as "leprosy"), or the eating of prohibited foods. Several legal texts in the Old Testament provide more detailed instructions on what constitutes impurity and rituals for decontamination (e.g., Leviticus 11—15, Deuteronomy 14). Becoming impure from various causes was a common occurrence for most people (e.g., attending the funeral of a parent, inadvertently eating unclean food, menstruation), so that rituals of purification were readily available to make oneself clean again. Impurity was not sin and could always be removed through various ritual washings, waiting periods, and offerings.

The function of these laws of purity or uncleanness in the social world of ancient Israel has been a much-debated issue. Some argue that the purity laws functioned as primitive rules of hygiene, as regulations against Canaanite religious practices, or as reflections of deeper ethical principles such as the sacredness of life. Anthropologists have viewed the purity laws as part of a social symbol system that classifies boundaries within the realm of nature in order to protect the society from destructive powers. For example, unclean animals are those who in some way mix or cross over perceived boundaries: fish without fins or scales, flying insects with more than two legs, animals that either do not chew the cud or do not have divided hooves. Purity regulations touch on matters involving food, sex and marriage, family relationships, business practices, physical anomalies, and abhorrent worship practices of other gods by other nations. No single principle or concept can explain all the aspects of the purity laws, but they all relate in some way to preserving certain boundaries of holiness within the community of God's people, which is sacred by virtue of God's presence in its midst.

In recent New Testament studies of the historical person of Jesus, some scholars have argued that a central feature of Jesus' mission was to disobey and dismantle the system of purity laws in Israel. These scholars argue that the purity laws stigmatized the outcasts, the poor, all Gentiles, and women as unclean; Jesus sought to break down the barriers between these groups and God through a revolutionary attack on the entire purity system within Judaism. However, other New Testament scholars have correctly pointed out that the purity laws did not make distinctions strictly along the lines of class, ethnicity, gender, or race. All segments of Jewish and Gentile society were capable of being rendered pure or impure. Jesus is certainly portrayed in the New Testament Gospels as reaching out to heal and restore people whose condition had rendered them unclean: he cleansed lepers, healed the woman who suffered from a flow of blood, raised the dead, and ate

31

with sinners. But in doing so, there is no evidence that he did not follow the usual rules and rituals for purification. For example, Jesus instructs a leper whom he heals to show himself to the priest to certify his cleanness and to make an offering "as Moses commanded" (Mark 1:40–44; Luke 5:14). Jesus does teach that it is what comes out of a person in terms of words, intentions, and actions that defile a person more than the kind of food that person takes in (Mark 7:14–23; Matt. 15:1–20). Here Jesus' emphasis is more on validating the underlying principle of the purity laws than on overturning the entire system (Frederickson, pp. 18–25, 42–47). As the early Christian church moved out of the orbit of Jewish society and became more and more a religion of Gentile converts to Christianity, the specific Jewish laws of purity became less and less applicable in the emerging Christian communities (cf. Acts 10; Galatians 2).

The notion of boundaries of holiness and purity and the threat of defilement and contamination is such an important feature of the book of Numbers that we need to pause to consider the meaning of purity for Israel as an ancient culture quite different from ours and its possible implications for our time. In nearly all premodern cultures and religions, purity codes and notions of boundaries between clean and unclean have been important parts of religion that defined and shaped reality. Anthropologist Mary Douglas notes:

> In all previous civilizations, religion defines reality and the concept of impurity shapes the world. For us a long scientific liberal tradition has made our culture secular and pluralist. The effort of tolerance so needful for living in a plural society leads us to repudiate the drawing of moral lines and social boundaries but it is of the essence of impurity to draw sharp lines. This may be why comparative religion starts with a prejudice against impurity and finds defilement difficult to understand. (Douglas, p. 24)

Our modern inability to appreciate or even understand how purity systems work is a barometer of how far away we are as a culture and society from having a notion of the reality of a holy God as a truly defining center of our lives and communities. We are not able nor should we try to reconstruct the ancient biblical purity system in our modern society. But as faithful people of God, we need to find ways by which the holy reality of a living and loving God at the center of our lives and our universe may more deeply shape and guide us as individuals and communities.

32   Although the biblical concerns for purity reflect many of the elements of purity codes in other religions, Mary Douglas points to an important and unique feature of the Israelite purity laws that stands

out to her as an anthropologist of world religions. Often the normal use of defilement in other religions is as a weapon of exclusion aimed at outsiders and certain marginal groups within a society. In contrast to this typical use of purity codes in other societies, Douglas observes that the purity laws of Leviticus and Numbers

> never use the principle of ritual purity to separate classes or races, foreigners or natives. This is very remarkable. . . . In the biblical creed defilement is not caused by contact with other people; it comes out of the body, or it comes out of moral failure. Everybody is liable to be defiled or to defile. This should be totally unexpected to the anthropologist used to purity codes in other religions. (Douglas, p. 25)

The Old Testament purity system implies that everyone is universally susceptible to impurity. "Biblical defilement is *not* from contact with foreigners or from lower classes. It is not used for keeping them outside or in lower ranks" (Douglas, pp. 25–26). The key concern of the biblical purity laws is that the holy and powerful God of Israel is really and intensely present in the midst of the community. God's presence there makes the whole camp holy and set apart as God's specially chosen people whom God loves with a steadfast love that endures forever. But the recurring sin and impurity of this people of God continually threatens the boundaries of holiness that give order and safety to the camp. These boundaries of purity protect the people from the divine death and destruction that explodes upon sinful human beings when they maliciously or even inadvertently encroach upon the awesome and powerful holiness of God.

It is this central tension that animates the drama and anxiety of Israel's march in the wilderness to the promised land in the book of Numbers: the tension between God's gracious yearning to be an intensely present and guiding power in the midst of God's holy people and the constant threat of death and annihilation that accompanies a holy God dwelling among a sinful people. To combine divine holiness and human sin in this way is like putting a huge fiery oven in the middle of a fireworks factory. The walls of the oven and careful rules and procedures may keep the fire and the explosive devices separate. But missteps in any of the protective measures will result in explosive danger and death to all who work within the walls of the factory. It is this fundamental tension in the interplay of God and humanity, the holy and the sinful, the divine and human natures, the Creator and the creature, that weaves its way through the biblical story, all the way to the mystery of the incarnation in Jesus. How is a holy and loving God to live and work in and through a sinful people as they march toward the promised land? That is the pivotal struggle of the Bible's story, but it is also the key to the good news of the gospel: "the Word became flesh and lived among us, and we have seen his glory . . . full of grace and truth" (John 1:14).

Impurity and Sins against the Neighbor (5:1–10)

We return now to the specific texts in Numbers 5 with a clearer picture of what is at stake in these laws of purity and in the concerns for the holiness of the Israelite camp. In 5:2–3, God commands Moses to instruct the people to put those who are unclean outside the camp. People with certain skin diseases, bodily discharges, or those who have touched a dead body are explicitly named (cf. Lev. 13, 15; Num. 19:11–20). God proclaims the reason clearly: "they must not defile their camp, where I dwell among them" (5:3). Numbers 5:4 reports the obedient response of the people, in line with the atmosphere of dutiful compliance throughout these beginning chapters of Numbers: "as the LORD had spoken to Moses, so the Israelites did."

Numbers 5 continues by shifting the focus from ritual impurity to sins done against a neighbor within the community. Numbers 5:5–10 instructs a person who sins against a neighbor to confess the sin and make full restitution plus 20 percent of the total loss. This corresponds to the law also found in Lev. 6:5. The law in Numbers 5, however, adds another dimension to the law not found in Leviticus. When the person who has been wronged is dead and has no relatives, the priest is to be paid the restitution along with the ram offered for atonement of the sin. What is striking about the law is the identification of wrongdoing against another human being as being the same thing as "breaking faith with the LORD" (5:6). Harming or unjustly taking from another person in the community is an act of human injustice, but it is also an act that breaks the relationship with God. This moral guilt, like ritual impurity, also threatens the holiness of the community. But also like ritual impurity, there are processes by which the guilt can be atoned for and forgiven. The involvement of the priest in the process of restitution provides a tangible reminder that the holiness of God is intricately connected not only with what goes on in the tabernacle but also with the everyday business and commerce of human interactions. To wrong another human being is to threaten the health and well-being of the whole community and its relationship to God.

The Case of Suspected Adultery (5:11–31)

Before chapter 5, the book of Numbers had concentrated on men only: male tribal leaders, male warriors in the census list, male clergy serving the tabernacle. The first two laws in chapter 5 introduce women into the picture for the first time in Numbers. In both of these laws, women are subject to the laws on an equal basis with men: "both male and female" (5:3); "a man or a woman" (5:6). This apparent equality suddenly dissolves in the next long and complex ordinance undertaken when a husband suspects his wife of infidelity. The structure of the judicial ritual is as follows:

I. *The Conditions of the Case (5:11–14).* The ritual applies if a husband is jealous and suspects his wife of adultery, whether she has actually committed adultery in secret (vv. 11–14a) or whether a spirit of jealousy has come upon the husband even if his wife is actually innocent and has not defiled herself (v. 14b).

II. *Preparations for the Ritual Ordeal (5:15–18).* The husband is to bring his wife before the priest along with an offering (v. 15). The priest dishevels the woman's hair and prepares the water of bitterness that brings the curse. The water is a mixture of holy water, dust from the floor of the sacred tabernacle, and the ink or parchment with which the curses are written (vv. 16–18, 23).

III. *The Administration of the Ritual Ordeal (5:19–26).* The priest speaks the oath with the curse: if the woman is guilty of adultery, then her uterus will drop and her womb will discharge when she drinks the water of bitterness (vv. 19–21). The woman accepts the oath upon herself by saying, "Amen, Amen" (v. 22). She then drinks the water, and the priest offers the grain offering (vv. 24–26).

IV. *The Two Possible Results of the Ritual Ordeal (5:28–29).* If guilty, the woman will experience bitter pain, her uterus will drop, and her womb will discharge. If innocent, the woman will be immune and able to conceive children.

35

> V. *Postscript: The Law for a Husband's Jealousy (5:29–31).* This is the law for cases in which a wife has actually defiled herself or when a spirit of jealousy has come upon the husband. The man shall be free from iniquity, but the woman shall bear her iniquity.

This text is highly disturbing to any modern reader sensitive to issues of mutual love and fairness in marriage relationships. The law reflects ancient cultural mores that most readers would find unacceptable today. Feminist scholars have rightly pointed out the seemingly unjust emphasis on the woman's guilt in adultery and the husband's ability to bring his wife to judgment on the basis of unproven jealousy (Bach, pp. 26–54). There is no provision here stating that a wife has a reciprocal right to put her husband through such an ordeal based on her jealousy. This reflects the underlying view that in ancient Israel a woman's sexual activity outside the bounds of marriage is an offense against a man, whether the woman's husband or father (cf. Deut. 22:13–29). The elaborate ritual of the woman drinking the priest's mysterious water of bitterness and the graphic effects it may have on the female's reproductive organs seem extremely repulsive and degrading to women. Much of the legal case seems to presume the woman's guilt, although the possibility of her innocence is acknowledged in 5:14 and 5:30. The woman's hair is disheveled as part of the ritual, signifying shame or mourning. The husband apparently bears no guilt if the ordeal proves that his accusation against his wife is wrong (5:31).

This is the only case of a trial by ordeal for a secret sin in the Bible, and it applies only to women. However, one near parallel is a series of curses for secret sins applied to all Israel, some of which involve illicit sexual activity (Deut. 27:15–26). The Israelites accept the curses upon themselves by saying "Amen" (just as the suspected adulteress does in Num. 5:22). The curses in Deuteronomy 27 subject the people to God's judgment in these secret cases since a human court cannot adjudicate a matter if no witnesses are available. The case of the suspected adulteress likewise takes the accusation of secret infidelity out of the hands of a human court and places it in the arena of divine discernment of guilt or innocence.

Several studies have wrestled with various aspects of this troublesome text. One disputed feature is the precise effect of the holy water upon a guilty woman: "her womb shall discharge, her uterus drop" (5:27). Some argue the consequence would be a spontaneous abortion or miscarriage of a fetus conceived by the illicit sexual activity. Others argue the result would be permanent or temporary sterility, either experienced immediately and in public or over the course of some time and in private. Others argue the ordeal would result in death, either from the poison itself or else by public stoning once the guilt was determined.

Jacob Milgrom provides a softer interpretation of the ritual ordeal, arguing that the trial by ordeal actually protects the woman from the lynch-mob mentality of an angry community or jealous husband. The priest takes the case out of the hands of a human court and places it under divine judgment. This, Milgrom argues, protects the woman if she is innocent. Moreover, the technical term for "committing adultery" used in the Ten Commandments of the Sinai covenant is never used in Numbers 5. Thus, the law in Numbers seems to create a less severe category for cases of secret or humanly unproven infidelity as opposed to proven adultery. The woman in Numbers 5 does not become subject to the death penalty as in cases of adultery judged in a human court (Milgrom, pp. 346–54). But these and other attempts to soften the ritual ordeal cannot erase the disturbing fact that a husband's mere unfounded suspicions can subject his wife to a humiliating ordeal without any sanction against the husband if his suspicions are proved wrong. The husband's concerns are heard, but the woman has no voice or opportunity to do anything other than to assent to the ritual with the words "Amen, Amen."

Another interpretive move made with this text is to theologize the ritual by linking the text of the suspected adulteress with the prophetic use of the unfaithful wife as a metaphor for Israel (Hosea 1—3; Isa. 50:1; 51:17–23; 57:3–14; Jer. 3:6–10; Ezekiel 16; 23). (Fishbane, "Accusations of Adultery," pp. 40–45; Douglas, pp. 160–69). The "jealousy" of the husband is linked with the "jealousy" of God (Exod. 20:5; 34:14; Deut. 32:12). The association of Israel's idolatry as adultery toward God is a frequent prophetic motif, but it also appears in Numbers 25 in the last act of rebellion by the old generation. The story in Numbers 25 joins an act of Israelite idolatry with an act of Israelite male adultery. Moreover, the Hebrew word *ma'al* used for the wife being unfaithful to the husband in Num. 5:12 is unique in the Bible. In every other use of *ma'al* in the Bible, the word is a technical term for human unfaithfulness to God rather than a human (Milgrom, p. 37). In fact, the term is used in the section just prior to the suspected-adultery law (Num. 5:6). In this passage, a man or woman who wrongs another has committed an act of "breaking faith" *(ma'al)* with God.

Scholars have also noted similarities between the ordeal of the woman drinking the water of bitterness and the story of Israel's golden calf apostasy in Exod. 32:20. There Moses mixes water with the dust of the golden calf, which had been ground to powder. The dusty water presumably functioned as a trial by ordeal and brought punishment upon the Israelites who were guilty of worshiping the idolatrous golden calf, just as the waters of bitterness brought judgment upon the unfaithful wife in Numbers 5. Jeremiah also uses the imagery of Israel bringing judgment upon itself by drinking the poisonous water of its idolatry:

> Let us go into the fortified cities and perish there; for the LORD our God has doomed us to perish, and has given us poisoned water to drink, because we have sinned against the LORD. (Jer. 8:14; cf. also Jer. 9:15; 23:15)

The theological echoes of this text throughout the Old Testament are suggestive, but they do not erase the problematic portrayal of women and the inequitable human marriage relationship implied by the sole focus on the husband's jealousy. At least in the theological echoes of Israel as unfaithful wife and God as jealous husband, the final word in both prophetic and narrative texts is typically one of forgiveness, restoration, and love renewed.

Some postbiblical Jewish expansions upon the law of the suspected adulteress added provisions which further degraded the woman in ways that went beyond the biblical text. Other expansions moved in a different direction. These expansions greatly restricted the husband's prerogatives, making the conditions for using the ritual more difficult to realize. There are no recorded instances of the trial by ordeal actually being carried out, and the ritual was officially abolished with the destruction of the Second Temple in Jerusalem (there being no more active priesthood, nor was dust from the tabernacle floor available for the water mixture).

The New Testament does not quote this text explicitly, but Jesus intervenes in a case where a community is set to stone a woman for adultery (John 8:1–11). Jesus levels the playing field between men and women and dissipates the crowd with his challenge, "Let anyone among you who is without sin be the first to throw a stone at her." Another intriguing echo of the Numbers 5 text is the story of Jesus and the Samaritan woman in John 4:1–30. Jesus comes for a drink of water from the well of Jacob and meets there a woman of Samaria. Jesus offers her a drink of "living water" and in so doing discerns her secret that she has had five husbands and now lives with a man who is not her husband. He does not condemn her. Rather, Jesus proclaims to her that he is the Messiah, and she becomes one of the first in John's Gospel to proclaim to her community the good news that the Messiah has indeed come. What was once the water of bitterness given to a woman suspected of adultery in Numbers 5 becomes the living water of the gospel. Like the water of bitterness, this water discerns sin and reveals the truth. But the living water of Jesus also offers forgiveness and new life to this woman from Samaria.

In terms of the relationship of human husbands and wives in the Bible as a whole, other texts of Scripture provide sounder principles and paradigms for the relationship of males and females than those implied in Num. 5:11–31. Even the two laws preceding the suspected adulteress law uphold both men and women as equally subject to them (Num. 5:3, 5). Our vision of humanity would be better served by a text like Genesis 1:27 that affirms both male and female as created in the image of God. Galatians 3:28 professes that in Christ "there is no longer male and female; for all of you are one in Christ." Such texts provide an inner-biblical basis for critique of the gender inequality in Numbers 5. But within the ancient culture of Israel, the ordeal ritual for the unfaithful wife was intended to be another means of safeguarding the holiness of the Israelite camp as it traversed the wilderness toward the promised land. Any disruption of human relationships, whether actual or perceived, endangered the whole community and threatened the continuation of God's holy presence in its midst (Num. 5:6).

Nazirite Vows (6:1–21)

We turn now to a law which again applies equally to men or women (6:2), the law of the Nazirites. The Hebrew meaning of Nazirites is "dedicated" or "consecrated ones." Nazirites were laypeople within the community who had been set aside as especially holy and dedicated to God. Such dedications to special service to God were made either by parents or by the Nazirites themselves. There were three main commitments observed by the Nazirite: refraining from alcohol, not cutting the hair, and avoiding contact with the dead. Avoiding contact with a corpse extended even to one's own father or mother at their funerals (Num. 6:1–7). The rigor of this latter obligation is comparable to that required only of the high priest (Lev. 21:10–12; cf. Lev. 21:1–4).

Several biblical figures were Nazirites. Joseph is named as a *nazir,* one set apart from his brothers (Gen. 49:26). Samuel is not explicitly called a Nazirite, but his mother Hannah dedicated him with a vow that suggests he was a Nazirite (I Sam. 1:11). The most well-known Nazirite in the Bible is Samson (Judg. 13:5). The story relates how

39

Samson gradually breaks his vows as he comes in contact with the carcass of a lion (Judg. 14:8–9), participates in drinking feasts with Philistines (Judg. 14:10), and allows his hair to be cut by Delilah (Judg. 16:15–22). Jesus is called a "Nazarene" or "Nazorean" in Matt. 2:23, a reference which may allude to his consecration to God from his birth as well as his home in Nazareth.

Numbers 6:1–8 spells out the nature of the Nazirite vows. Verses 9–12 set up conditions for remedying the accidental violation of the Nazirite vow against contact with the dead. The ordinary layperson could be made pure from corpse contamination by washing in a special mixture described in Numbers 19. Nazirites, however, require a more elaborate regimen of special cleansing from such contamination. The special instructions in 6:9–12 highlight the Nazirites' special holiness. Verses 13–21 prescribe the ritual for terminating the Nazirite vow, which need not be lifelong but may be of limited duration (cf. Acts 18:18; 21:17–26). Any commitment or vow made to the holy God of Israel, whether by a priest or a Nazirite, is a matter of utmost seriousness and discipline, for it affects the holiness of the entire community.

Numbers 6:22–27
The Ultimate Word Is Peace:
The Priestly Blessing of the Community

The words of Num. 6:22–27 are perhaps the most well known of the entire book of Numbers. They record the words of God's blessing or benediction that the priests are to proclaim to the community of God's people. This priestly blessing continues to be used as part of worship services in many different Christian and Jewish traditions. The Mishnah, an authoritative compilation of Jewish interpretation of biblical law, prescribes the priestly or Aaronic blessing from Numbers 6 to be spoken at the end of the synagogue service. Many Christian traditions regularly use the benediction at the end of their Sunday worship. Some traditions also use the blessing at the end of the baptismal service in which the name of God is invoked along with these words of blessing.

The importance of this Aaronic or priestly blessing in ancient Israel has been confirmed by recent archaeological findings from the First Temple period in Jerusalem. Two silver cylinders were discov-

40

ered in burial caves dating from 600 B.C.E.; the blessing from Numbers
6 was written on the two silver scrolls. These are the earliest known
fragments of any biblical texts, antedating the Dead Sea Scrolls biblical
manuscripts by about 400 years. This archaeological discovery confirms the antiquity and prominence of the priestly blessing from Numbers 6 in the religious life of Israel.

The blessing is couched in poetic Hebrew style, an elevated form
of speech characterized by parallelism, terseness, and the use of metaphors. In Hebrew, the first line of the blessing in verse 24 consists of
three words, the second line of five words, and the third line of seven
words. The progression in the number of words mirrors the outward
movement and flow of God's blessing through the single priest to the
broader community. Each of the three lines in the blessing consists of
two clauses. The first clause invokes God's movement toward the people (bless, make the face to shine, lift up the face), and the second
clause names the results of these three divine movements toward the
people (keep you, be gracious to you, give you peace) (Miller, pp. 240–
51; Fishbane, "Forms and Reformulation," pp. 115–21). The LORD
(Yahweh) is explicitly named as subject in the first clause of each of the
three lines. That God is the source of blessing is accentuated again in
the concluding statement in verse 27. God proclaims, "*I* will bless
them;" the "I" is emphatic in Hebrew. Although Aaron and his priestly
sons speak the blessing (6:23), the blessing remains under God's control and God's discretion.

The first line of the benediction in verse 24 speaks of God's action
of blessing and its consequence of keeping. Blessing includes the giving of God's gifts of posterity, land, health, the ongoing presence of
God, and all other things that make human life possible and full (Deut.
28:2–14). This blessing activity leads to God's keeping, which guards
and protects from evil. Psalm 121 is an expanded commentary on the
theme of God's keeping of Israel. The verb "to keep" using God as
subject occurs six times in the psalm's eight verses. The psalm concludes with these verses:

> The LORD will keep you from all evil;
>   he will keep your life.
> The LORD will keep your going out and your coming in
>   from this time on and forevermore.

According to the psalmist, God's ongoing vigilance is constant and reliable, extending to every dimension of the psalmist's life.

The second line of the blessing in verse 25 employs the metaphor
of light to refer to God's face as it shines benevolently upon the

nations. Light connotes clarity, revelation, the warmth of sunshine, rescue from cold darkness, renewal of life, and the brightness of joy. This bright shining of God's face upon Israel is a theme in an exuberant psalm of praise that celebrates God's fertile blessing and deliverance in times of trouble. Psalm 67 begins with these words:

> May God be gracious to us and bless us
>   and make his face to shine upon us,
> that your way may be known upon earth,
>   your saving power among all nations.
>   (Ps. 67:1–2)

The psalm's focus on all the nations and all creation suggests that the image of God's shining face evokes the wider theology of God as Creator of all. As the life-giving rays of the warm sun extend over all the world, so the blessing of God's shining face radiates out to the ends of the earth. Psalm 67 concludes:

> The earth has yielded its increase;
>   God, our God, has blessed us.
> May God continue to bless us;
>   let all the ends of the earth revere him.
>   (Ps. 67:6–7)

The shining of the divine face leads to God's being gracious, dealing with people not according to their sins but with freely given love and compassion (Ps. 123:2–3; Exod. 33:19).

The third line of the blessing in verse 26 brings the passage to a crescendo. The Aaronic blessing moves from the general blessing of the first line to the shining of God's face, which like the sun extends to all the nations, in the second line. The third line of the blessing moves from the passive shining of God's face to God's more active movement of lifting up the divine face and sending peace and blessing specifically upon God's people. This gracious nod of God toward the community signifies favor and acceptance, even when not deserved. In Gen. 32:20, Jacob hopes his brother Esau will lift up his face and accept him after their separation and estrangement since their youth. In Job 42:8–9, God instructs the foolish friends of Job to offer a sacrifice and hope that God will lift up the divine face and look with favor upon Job's prayer of intercession on their behalf.

The ultimate goal of God's blessing is summed up by the final word of the benediction, the Hebrew *shalom,* or peace, which is the outcome of God's lifting up the face and is the ultimate word of the benediction as a whole. Peace or *shalom* denotes a rich array of benefits: prosperity (Ps. 37:11; Prov. 3:2), longevity, happiness in a family

42

(Ps. 128:6), safety, security (Ps. 4:9; 122:6–8), good health (Ps. 38:4), friendship (Jer. 38:22), and general well-being. In the Psalms, peace and righteousness go together:

> Steadfast love and faithfulness will meet,
> Righteousness and peace will kiss each other.
> (Ps. 85:10)

The king of Israel is seen as God's instrument of bringing peace to God's people from enemies. But the king's peace and prosperity also join with righteousness and justice to ensure that all in the community may experience well-being (Ps. 72:3, 12–14). This royal image of a king blessing the nation is also applied to God, whose powerful voice of blessing tames the threatening waters of chaos in Psalm 29:

> The LORD sits enthroned over the flood;
> The LORD sits enthroned as king forever.
> May the LORD give strength to his people!
> May the LORD bless his people with peace!

The granting of God's peace extends to the individual, to the worshiping community, to the nation, and even to all creation.

This powerful word of peace is God's ultimate word, which concludes the worship service of many congregations. Within the literary context of the book of Numbers, the word of peace and blessing is also a word spoken at the end of the life of the old wilderness generation in Numbers 22—24, where God turns a curse into a blessing. Moreover, the concluding chapters about the new generation in Numbers 26—36 are filled with positive words of hopeful anticipation for the entry into the promised land.

The book of Genesis ends with Jacob's last words to his twelve sons couched in the form of a blessing (Genesis 49). Moses' last words to Israel at the end of his life and at the end of Deuteronomy are extended words of blessing for the twelve tribes of Israel (Deuteronomy 33). Most of the major prophetic books of the Old Testament end with words of promise and blessing in spite of earlier words of judgment. Whether in the congregational practice of worship or in the literary shape of Numbers or in God's ultimate will for God's people throughout the biblical story, the word of blessing and hope is God's final word. The provisions for the priestly blessing of the community round out this section of Numbers with its obedient concern for the holiness of the camp and the enjoyment of God's blessing in Israel's midst. The Israelites bear the name of God as a community with God's presence in its midst, a presence and a name whose ultimate will is peace, mercy, and blessing (Num. 6:27).

43

Numbers 7—8
The Ministry of Stewardship:
The Offerings of Possessions and People
in Service to the Worship of God

The dating formula which begins Numbers 7:1 introduces a narrative flashback to a time one month in the past. Numbers 7:1 turns the clock back to "the day when Moses had finished setting up the tabernacle, and had anointed and consecrated it." The anointing of the altar and the consecration of the priesthood had taken place back in Leviticus 8, and the tabernacle had been completed already in Exodus 40 "in the *first* month in the second year, on the first day of the month" since leaving Egypt (Exod. 40:17, emphasis added). The first chapter of Numbers had begun one month later, "on the first day of the *second* month, in the second year after they had come out of the land of Egypt" (Num. 1:1). The flashback to a month earlier (in 7:1) continues until 10:11, where we return again to the point at which Num. 1:1 began—"the second year, in the second month."

Most scholars see this section in Numbers 7—10 as a late editorial addition of a miscellaneous collection of material. But the narrative effect of this flashback is to rehearse the careful preparations that all the tribes of Israel have obediently made in regard to the tabernacle, its personnel, and other cultic matters. The flashback forces the reader to slow down, to wade through the repetitive lists of tribes and their offerings, to sit through the consecration of the Levites, to take time to celebrate the second Passover, and to prepare the lampstand and silver trumpets. We may want to get on with the journey to the promised land. But this attention to matters of the sanctuary, priests, Levites, and the worship life of the people reminds the reader that Israel's hope and trust is properly centered on God's presence in their midst.

An apt analogy might be to think of a congregation as it plans its future mission and budget. Some members press for money-saving efficiency, time management, quick results, business tactics, and programmatic gimmicks that bolster this month's bottom line—a bottom line defined by dollars, new members, number of pastoral visits, or other quantifiable evidence of progress on the journey. While such issues may have a role to play in a church's life, ministry derives its long-term power and health from primary attention to the vibrant teaching and preaching of God's word, the administration of the sacraments, and the active ministry of love and service through the daily lives and vocations of church members. It may be difficult to quantify progress resulting from sustained Bible study or faithful preaching or regular participation in the Lord's Supper. But the careful attention to matters of worship and God's presence and power in the book of Numbers reminds us of the need to keep our focus on that which gives long-term life and strength to a community of faith: Scripture, worship, prayer, fellowship, service, and the profound sense of the presence of God at work in the heart of the community.

Numbers 7 continues the depiction of Israel as an obedient people in thankful response to the gracious sign of God's presence in their midst in the tabernacle, its priests, and its worship life. Numbers 7:1–9 records the one-time gift of six covered wagons and twelve oxen given by the leaders of all twelve tribes to the three clans of the Levites—the Merarites, the Gershonites, and the Kohathites. In chapter 4, the Merarites were assigned the larger bases and frames on which the tabernacle stood; chapter 7 reports that they receive four of the wagons to transport this bulky material. The Gershonites carried the curtains and other outer trappings of the tabernacle, so they receive two of the wagons. Since the Kohathites took care of the most holy objects, they had to carry them carefully by hand on their shoulders, so they receive no wagons. Each group is given in proportion to its needs and tasks.

Numbers 7:10–88 presents a lengthy narrative of a twelve-day ceremony in which the twelve tribal leaders present offerings for the dedication of the altar. The intention is to supply all the sanctuary's needs in the course of a twelve-day festival. Over the course of the twelve days, each tribe has a day to present its offering. The sequence of the tribes as they offer their gifts follows the sequence of the camp established in Numbers 2, beginning with Judah and continuing through all twelve tribes.

The striking part of this ceremony of tribal gifts is that the contents of the offering are enumerated in meticulous detail, yet the offerings for each tribe are exactly the same each time! There is absolutely no deviation in the long list of offerings made by every tribe: a silver plate and basin with oil and flour, a gold dish with incense, a bull, a ram, a lamb, a goat, two oxen, five rams, another goat, and five more lambs. The narrator could have listed what the first tribe gave and then just told us that the other tribes brought the same. But the text wants to give equal recognition to each of the tribes. Every tribe is equidistant from the tabernacle in the center of the camp. Every tribe contributes

45

exactly the same offering to the tabernacle. No tribe has any more claim to the divine center of power than any other.

This affirmation of tribal equality is a powerful claim made by what seems to be a monotonous catalog of the twelve-tribe gift list. Israel's history had been peppered by tribal jealousies and struggles, having already begun in Genesis with the sons of Jacob hating their brother Joseph. But the battles among the twelve tribes had erupted into far more than mere family feuds. Judah and Ephraim became separate nations, sometimes at war with one another (e.g., Isaiah 7). After the return from exile in Babylon, there were fierce struggles among groups within Israel over which group had the right of leadership in Jerusalem and at the temple (Isaiah 66; Mal. 1:6–14).

The book of Ezra recounts the rebuilding of the Jerusalem temple and includes material similar to these opening chapters of Numbers: census lists of clans and priestly families returned from exile (Ezra 2); rebuilding and dedication of the central place of worship, the temple in Jerusalem (Ezra 3—6); celebration of Passover (Ezra 6:19–22); a list of tribal or family leaders and of Levites (Ezra 8); and a list of gifts for the temple (Ezra 8:24–30). Written in the same postexilic time frame as Ezra, Nehemiah 4 recounts the hatred between the returned exiles in southern Judah and the Samaritans who had roots in the old northern tribe and nation of Ephraim. Mary Douglas argues that the book of Numbers is aimed at this particular postexilic period in Israel's history. The priests who wrote the book of Numbers, she argues, are writing a critique of the exclusivity of the Ezra/Nehemiah separatist program, which favored returned exiles and people from Judah over other groups who had roots in the northern tribes (Douglas, pp. 35–41). Douglas is right to note the concern of Numbers to include all the tribes of Israel at every stage. As we move through the book, we will see that all the tribes are implicated not only in the positive acts of obedience at the beginning of Numbers but also in the rebellions that come later. In the end, no single tribe escapes responsibility for rebellion and disobedience. But it is likely that this more inclusive vision in Numbers that mourns the separation of northern Ephraim and southern Judah had a longer history than just the period of Ezra and Nehemiah. The vision of tribal equality may have had a particular intensity around the building of the Jerusalem temple and the leadership of its worship in the postexilic period, but the yearning for reconciliation among the Israelite tribes was a longstanding tradition.

46   Numbers 7:89 concludes the chapter with a brief note about Moses and the voice of God. Now that the sanctuary has been stocked and the tabernacle and altar consecrated, God regularly speaks to

Moses from within the tent of meeting or tabernacle. God's voice comes "from above the mercy seat that was on the ark of the covenant from between the two cherubim." The cherubim—or cherubs—are not the chubby little winged children depicted in traditional Christian art. The cherubim are hybrid animals with wings, often associated in the ancient Near East with the presence of God; the cherubim in the tabernacle are carved figures that are part of the golden cover of the sacred ark of the covenant (Exod. 25:17–22). In the Jerusalem temple, which in many ways mirrors the tabernacle of the wilderness, God's presence is understood as invisible but enthroned upon the golden cherubim. The ark of the covenant is the footstool of God (Ps. 99; II Kings 19:15).

Numbers 7:89 provides the assurance that Moses will continue to receive new insights and commands from God. The voice of God is not seen, but it is heard. The divine voice is localized in a special place of worship from which God has promised to speak. The sanctuary becomes a place not just for ritual maintenance of the status quo, but a special locus for the voice of God to carry on a living dialogue with Moses and the people of God. Just as the tabernacle is mobile and moves into new territories and situations on its wilderness journey, so God's voice guides Moses when new questions arise and new circumstances emerge (e.g., Num. 11:16–30; 27:1–11). When King David offered to build God a permanent temple to house the tabernacle, God was reluctant and seemed to prefer the freedom and mobility of the desert tent of meeting (II Samuel 7). David's son, Solomon, built the temple in Jerusalem, but it came to be destroyed and then rebuilt and destroyed again. God's presence resisted being captured in one permanent house, retaining its divine freedom and portability to move with the vagaries of history and the actions of God's people.

The meticulous obedience of the people in Numbers 7 is followed by evidence of the obedience of Aaron and the Levites in chapter 8. In 8:1–4, God commands Aaron to light the seven lamps in the sanctuary and to ensure that the light beams forward in front of the lampstand. The tabernacle lampstand was golden, had three pairs of branches, and elaborate floral decorations (Exod. 25:31–40; 37:17–24). The lamp's branches and floral designs are suggestive of the sacred tree that symbolizes fertility and life in the ancient Near East. The lampstand expresses visibly the life-giving power and light of God's unseen presence in the midst of the community.

The lampstand tradition continued in somewhat modified form in Solomon's Temple in Jerusalem where ten golden lampstands stood (I Kings. 7:49). After the temple was destroyed and then rebuilt in the

47

sixth century B.C.E., those who furnished the new temple apparently went back to the old tabernacle tradition of a single golden lampstand with an olive tree motif (as revealed in Zechariah's temple vision in Zech. 4:1–6, 11–14). This branched lampstand—or menorah—became an important symbol in the celebration of the Jewish festival of Hannukah, alternately called the Festival of Dedication or the Festival of Lights, and typically celebrated in early or mid-December. This festival recalls the purification and dedication of the Jerusalem temple after being desecrated by pagans and then recaptured by the Jewish Maccabees, as recounted in the deuterocanonical book of II Maccabees. The apocalyptic book of Revelation, with its vision of the heavenly temple and the cosmic struggles between the saints and enemies of God (Rev. 11:14), continues the tradition of the lampstand and tree branches into the New Testament.

Numbers 8:1–4 notes God's command for Aaron to light the seven lamps in the sanctuary. Verse 3 states that Aaron did exactly as God commanded; verse 4 again emphasizes Aaron's careful conformity to God's instructions for constructing the lampstand. Both of these reports about the positioning and the construction of the lamp fulfill commands given earlier in Exod. 25:31–36 (instructions for construction) and Exod. 25:37 (instructions for positioning the lamp). It is as if the writer has a list of the commands made in Exodus and is checking them off to assure the reader that the instructions are being fulfilled. The same is true of Num. 7:89 concerning the voice of God speaking from above the mercy seat between the cherubim; God promises Moses in Exod. 25:22 that this is where God will be, but it is not until Num. 7:89 that the promise is actually fulfilled. Israel seems to be keeping its side of the covenant, and God is fulfilling the promises that the divine presence and guiding voice will be in the midst of the camp. It seems all is well.

The next section, Num. 8:5–26, describes the purification and dedication ceremony for the Levites. Chapters 3, 4, and 7 described the census of the Levites, their duties in tending and carrying the tabernacle and its furnishings, and the gift of oxen and wagons for transporting the tabernacle. All that is now required is the Levites' official purification and dedication to their tasks. The ceremony is a sign that another milestone has been passed on the way toward the actual inauguration of the march of the holy camp of Israel.

The Levites' ceremony involves a two-step process. First, their bodies go through a ritual of purification (8:5–7). The ritual includes shaving hair, washing the body, laundering clothes, and being sprinkled with the "water of purification" (perhaps the special mixture of purifying water from chapter 19). These purifying rites are associated elsewhere in the Bible with cleansing contamination from a person. Leviticus 14:8–9 prescribes the actions of shaving, body washing, and clothes washing after one is declared clean from skin disease. Numbers 19 commands clothes and body washing after contact with a dead body. The Nazirite has to shave his head after contact with a corpse and at the termination of his Nazirite vow (Num. 6:9). Similarly, attention to ritual purification is essential for the Levites. They provide a buffer zone of holiness between God's presence in the tabernacle and the rest of the Israelite tribes, and they carry the tabernacle when Israel is on the march.

The second step in the purification and dedication ceremony is the presentation of the Levites before the tabernacle by Aaron (8:8–19). In this part of the ceremony, the Levites are presented as a living sacrifice made on behalf of the whole people of Israel. The scene is dramatic and carefully structured. Aaron is the priest who officiates at the sacrifice. All the Israelites surround the Levites and lay their hands upon them. The Levites in turn lay their hands upon the bulls, which are then sacrificed. The ritual's meaning is clear. The Levites in their service to Aaron and the priests are thereby dedicated to God as a living sacrifice. They are the substitute for all the firstborn of Israel who rightfully belong to God, a principle established when God struck down all the firstborn in Egypt during the last plague of the exodus (8:14–19). By their dedication to God, the Levites make atonement for Israel's firstborn "in order that there be no plague among the Israelites for coming too close to the sanctuary" (8:19).

The model of the living sacrifice of the Levites surely provides some of the background to the apostle Paul's exhortation in Romans 12:1–2:

> I appeal to you therefore, brothers and sisters, by the mercies of God, to present your bodies as a living sacrifice, holy and acceptable to God, which is your spiritual worship.

Paul continues by urging everyone in the community not to think more highly of themselves than they ought to think. He then applies the model of a body to the Christian community, a model that also fits with the picture of Israel as a camp with priests, Levites, and twelve tribes in various positions around the tabernacle, each providing the different services and gifts necessary for the community:

> For as in one body we have many members, and not all the members have the same function, so we, who are many, are one body in Christ, and individually we are members one of another. (Rom. 12:4–5)

49

Like the camp in the wilderness, the church in the world is supported and sustained by God's gifts provided through the varied ministries and gifts of all its members.

In line with the whole tone of the flashback in Numbers 7—10, the commands for the dedication ceremony for the Levites are spelled out in 8:5–19, then we are told that Moses and Aaron and all Israel "did with the Levites just as the LORD had commanded Moses concerning them" (8:20). The assurance that every instruction was obeyed is reiterated again in 8:22. The chapter concludes with the age requirements for the Levites' service in the tent of meeting. They are to begin at twenty-five and retire at fifty years of age (8:23–25). Numbers 4:47 had set a different age range for the Levites—from thirty to fifty years of age. There is no obvious reason for the discrepancy, other than a difference of traditions at various times in Israel's history.

One final statement in Num. 8:26 stresses the distinction between the Levites, who "assist" their brothers, and the full priests, who are Aaron and his sons. The Levites themselves "shall perform no service" in terms of actual sacrifice and worship in the tabernacle (Num. 8:26). The Levites' dedication ceremony has some similarities to the priestly ordination service in Leviticus 8—9, with the ritual cleansing and offerings. But there the priests were anointed with blood and oil, dressed in special priestly garments, and they underwent more elaborate rituals than the Levites. The Levites, at least in the view of the tradition represented in Numbers, are servants to the priests, not full priests themselves. Each group has its important role, one no less important than another. But strict boundaries maintain the order of the camp so that the powerful holiness and blessing of God is carefully mediated through the priests, assisted by the Levites, to the whole community.

Numbers 9—10

A Second Passover and a New Beginning:
The Inauguration of the March
of the Holy Camp of Israel

The Second Passover (9:1–14)

50

Numbers 9—10 continues the flashback sequence of scenes begun in chapter 7. Numbers 7 had portrayed the obedience of all twelve tribes in bringing gifts to the tabernacle. Numbers 8 affirmed the obedience of the priests and Levites. Now in Numbers 9 we return again to the obedience of the people as a whole. That obedience is expressed in the celebration of the most important festival in Israel, the Passover. As in the two preceding chapters, the account in Numbers 9 is a direct fulfillment of a divine command first proclaimed in the book of Exodus, in which instructions for the Passover are given: "You shall observe this rite as a perpetual ordinance for you and your children" (Exod. 12:24).

The first Passover, in Exodus 12, had been the prelude to a new beginning in the exodus out of Egypt. The last of the ten plagues killed all the firstborn of Egypt but passed over the houses of the Israelites whose doorposts were marked with the blood of the passover lamb. This last plague finally convinced the Egyptian Pharaoh to set Israel free from its slavery. As a result, a new chapter began in Israel's life as the people of God. This second Passover in Numbers 9 signals the reconstitution of Israel after the golden calf debacle has endangered Israel's status as God's holy people. This second Passover in Numbers marks as radical a new beginning as did the first Passover in Exodus. Numbers 9:4–5 echoes the recurring theme of the opening chapters of the book: the people of Israel dutifully comply with every command that God speaks to them through Moses.

The subject of the Passover provides an occasion for a new legal decision regarding persons unable to observe the festival at the appointed time. These discussions between God and Moses presumably occur in the tabernacle, according to Num. 7:89. Two problematic situations are raised. What if someone comes in contact with the dead and is thereby rendered ritually unclean or impure? Is the Passover of such importance that the unclean person should still observe the festival on the appointed day—the fourteenth day of the first month (vv. 6–7)? And what if someone is traveling on a journey during the appointed time for the Passover (v. 10)? God decrees that a special supplemental Passover on the fourteenth day of the *second* month should be held for those not able to celebrate on the normal date of the fourteenth day of the *first* month (vv. 9–11). This concession should not, however, be seen as a license for laxity in observing the Passover (v. 13). Indeed, the Passover is so significant that even foreigners who live among the Israelites should celebrate it (v. 14).

Some scholars argue that the two dates for the Passover, one in the first month of the year and the other in the second, represent two different traditions in Israel's history, one from northern Israel or Ephraim and the other from the southern kingdom of Judah. The story of Hezekiah's Passover in II Chron. 30:1–3 may carry a hint of these divergent traditions. In any case, the two traditions have now been merged and reshaped to emphasize the significance of Passover and Israel's careful observance of it in obedience to God's command. This Passover tradition is one that all Israel shares together.

The New Testament Gospels portray Jesus as instituting the Lord's Supper at a Passover meal on the night before his trial and death on the cross: "On the first day of Unleavened Bread, when the Passover lamb is sacrificed . . ." (Mark 14:12). Just as the two Passover meals in Exodus and Numbers mark the eve of a new chapter in God's relationship to Israel, the Passover meal that Jesus celebrates with the disciples is the eve of God's new act of salvation in and through Jesus' death and crucifixion. In John's Gospel, John the Baptist declares Jesus to be "the Lamb of God, who takes away the sin of the world" (John 1:29, 35). I Peter 1:18–19 speaks of "the precious blood of Christ, like that of a lamb without defect or blemish."

The law concerning the eating of the Passover lamb in Numbers 9:11–12 instructs the celebrants to eat the lamb with unleavened bread and bitter herbs. The bread contains no yeast and is unleavened, since the Israelites could not wait for the bread to rise as they hurried to flee from Egypt. The bitter herb (e.g., horseradish) was a strong reminder of the bitterness of the slavery that Israel endured in Egypt. Numbers 9:12 recalls one other instruction concerning the roasted lamb of the Passover: "They shall leave none of it until morning, nor break a bone of it." John's Gospel account of Jesus' death on the cross includes a scene that cites this verse from Numbers 9. There is a concern that the dead bodies of the three people crucified (Jesus and the two robbers) be taken down from their crosses before the sabbath begins at sundown on Friday. Permission is therefore granted to break the legs of the three men to hasten their death. But when the soldiers come to Jesus, they see that Jesus is already dead and thus do not break his legs (John 19:31–33). John's Gospel then quotes Num. 9:12: "These things occurred so that the scripture might be fulfilled, 'None of his bones shall be broken'" (John 19:36). Here the Gospel writer again draws upon all the richness of meaning and imagery associated with the Old Testament Passover as a significant marker of transitions and new beginnings in God's journey with Israel as the people of God.

The Cloud of God's Presence in the Midst of the Camp (9:15–23)

This section continues the theme of Israel's obedient following and is a sign that the actual march from Sinai to Canaan is about to begin. The picture of God's presence veiled in a cloud and its association with the tent of meeting here in Numbers is a reshaping of the traditions found in Exodus. In Exod. 13:21–22, the cloud is shaped like a pillar that moves in front of the people and guides them in the flight from Egypt after the celebration of the first Passover. Just as the cloud marks a new chapter in Israel's life in the exodus, so too the appearance of the cloud motif after the second Passover in Numbers 9 marks a new and pivotal transition in the life of Israel. The march toward the promised land of Canaan after the reorganization of the holy camp is about to begin.

The cloud in Num. 9:15–23, however, does not go in front of the people as it did in Exod. 13:21–22. Rather, in line with Exod. 33:7–11, the cloud of God's presence is now closely tied to the tent of meeting or tabernacle. In Exod. 33:7–11, the tent of meeting was outside the camp because of the sin of the golden calf that had rendered the community unclean. But now Israel has been granted a second chance and elaborate provisions have been made throughout Leviticus and Numbers that allow the tent of meeting and the cloud of God's presence to stand in the middle of the camp.

The central theme of this section and of all the opening chapters of Numbers is sounded in a refrain repeated three times (vv. 18, 20, and 21): "At the command of the LORD the Israelites would set out, and at the command of the LORD they would camp." These and other verses in this section contain a chorus of affirmations of Israel's diligent obedience in following God's instructions.

Blowing the Silver Trumpets: The March Is About to Begin (10:1–10)

The image of the cloud and God's leading of the people in Numbers 9 is complemented by the leadership and guidance provided by the sons of Aaron through the blowing of the silver trumpets. Numbers 10:2 suggests two functions for the trumpets. One is to summon the congregation to a gathering. When both trumpets are blown, the whole congregation is to assemble around the tabernacle in the middle of the

53

camp (v. 3). When only one trumpet is blown, only the leaders are to gather (v. 4). (A provision that may have been added secondarily establishes the procedure for gathering the people together when they are settled in the promised land (vv. 9–10). A special alarm signal will call the people together at times of war. The trumpets will also summon the people at more joyous times of religious festivals, as a remembrance of God's faithfulness.) This first function of the trumpets associated with life in the promised land lifts our attention for a moment to the distant goal toward which all these preparations for the march through the wilderness point—settlement and life in the land of Canaan.

The second function of the blowing of the trumpets turns the reader's focus back to the immediate context. The trumpets are a signal for breaking camp and beginning the march. The brassy sound of the trumpets gives notice to the twelve tribes to move out according to the order assigned in the arrangement of the camp in Numbers 2 (10:5–6). This second function raises our anticipation for the long-awaited march that is set to begin immediately in Num. 10:11.

The trumpet's call to gather the people of God and to announce a new beginning continues throughout much of the Old Testament and into the New Testament. The trumpets are mentioned only one more time, in Num. 31:6, where they sound the alarm for holy war against the Midianites. In Chronicles, priests blow the trumpets during processions of the ark, at the dedication of Solomon's temple, as an alarm to call people to war, and at the restoration of worship at the temple after the reforms of King Hezekiah (I Chronicles 15—16; II Chronicles 13, 15, 29). The trumpet call becomes especially prominent in apocalyptic literature, in which the trumpet calls together the elect, announces the beginning of a new age, and signals the beginning of the cosmic battle between God and God's enemies. For instance, in Zech. 9:14, God sounds the trumpet and begins the march to fight the enemies of God's people. Matthew 24 speaks in an apocalyptic context of the Son of man gathering the community of the elect: "And he will send out his angels with a loud trumpet call, and they will gather the elect from the four winds, from one end of heaven to the other" (Matt. 24:31). The apostle Paul describes the day when God will raise the dead with the final trumpet call:

> We will not all die, but we will all be changed, in a moment, in the twinkling of an eye, at the last trumpet. For the trumpet will sound, and the dead will be raised imperishable, and we will be changed. (I Cor. 15:51–52)

The seven angels of the apocalyptic vision of the book of Revelation blow seven trumpets that signal seven assaults or judgments against the enemies of God (Revelation 8—9). Similarly, the trumpets blowing in the holy camp of Israel in the wilderness becomes a prototype for Israel's worship in the Jerusalem Temple and for the gathered community of the new age on whose side God fights apocalyptic conflicts with evil, death, and all forces that oppose the life-giving will of God.

The Actual Inauguration of the March of the Holy Camp of Israel (10:11–36)

At long last, the camp of the twelve tribes of Israel with God's presence in its midst begins its climactic march from the wilderness of Sinai toward the promised land. The preparations for the march that preserve the holiness and purity of the camp have been elaborately and painstakingly carried out. The plodding and repetitive style of the narrative in Numbers thus far has created in the reader a sense of impatience and anxious anticipation. Now finally the twelve-tribe camp picks up and moves. "They set out for the first time at the command of the LORD by Moses" (10:13).

The flashback to a month before the beginning of the book of Numbers had begun in Numbers 7 and continued through Num. 10: 10. Numbers 10:11 resumes the chronological sequence and story line of Num. 1:1. According to 10:11, the tribes set out nineteen days after the day the census was taken (Num. 1:1) and eleven months after arriving at Mount Sinai (Exod. 19:1). Numbers 10:14–28 recounts in some detail how the tribes start out the wilderness trek precisely in the order laid out in chapter 2. Moreover, the Levites obediently carry out their tasks of taking down the tabernacle and transporting it in accordance with the instructions in chapter 3.

Numbers 10:29–32 is usually thought to be a much older narrative tradition than the material in the previous chapters. The Hebrew text in verse 29 suggests either that Hobab is the "father-in-law" of Moses, or that Hobab is the son of the "father-in-law" of Moses named Reuel. Reuel is named as the father-in-law of Moses in Exod. 2:18, but Hobab is called Moses' father-in-law in Judg. 4:11. Apart from the ambiguity of verse 29 itself, another difficulty arises, since the name of Moses' father-in-law in Exod. 3:1 and 18:1 is neither Reuel nor Hobab but Jethro. Did Moses have more than one wife and thus more than one father-in-law? Is Hobab simply an alternate name for Jethro from a

55

different tradition? Or does the Hebrew term for "father-in-law" have a wider range of meaning, such as "any relative by marriage"? The correct explanation is difficult to decide. In any case, Moses asks Hobab to be a guide for Israel. Since Hobab belongs to the desert tribe of the Midianites, he is apparently well-acquainted with the desert and can offer expertise in charting the way Israel should travel. Initially, Hobab refuses to go along with Moses and the Israelites. Moses is known as one who will not easily take "no" for an answer, even from God (Exod. 32:10–14; 33:17)! Thus, Moses insists that Hobab go with them, and Moses promises that God will be gracious to him, a foreigner, as God will be to Israel (vv. 30–32). Hobab's response is apparently positive, although it is not explicitly recorded here. The book of Judges twice mentions descendants of Hobab living with the Israelites in the land of Canaan (Judg. 1:16; 4:11).

The mention of a human guide, Hobab, is balanced in the verses that follow by a reaffirmation of the role of the ark of the covenant (Num. 10:33) and the cloud (v. 34) as instruments of divine guidance for Israel's journey. The cloud of God's presence and the priest's trumpets are paired as complementary divine and human signs to set up or break down the camp (9:17; 10:2). In a parallel way, the human guide who is a foreigner and the divine presence in the cloud and ark are paired as complementary sources of guidance and direction for the people. A subtle interaction exists here between the divine and human. Moreover, Numbers exhibits an openness to wisdom and guidance from those who come from outside Israel.

At least one scholar has argued that Moses' turning to Hobab the Midianite for guidance is an act of unfaith and rebellion against God's guidance through the ark and cloud. But there is no hint that what Moses does here is wrong, and the tenor of this whole section in Numbers is one of uninterrupted obedience by all Israel, including Moses. The welcoming of Hobab's voice and wisdom into Israel's community suggests the need for God's people to be open to hear and learn from voices that may not be part of their fellowship. Certainly God's people derive primary guidance from the voice of God present in their midst. But in order to hear the full wisdom that God has built into all creation (Prov. 8:22–36), we need to listen to the voices of others—strangers, outsiders, and those on the fringes of our community. The book of Numbers wrestles in many of its stories with discerning truth and falsehood, wisdom and folly. Sometimes an internal voice from within the Israelite community, like Korah the Levite, speaks a rebellious word that misleads (Numbers 16). Sometimes a foreigner like Hobab the Midianite or Balaam the pagan seer (Numbers 22—24) can speak the truth and offer genuine words from God. Yet sometimes the words and actions of foreigners and outsiders lead Israel astray. Numbers 25 recounts how Hobab's fellow Midianites entice Israel into idolatry and lead them into death and destruction. Balaam, who blessed Israel in Numbers 22—24, is also named as the one responsible for urging the Midianites to lead Israel into apostasy (Num. 31:8, 16). Thus, every word and every voice must be tested, and discernment must be exercised. But God's people need to be attentive to the dialogue with outsiders and strangers, for wisdom and guidance can be found there as well.

The implications of this welcoming of the wisdom of an outsider in the book of Numbers are important for contemporary church life and our Christian faith. They open the door and encourage ecumenical and interfaith dialogues and cooperation. The best wisdom of science and the humanities may be accepted and applied, when appropriate, to our understanding of the world, of human beings, of the Bible, and of God. Voices of groups who have been marginalized in our society or the church (e.g., the poor, women, racial minorities, children) must be heard if we want to hear the full voice of God in our world. We must be open to being changed by the encounter with the other in whatever form it may take. Israel's journey through the wilderness surely took different turns and had a different shape because of the wisdom of Hobab's guidance. Our journeys with the stranger may take us to places and ways of seeing the world we would never have imagined.

In Luke 24, the journey of two disciples on the road to Emmaus turned their world upside down when they met a stranger. This stranger walked with the disciples and guided them through the Scriptures. When the stranger left, the disciples finally realized that he had been Jesus. The one whom the disciples had seen killed on a cross was alive in their midst (Luke 24:13–35). Their world would never be the same because they had carried on a dialogue with the voice of this stranger on the road. Hobab, Balaam, the stranger on the Emmaus road—such stories remind us of the importance of seeking out the voices and the wisdom of strangers along with the guidance God provides through our own communities and traditions.

Numbers 10 concludes with two brief portions of poetry, one offered when the ark sets out with the camp and the other spoken when the ark comes to rest. The poetic lines in 10:35 underline the function of the divine presence over the ark as a divine warrior leading Israel into battle. This ark tradition in a holy war context is well attested elsewhere in the Old Testament (Pss. 68:1; 132:8; I Sam. 4:1—7:2; II Sam. 6:1–19). These traditions often speak of God as "the LORD of hosts,"

57

that is, the leader of a heavenly army who fights alongside Israel and gives victory to Israel's human and earthly army. Without God's presence fighting with Israel, no victory is possible. The concluding words of Moses in verse 36 celebrate the return of the ark and "the ten thousand thousands of Israel" to the camp. This makes an appropriate inclusio for the section of Numbers 1—10 by recalling the many thousands of Israelites counted in the first census in Numbers 1. Both of these short poetic pieces are regarded as ancient poetic texts with an almost liturgical flavor. They reinforce the impression of the inauguration of the march as a liturgical procession of God's holy and obedient people through the wilderness, with the divine warrior in its midst.

The sense we have gained, throughout these first ten chapters of Numbers, of Israel as a totally obedient people is about to be abruptly and surprisingly shattered. The reader of Numbers 1—10 has been lulled into a false sense of complacency about Israel's ability to do all that God commands. These opening chapters of Numbers are filled with words of dutiful obedience. The almost unreal and idealistic picture of Israel drawn here may tempt us to put the book down or skip over the rest, since we think we know where all this is going. God gives a command, and the people obey it. Over and over again. There has been virtually no forward movement of plot, only a momentary sliding back into the flashback of Numbers 7—10. The narrative seems so monologic, so predictable, so unlike our turbulent world of conflict and struggle.

But there has been another voice, another subplot seething under the calm surface of a wonderfully obedient and confident Israel. Sprinkled among all the command and fulfillment assurances have been subtle but ominous glimpses into a divine danger and power that lies just below the surface. Brief warnings about the possibility of death are tucked here and there throughout the laws and narratives. Anyone who comes near the tabernacle shall be put to death (3:10). Remember what happened to Nadab and Abihu, the priestly sons of Aaron, when they died before the Lord while offering illicit fire at the altar (3:4). The Kohathites, the Levites responsible for the holiest items of the tabernacle, must not touch the holy things or they will die (4:15). Moses warns the Israelites that they must not let the whole clan of the Kohathites be destroyed (4:18). The Levites exist as protection around the tabernacle "in order that there may be no plague among the Israelites for coming too close to the sanctuary" (8:19). Do we really have to worry about these things? Everything seems to be going so smoothly. Then the Kohathites are warned not even to *look* at the holy things or they will die (4:20). What is so hazardous and powerful that one cannot even look at it? Then we trip over those references about becoming unclean through contact with dead bodies. Everyone who has touched a corpse is expelled from the camp (5:2). Nazirites are enjoined not to get close to a dead person, not even their parents (6:6–7). A whole other Passover is offered for people who have become unclean by corpse contamination (9:6–11). Where are all these dead people? Are these laws anticipating something we as readers do not yet know about? Finally we hear of the Passover and are reminded of God's tragic killing of all the firstborn children of Egypt in a plague (8:17; 9:1–14).

Perhaps things are not as safe, predictable, and monotonous as they seemed at first. There is in fact a dialogue of two narrative voices in Numbers 1—10. One dominant voice speaks optimistically of repetitive compliance, calm order, and unquestioning faithfulness. The second narrative voice speaks in muted but foreboding tones of lurking powers, divine dangers, and deathly possibilities. This latter voice is all the more threatening because its source lies at the center of the camp of Israel, no longer at its edge at a safe distance outside the camp (cf. Exod. 33:7–11). The source is God's holy presence. Yet God's presence in Israel's midst is the expression of God's love and mercy, something that Moses negotiated hard to get. It was a hard bargain because God knew the potential risk of mixing divine holiness and human sin. A holy God is a fearful threat to a sinful people, but God's presence is Israel's only hope. With all the laws of Exodus and Leviticus and Numbers and all the careful boundaries and the arrangement of the camp with the Levites as a buffer zone, perhaps the tragedy of the golden calf can be prevented from ever happening again. The presence of God in the midst of Israel's camp is both a gracious glow of life-giving light and a powder keg threatening to go off at any moment. As we move into Numbers 11—20 and the next section of our commentary, we will see that the fuse is about to be lit.

II. An Abrupt Slide into Rebellion: The Death of the First Wilderness Generation Begins

NUMBERS 11—20

The abrupt shift from the picture of total obedience in Numbers 1—10 to the repeated rebellions beginning in chapter 11 represents an unanticipated turnabout in the flow of the story. Numbers 11:1 recounts the first complaint and rebellion by the people thus far in the book. It is a rebellion for which readers are unprepared. Such a dramatic shift from blissful obedience to the abrupt disintegration of relationships occurs elsewhere in the Pentateuch in only two other contexts. One is the sudden transition from Genesis 2 to Genesis 3. The paradise of the Garden of Eden in Genesis 2 is suddenly shattered by the tale of disobedience and death that begins with a dialogue between the woman and a snake in Gen. 3:1: "Now the serpent was more crafty than any other wild animal that the LORD God had made." Paradise is lost, never to be regained (Gen. 3:24). The second unanticipated shift from obedience to rebellion occurs between God's giving of the laws and covenant to Moses on Mount Sinai in Exodus 19—31 and the sudden fall of the Israelites into idolatry in the golden calf story of Exodus 32. In these two stories in Genesis and Exodus, the reader experiences the abrupt shift of tone in the narrative as a literary effect that mirrors the wrenching fracture in the relationship between God and God's people. The reader has a similar disorienting experience in moving from the obedience preceding Numbers 10:36 to the sudden succession of rebellions that begins in 11:1.

Throughout Numbers 11—20, God's people continually rebel, and God punishes Israel with plagues and military defeats. God offers signs of forgiveness and compassion, but the people in each case resume their rebellious ways. First, there is a general rebellion of the people in Numbers 11. Next, in Numbers 12, there is a rebellion for the first time in the wilderness by two leaders of the people, Aaron and Miriam. This is followed in Numbers 13—14 by the most serious revolt against God—in the spy mission into the promised land. The spy story defines the central theme and structure of the entire book of Numbers as the tale of the death of the old wilderness generation and the birth of the new generation of hope on the edge of the promised land. After a word of hope is offered in chapter 15, the people and even the Levites resume the cycle of revolts and disobedience. The spirit of rebellion and unfaithfulness extends even to Aaron and Moses in the narrative of chapter 20. The death of Aaron the priest and the succession of his son Eleazar as the new high priest in 20:22–29 is a precursor of the coming end of the entire first generation of Israelites who came out of Egypt and the dawning of a whole new generation of hope.

Numbers 11—12
The Spreading Rebellion against God:
From the Fringes to the People to the Leaders

Fire at the Fringes: The First Rebellion (11:1–3)

As we have noted, Numbers 11 marks a dramatic shift from the positive tone in chapter 10. There the people looked forward to the promised land and were assured of God's care and protection (10:29). Numbers 11:1–3 recounts the first instance of the people's discontent and complaining against God in the book thus far. The motif of the people's complaining to Moses and God in the wilderness is not new; a number of complaint or murmuring stories occur in the book of Exodus before the giving of the commandments and the covenant at Mount Sinai and before the golden calf story. The complaints that Israel makes to God in the book of Exodus are treated as legitimate needs: the people need water (Exod. 15:22–26), the people need food (Exod. 16), and the people again need water (Exod. 17:1–7). In each case, God takes the complaints seriously and fulfills the needs of the Israelites by turning bitter water into sweet water, by providing manna and quail for food, and by causing water to flow from a rock.

In the book of Numbers, however, the Israelites raise their voices in complaint about similar needs, but here things turn out differently. The complaints are treated as acts of faithlessness. The whining of the Israelites rouses God's anger and punishment, which is mitigated only by Moses' aggressive intercession. It is instructive to set the Exodus material up to the Sinai covenant in chapters 15—19 next to the

61

parallel Numbers material following Sinai in chapters 11—20 and to note the similarities, as well as the crucial differences. The two sets of pre-Sinai and post-Sinai texts may be sketched as follows:

Exodus—*Before Sinai*	Numbers—*After Sinai*
Miriam's song of praise—15:20–21	Miriam and Aaron rebel—12
complaint about water, bitter water made sweet, the LORD heals—15:22–26	unspecified complaint—angry fire of the LORD kills—11:1–3
manna/quail—16	manna/quail—11:4–15, 31–35
water from the rock—17:1–7	water from the rock—20:1–13
leaders appointed to ease Moses' burdens—18	leaders appointed to ease Moses' burdens—11:16–30
Israel attacks Amalek and is victorious—17:8–16	Israel attacks Amalek and is defeated—14:39–45

Other echoes between Exodus and Numbers include notations about a three-day journey toward Sinai (Exod. 15:22) and a three-day journey away from Sinai (Num. 10:33); advice from Moses' father-in-law Jethro (Exod. 18:1) and advice from Moses' father-in-law Hobab (Num. 10:29); and a note about a spring of water in Numbers 21:16–18, which may hearken back to the water miracle in Exodus 15:22–25.

Some scholars have attempted to sketch out precisely paired chiastic or other parallel structures between the Exodus and Numbers material (e.g., Schart, pp. 49–53). But the episodes are not rigidly paired; the two sets of texts are sometimes in different sequence and are interrupted by insertions of other material. Significant parallels do exist, however, and it is sufficiently instructive to note the correspondences and the key differences between Exodus and Numbers. If we move through the two columns of texts presented above, we observe that in each case the positive scenario in Exodus becomes an act of rebellion, failure, or defeat in Numbers. Miriam sings God's praise in Exodus, but she joins her brother Aaron in a rebellion in Numbers. Exodus 15:22–26 recounts God's gracious transformation of bitter water into sweet, drinkable water and God assures Israel that "I am the LORD who heals you" (Exod. 15:26). The image of sweet, cool water is countered in Num. 11:1–3 with an image of the LORD's hot anger at a place called "Burning" because "the fire of the LORD burned against" Israel. Manna and quail are gratefully received as divine gifts of food in Exodus 16. But in Numbers 11 the Israelites complain about the monotony of the manna (11:6), and the abundance of the quail makes the people deathly ill. The dead are buried in "Graves of Craving" (11:33–34). In Exodus 18 when Jethro counsels Moses to appoint additional leaders to assist him, Moses does not seem to realize there is any problem until Jethro tells him. In contrast, God's appointment of assistant leaders in Numbers 11:16–25 is made in response to Moses' desperate plea to God that the people "are too heavy for me." Moses begs God to "put me to death at once" (11:14–15). Finally, the Israelite victory over Amalek in Exod. 17:8–16 contrasts with the Israelite defeat at the hand of the Amalekites and Canaanites in Num. 14:39–45.

The contrasts between the parallel sets of narratives *before* Sinai in Exodus and *after* Sinai in Numbers raises obvious questions that beg to be answered. What has happened in the interim between Exodus 15—18 and the Numbers 11—20? What has caused this shift from divine accommodation in Exodus 15—18 to divine punishment of the complaining people in Numbers 10—20? What has happened between these two texts is that God has established the covenant with Israel at Mount Sinai. Before Sinai, Israel was like a newly adopted child who did not yet know the rules of the household. God, the divine Parent, bent over backwards to satisfy the legitimate needs of an Israel immediately out of Egypt. But by the time we reach Numbers, the people of Israel know their responsibilities in the law and the commandments. Israel must take responsibility and is answerable for its relationship to God. Moreover, Israel has already rejected God once in the dramatic golden calf story in Exodus 32; God nearly abandoned Israel then. God's powerful and holy presence in the midst of sinful Israel was a divine concession to Moses' urgent pleas (Exodus 32—34). But the holiness of God cannot tolerate unfaith and rebellion without deathly consequences for Israel as a people. Israel now knows the law and is accountable for it, beginning with the first and most important of the Ten Commandments: "You shall have no other gods before me."

Thus, the unspecified complaint in Num. 11:1–3 becomes a schematic summary of the basic outline of the complaint stories to follow. The people complain; God's anger is kindled; Moses intercedes; and the punishment is stopped. God's anger in Num. 11:1–3 is hot, and the punishment is in the form of fire that "the LORD burned against them" (11:1). But the fire consumes only some outlying parts of the camp. Before the divine fire spreads any further toward the center of the Israelite camp, Moses prays on behalf of the people and the fire diminishes. The name of the place is then called Taberah, which in Hebrew means "Burning." At this point in the narrative the reader may wonder whether this is only a minor and temporary setback, since the fire touches only the fringes of the community. Perhaps there will be a return to the monotone of commands and obedience that was the theme of Numbers 1—10. We do not have to wait long to find out that such an

63

optimistic scenario is not what is in store; we quickly arrive on the heels of yet another rebellion story in 11:4–35.

Food, Sharing Leadership, and the Graves of Craving: Another Rebellion (11:4–35)

This second rebellion story combines the motifs of provisions of quail and manna in Exodus 16 with the motif of Moses' need for additional leadership assistance in Exodus 18. In Exodus 16 and 18, the Israelites had just come as destitute slaves out of Egypt into the wilderness. God graciously provided manna and quail to the people because they had a legitimate need for food (Exod. 16:12). Moses seemed content and did not realize his own need for help in carrying out his leadership tasks until his father-in-law Jethro saw a problem and offered a solution (Exod. 18:13–27). But after Sinai and all the provisions God had given to the Israelites in the desert, the same needs and complaints arise, yet they take on a different complexion. Legitimate pleas for mercy become subversive acts of unfaith punishable by death.

Numbers 11:4 begins with a rabble or disorderly mob stirring up the people's desire for meat and other foods they had enjoyed in Egypt. This rabble or riffraff (Hebrew 'asafsuf) is a term that refers to the non-Israelites who joined Israel's flight out of Egypt; in Exod. 12:38 they are called "a mixed crowd" (cf. Lev. 24:10). One Jewish rabbinic interpretation links this non-Israelite fringe group with the preceding rebellion in Num. 11:1–3 in which God's fire burned only the outlying parts of the camp; it is this fringe group who is responsible for both rebellions. In the second rebellion about food, however, this non-Israelite fringe group succeeds in stirring up the Israelites themselves (11:4). Thus, the discontent of the community seems to be spreading from the margins in toward the center of the camp.

The quail provided in Exodus 16 had apparently been a one-time treat; it was manna that had become the stable diet for the forty years of the wilderness wandering (Exod. 16:35). The rabble recalls the fish, the cucumbers, the melons, the leeks, the onions, and the garlic that they had in Egypt. The list reflects a wide variety of foods: meat, vegetables, fruits, and spices, all the ingredients of an interesting and varied diet. But the manna provided sufficient if somewhat monotonous nutrition to sustain the people of Israel until they reached the promised land of Canaan. Once in Canaan they could eat the produce of the land, and the manna would cease (Josh. 5:12).

The manna was a basic, temporary food with which the Israelites

64

could make cakes; enough was provided with the morning dew to sustain the Israelites for that day and no more (Num. 11:9; cf. Exod. 16:13–30). The daily manna taught Israel to trust God to provide what was needed for one day at a time. The manna story lies behind the petition of the Lord's Prayer that Jesus taught to his disciples: "Give us each day our daily bread" (Matt. 6:9; Luke 11:3). The primary lesson that God sought to teach Israel through the daily manna (Exod. 16:4) is perhaps best summed up by the words of Jesus in Matt. 6:31–34:

> Therefore do not worry, saying, "What will we eat?" or "What will we drink?" or "What will we wear?" For it is the Gentiles who strive for all these things; and indeed your heavenly Father knows that you need all these things. But strive first for the kingdom of God and his righteousness, and all these things will be given to you as well. So do not worry about tomorrow, for tomorrow will bring worries of its own. Today's trouble is enough for today.

Israel understood the manna as a wondrous gift provided by God, a miraculous food from heaven. Researchers in modern times have suggested that perhaps the manna is actually to be identified with a natural substance eaten by people living in the desert in northern Arabia:

> There forms from the sap of the tamarisk tree a species of yellowish-white flake or ball, which results from the activity of a type of plant lice. . . . The insect punctures the fruit of the tree and excretes a substance from this juice. During the warmth of the day it melts, but it congeals when cold. It has a sweet taste. These pellets or cakes are gathered by the the natives in the early morning and, when cooked, provide a sort of bread. The food decays quickly and attracts ants. The annual crop in the Sinai Peninsula is exceedingly small and some years fails completely. (Kselman, p. 505)

Whether or not this sap from the tamarisk tree is the original source of the desert manna in Exodus and Numbers, the present form of the biblical text underscores the ultimate divine origin of the manna. Moreover, enough manna appears each day to satisfy the legitimate needs of the two million or so Israelites on their desert journey. The manna is surely a wondrous gift from God, regardless of its origin.

It is the refusal to be satisfied with the gifts God has given that leads the rabble to stir up a mood of disgruntled dissatisfaction among the Israelites (11:4–9). The disquiet among the people leads to both Moses and God becoming angry (11:10). Then in a rare act of complaint, Moses himself laments the burden of leadership that God has placed on his shoulders (11:11–15). The conversation between God and Moses that ensues is an ironic twist on the dialogue between God

65

and Moses surrounding the golden calf incident in Exodus 32—34. After the golden calf episode, God decided to abandon Israel and go off with Moses alone and make of him a great nation (Exod. 32:9–10). Moses changed God's mind, convincing God to let the people go to the promised land (Exod. 32:11–14). God agreed to allow the Israelites to go on to Canaan, but God refused to travel with the Israelites in their midst (Exod. 33:1–3). Again, Moses changes God's mind, this time by appealing to the personal relationship between Moses and God. Moses pleads with God:

> If your presence will not go, do not carry us up from here. For how shall it be known that I have found favor in your sight, I and your people, unless you go with us? In this way, we shall be distinct, I and your people, from every people on the face of the earth. (Exod. 33: 15–16)

God responds, "I will do the very thing that you have asked; for you have found favor in my sight, and I know you by name" (Exod. 33:17). Moses used the special intimacy of his relationship with God as a lever to keep himself, the Israelites, and God together and their relationship alive.

Now as we come to Numbers 11 and hear again Moses' appeal to the favor he has found in the sight of God, what Moses asks for is quite different. Moses complains to God about these whining Israelites, asking why God has treated him so badly: "Why have I not found favor in your sight, that you lay the burden of all the people on me" (11:11). Moses is exhausted and exasperated. In the Exodus dialogue with God, Moses always emphasized the intimate tie between himself and the people of Israel. Moses always ensured that the personal favor he had in God's eyes also extended to the people as a whole. But here in Numbers 11, Moses severs himself from the Israelites:

> Did I conceive all this people? Did I give birth to them, that you should say to me, "Carry them in your bosom, as a nurse carries a sucking child," to the land that you promised on oath to their ancestors? (11:12)

The female and maternal imagery is striking. The implication of Moses' words is that God is the mother who conceived and gave birth to Israel. God is the one who ought to take responsibility for carrying Israel as a wet nurse cares for a breast-feeding child. Such female imagery for God is unusual in the Old Testament, but it is not unique (Deut. 32:18; Isa. 42:14; 66:13).

66

Moses is unable to take the stress of leading this people and seeing to their needs as they cry for meat. Moses cries out, "I am not able to carry all this people alone, for they are too heavy for me." The problem is that Moses feels alone in his responsibility, which weighs heavy upon his shoulders. The stress leads him over the edge. Moses appeals to his special and intimate relationship to God so God will grant the favor of putting Moses to death, separating him from the Israelites and from God:

> If this is the way you are going to treat me, put me to death at once—if I have found favor in your sight—and do not let me see my misery. (Num. 11:15)

Moses' plea for his own death is a dramatic contrast to Exodus 32—34, in which Moses strove mightily to keep himself, Israel, and God alive and together.

God immediately responds to Moses by commanding him to gather seventy elders at the tent of meeting. There God will "take some of the spirit that is in you and put it on them"; the seventy elders will assist Moses in leadership "so that you will not bear it all by yourself" (11:17). Leaders and prophets often have a special spirit that sets them off as rulers or guides for the community (for example, the prophet Balaam in Num. 24:2–3; the leader Joshua in Num. 27:18; the judge Othniel in Judg. 3:10; the prophet Ezekiel in Ezek. 2:2). The tradition of seventy elders is found already in Exod. 24:1, where they join Moses on Mount Sinai. One rabbinic interpretation, troubled by this new appointment of seventy elders, concludes that the first group of seventy elders from Exodus was killed by divine fire in the first rebellion at Taberah in Num. 11:1–3. That left Moses to rule alone, and so God appointed a new group of elders. However, it is more likely that these stories are simply alternate traditions. The notion of a group of seventy elders continued in Judaism in the form of the seventy members of the Sanhedrin, the supreme judicial and religious body for Jewish life in Palestine during the time of imperial Roman rule. In the New Testament Gospel of Luke, Jesus sends out a group of seventy evangelists to assist him in his mission to preach and to heal (Luke 10:1–20).

In the case of Moses' complaint about the demands of leadership in Numbers 11, God accepted Moses' grievance as legitimate and produced a remedy. A similar scenario occurred early in Moses' career when he was first called to lead Israel out of Egypt. But God is not as gracious with the people's demand for meat and their yearning for Egypt as God was with Moses. God resolves to give the Israelites exactly what they have requested: meat, lots and lots of quail meat, not for a day or a week but for a whole month "until it comes out of your nostrils and becomes loathsome to you—because you have rejected the LORD who is among you" (11:19–20). Moses hears this divine announcement as one more impossible burden he must carry out: Where is Moses going to get a month's worth of meat for 600,000 warriors and their families? God rebukes Moses, "Is the LORD's power limited?" (11:25). The Hebrew is literally, "Is the LORD's hand too short?" Doesn't Moses know that God is able to fulfill all promises? God instructs Moses to wait and see. Let God be God. "Now you shall see whether my word will come true for you or not" (11:23).

God stops talking and begins to take action through the spirit of God. The Hebrew word for "spirit" also means "wind," and this dual meaning helps to bind together the two actions of God in verses 24–35. In the first action (vv. 24–30), God takes some of the spirit of Moses and places it upon the seventy elders. The elders stand at the tent of meeting in the holy center of the camp so that they may share the burden of the leadership of the twelve tribes. The seventy prophesy with words from God when the spirit first comes upon them, "but they did not do so again" (11:25). The elders' one-time ability to prophesy is in contrast to the unique prophetic role of Moses, who speaks directly with God in an ongoing way (cf. Num. 12:6–8).

As God gives the spirit to the seventy elders, some of the spirit apparently spills over onto two people who are still among the tents of the twelve tribes, not standing with the other elders at the tabernacle. Their names are Eldad and Medad, and they begin prophesying as messengers of God's word in the camp. Moses' assistant, Joshua, hears the prophesying and demands that Moses stop this runaway expression of God's spirit and claim to authority. But Moses assures Joshua that he welcomes the work and insights of God's spirit from among the people as well as the seventy leaders:

> Are you jealous for my sake? Would that all the LORD's people were prophets, and that the LORD would put his spirit on them!

The character of Moses' leadership is carefully drawn here. He welcomed assistance from the institutionally appointed seventy elders. But Moses also sought to share authority and receive wisdom from people of the spirit among those outside the institutional leadership of God's people. Prophetic voices throughout Israel's history spoke from outside the centers of power. Voices of the spirit regularly challenged kings, priests, judges, and others who misused their power and who led Israel to stray after gods and allegiances other than the true God of Israel. Prophets like Amos or Jeremiah spoke a true word of God from the margins of their societies. God's people need continually to be attentive to genuine voices of the spirit who speak God's words of judgment and hope, even though they may not be part of the established channels of institutional power.

In the second divine action (vv. 31–35), God sends forth a "wind" (same Hebrew word as "spirit" above). The wind of God brings enormous flocks of quail from the sea, and the birds fall to the ground all around the camp. The Israelites wade hip deep in dead birds and feathers, which spread out for miles and miles (a day's journey in any direction). The Israelites work for two days and nights greedily gathering as much quail meat as they can. They finally sit down to eat and anxiously anticipate the first taste of meat they have had in months. But while the meat is still between their teeth, God strikes the people with "a very great plague," killing the people who so hungered to eat the meat of quail. The place received the name Kibroth-hattaavah, "Graves of Craving," "because there they buried the people who had the craving" (11:34).

Numbers 1—10 was a narrative of total obedience and compliance. Numbers 11 introduces us to a brief rebellion that results in the angry fire of God, though just on the fringe of the community (11:1–3). Then a rabble of non-Israelites stirs up the people to desire meat, and God's judgment now infiltrates into the camp of the Israelites (11:4–34). But Moses has been given assistance from the seventy elders, and we think perhaps they will be able to help Moses keep the community on track and avoid any further rebellions. Or at least the rebellions will continue to be confined to the outer margins of the camp. That hope is soon dashed as we move to Numbers 12.

The Rebellions Spread to the Inner Circle:
The Jealousy of Miriam and Aaron (Numbers 12)

Thus far, only the people and not the leaders have joined in the rebellions. Numbers 12, however, introduces the complaint of Miriam and Aaron against Moses. Aaron is the high priest of Israel. Aaron, a brother to Moses, has been with Moses as a leader since Moses was first called to guide Israel out of Egypt (Exod. 4:14–17). We have heard less of Miriam, but she appeared earlier in key roles in the Exodus narrative. She is named a prophet and a sister of Aaron (and thus a sister to Moses) in Exod. 15:20–23. Miriam led the women of Israel in song and dance and the praise of God after the successful flight out of Egypt and the defeat of Pharaoh and his army (Exod. 15:20–21). Tradition also associates Miriam with the unnamed older sister of Moses who kept a

69

lookout as the infant Moses floated down the river in a basket. It was this sister of Moses who brought together Moses' mother and Pharaoh's daughter in a conspiracy to defy Pharaoh's order to kill all Israelite male babies (Exod. 2:1–10). Finally, Micah 6:4 lists all the gracious gifts which God gave Israel during its journey through the desert, including Israel's three leaders: "I sent before you Moses, Aaron, and Miriam." Thus, Miriam is a leader of the people, a prophet, a singer of the praise of God, a courageous savior of baby Moses, and a sister to both Aaron and Moses.

The preceding episode (11:26–30) had opened the door to the possibility of legitimate prophets and revelation outside the official or institutional leadership of the tribes. Eldad and Medad had prophesied in the camp, and Moses welcomed them as genuine channels of God's word. Numbers 12 wrestles with the limits of such revelation. The implicit question in chapter 12 is this: Can prophetic or any other revelation override Mosaic revelation? Is prophecy subordinate to the authority of Moses and the Mosaic tradition? Some scholars argue that behind this story lies a conflict between specific priestly or prophetic groups in Israel's history. The evidence for such clashes among groups is far from clear. The story in its present form treats the broader issue of the relationship of Mosaic tradition to prophecy in general.

The scene begins in Numbers 12 with Aaron and Miriam speaking against Moses "because of the Cushite woman whom he had married" (12:1). We know few details of Moses' married life. Moses had married Zipporah, a woman from the Midianites, a group of desert tribes located in the Syrian and Arabian deserts (Exod. 2:15–22). Moses had sent Zipporah away, but then her father Jethro had brought her back to Moses (Exod. 18:2). We hear of no other wives of Moses except for this reference in Numbers 12:1. Who is this Cushite woman? What is it about her that upsets Aaron and Miriam?

Several solutions have been offered. Some argue that Cush or Cushan is simply another name for Midian. Habakkuk 3:7 places Cushan and Midian in poetic parallelism, suggesting that they are the same region. If so, the Cushite woman is simply Zipporah, the Midianite wife. However, others argue that Cush is another nation either north and east of Israel (northern Syria) or south of Egypt in a region called Nubia or Ethiopia (Gen. 2:13; 10:6; II Kings. 19:9). The Septuagint, the Greek translation of the Old Testament, assumes that Moses' wife is Ethiopian. This possibility has led some scholars to wonder whether the blackness of her skin color was the issue in Miriam and Aaron's objection against the Cushite woman. If racial prejudice is at work in their attack on Moses' wife, then Miriam's skin turning white with skin disease may be seen as just punishment for her attack on the black skin color of Moses' wife. Against such claims, however, Cain Hope Felder has argued that racial prejudice against African people is more a modern European prejudice and ought not to be read into the biblical text here (Felder, chapter 3). Renita Weems agrees that the blackness of the Cushite's skin was not the primary issue. Rather, the real cause of the objection was a shift in the family relationships whereby the new wife of Moses and sister-in-law of Miriam and Aaron had more influence with Moses than his siblings (Weems, pp. 72–74).

The precise identity of Moses' Cushite wife and the nature of Miriam and Aaron's objection against her remain unclear. Whether their attack on Moses' wife is simply a smoke screen or whether it is related to the objection that follows, it is clear that the primary issue emerges in Numbers 12:2. There Miriam and Aaron ask, "Has the LORD spoken only through Moses? Has he not spoken through us also?" These two rhetorical questions challenge Moses' unique role as the supreme channel of God's word to the Israelites. Aaron and especially Miriam do have some legitimate claim to a prophetic role of mediator of God's word (Exod. 4:16; 15:20). But the narrator of the story immediately inserts a parenthetical note to the reader that Moses "was very humble, more so than anyone else on the face of the earth" (12:3). The word "humble" does not refer so much to a general personality trait of meekness as it underscores Moses' devotion or humility before God (Gray, p. 123; cf. Zeph. 2:3). The narrator's parenthetical comment instantly undercuts Miriam and Aaron's complaint and seeks to persuade the reader to stand with Moses in his defense against his siblings.

God also immediately appears in defense of Moses as God calls the three leaders to the tent of meeting for a consultation. In elevated poetic speech, God emphasizes the role of Moses as the unique and supreme vehicle of divine revelation. God does speak through other prophets, but only in the veiled form of visions and dreams (I Sam. 9:9; Deut. 13:7). Moses is different. Moses is God's servant, entrusted with all of God's house. God's words strain to describe the intense intimacy of God and Moses. God speaks with Moses "face to face" (literally in Hebrew, "mouth to mouth") and "clearly, not in riddles." Moses "beholds the form of the LORD" (12:6–8). Communication between God and Moses is clear, direct, and unmediated. Exodus 33:11 had earlier stated that "the LORD used to speak to Moses face to face, as one speaks to a friend." Deuteronomy 34:10 underlines the uniqueness of Moses as it describes his death outside the promised land: "Never

71

since has there arisen a prophet in Israel like Moses, whom the LORD knew face to face." Moses' face was shining with a holy aura after speaking with God (Exod. 34:35).

Even so, there were some limits and distance in Moses' remarkably intimate relationship with God. In the dramatic scene in Exod. 33:17–23, God's form moves past Moses who is hidden in a cleft of the rock until God has passed by. Then Moses is allowed to see only God's back and not God's face. God tells Moses, "You cannot see my face; for no one shall see me and live" (Exod. 33:20). Thus, the tradition affirms that Moses "spoke with" and "knew" God face to face in unparalleled intimacy. But there remained distance—Moses did not "see" God's face but only the back of God's form.

The New Testament expressions of Jesus' intimacy with his heavenly Father appear to build upon the image of Moses' close relationship with God. The Gospel of John in particular speaks of the closeness of Jesus and the Father. "No one has ever seen God. It is God the only Son who is close to the Father's heart, who has made him known" (John 1:18). Jesus is the only one who "has seen the Father" (John 6:46). Moreover, Jesus says, "Whoever has seen me has seen the Father" (John 14:9).

The difference between Moses' direct communication with God and other prophets to whom God spoke only in dreams and visions finds a parallel in the function of Jesus' parables about the kingdom of God. Jesus' disciples ask Jesus why he spoke to the crowds in parables, those brief metaphors of sowers, mustard seeds, treasure hidden in a field, pearls of great price, yeast, or salt. Why does Jesus speak in these enigmatic images that reveal but also hide the mysteries of the kingdom of God? Jesus replies:

> To you it has been given to know the secrets of the kingdom of heaven, but to them it has not been given. . . . But blessed are your eyes, for they see, and your ears, for they hear. Truly I tell you, many prophets and righteous people longed to see what you see, but did not see it, and to hear what you hear, but did not hear it. (Matt. 13: 10–11, 16–17; cf. Mark 4:10–12; Luke 8:9–10)

As with Moses, God spoke through Jesus, clearly and not in riddles, to his closest disciples. And yet in the interim between Jesus' death and resurrection and the glorious coming again of the risen Christ at the end of the age, the apostle Paul testifies to the veiled character of our knowledge of God:

> For now we see in a mirror dimly, but then we will see face to face. Now I know only in part; then I will know fully, even as I have been fully known. (I Cor. 13:12–13)

Moses stood in the dialogical tension between having unparalleled access and nearness to the mystery of God's presence and love and yet experiencing some distance from it, seeing only the back of God's form and not God's full face. Likewise, the New Testament testifies to the Christian life as one of a special intimate knowledge of God in and through Jesus. But until God's kingdom comes in all its glory, we struggle and die as Moses did on this side of the Jordan River, able to see the promised land "in a mirror dimly" but finally not able to enter it in this life (Deut. 34:1–12).

As we return to the confrontation between God and Miriam and Aaron, God asks a rhetorical question in response to Aaron and Miriam's initial rhetorical question in Num. 12:2. God asks, "Why then were you not afraid to speak against my servant Moses?" Before they answer, God's anger is kindled against "them" (both Miriam and Aaron) and God departs (12:9). God's anger had been kindled earlier in 11:1 and 11:33, both times with deathly consequences upon those who rebelled. So when we read that God's anger is kindled and then God departs, we expect dead bodies to be left after the dust settles. What is left, however, is not immediate death. Miriam is afflicted with a skin disease so that she is "white as snow" (12:10).

Aaron sees in horror what has happened to Miriam. Afraid that he will likewise be struck by a skin disease that would endanger the purity of the high priest and therefore the cult and God's presence among the Israelites, Aaron turns to Moses with a plea for mercy. Aaron's action of turning to Moses as the only one who can help is in itself an ironic confirmation of what Aaron and Miriam had earlier denied—Moses' unique relationship to God. Moreover, Aaron addresses Moses as "my lord," a further affirmation of Moses' status in relation to Aaron. Aaron confesses his and Miriam's sin: "Do not punish *us* for a sin that *we* have so foolishly committed" (12:11). Unlike the golden calf incident in which Aaron never acknowledged his sinful role in the idolatry (Exod. 32:21–24; cf. 32:1–6, 25), Aaron here accepts responsibility along with Miriam. Aaron then intercedes on behalf of his sister Miriam, whose ghastly appearance is "like one stillborn, whose flesh is half consumed when it comes out of its mother's womb" (Num. 12:12). Although not fully dead, Miriam's life has been diminished to the point of one who is stillborn. She waits to be reborn.

Moses hears Aaron's plea and cries to God on behalf of Miriam, "O God, please heal her" (12:13). As Miriam had saved Moses as a baby in Exodus 2, now Moses returns the favor and intervenes to save his sister in Numbers 12. God apparently responds to Moses' simple prayer by healing Miriam. Those with skin diseases were typically

73

banished and put outside the camp (Num. 5:2). The laws concerning skin disease in Leviticus require seven-day periods of quarantine (Lev. 13:5) and then a seven-day ritual of purification (Lev. 14:1–20). God's response to Moses suggests Miriam should be shut out of the camp for seven days. The seven days, however, do not appear to be a period of quarantine or ritual purification in accord with the laws in Leviticus; the seven-day banishment is a sign of the shame she has brought upon herself by rebelling against Moses and thus against God, her heavenly Parent (Milgrom, p. 98). Like a parent spitting in a child's face as a sign of shame (Deut. 25:9; Isa. 50:6), so God orders that Miriam bear her shame by being shut out of the camp for a week. Miriam is punished, but God removes her lifelong skin disease and instead she suffers the lesser punishment of a seven-day banishment for her shame. Out of respect for Miriam, who is one of their leaders, the people wait for the seven days until Miriam returns to the camp. After her return, they then pull up stakes and move from Hazeroth to the wilderness of Paran (12:15–16).

One critical question remains to be answered. Why did Miriam alone suffer the punishment of diseased skin and not Aaron, when he was as clearly involved as Miriam in the leaders' revolt against Moses? Several possible answers have been given. It may be that this story first circulated with Miriam as the only opponent of Moses, not Aaron. Miriam is listed first before Aaron in 12:1, and Aaron may have been added secondarily to the story. Another explanation is that the writer simply could not tolerate having the high priest rendered unclean by the skin disease. The priests were under much more stringent requirements for ritual purity than others (Lev. 21). A priest of Aaron's line was explicitly prohibited from eating from the sacred offerings of food if he suffered from a skin disease (Lev. 22:4). Even so, if Miriam was shut out from the camp not because of the uncleanness of her skin disease but as an act of shame, why should Aaron not have endured the same shame? Finally, the story may imply that Aaron was indeed about to be inflicted with the same skin disease as Miriam. But his confession of his sin and responsibility and his intercession to Moses on Miriam's behalf may have stopped the spread of the disease to his body. Some combination of the above factors may account for the imbalance in the punishment which Miriam bore. In any case, women in male-centered cultures will find in Miriam's example a resonance with their own experience of injustice. The unfairness of Miriam's burden of suffering continues to find echoes in cultures where women work more, own less, and suffer greater abuse than their male counterparts. But as we will argue in Numbers 20 in the stories of Moses and Aaron's rebellion

74

and the deaths of Aaron and Miriam, the figure of Miriam will ultimately be granted equality with her two brothers, co-leaders of the people of Israel. They all will join with the rest of the old wilderness generation and die outside the promised land. The judgment will be all-inclusive, even as the promise will be all-inclusive of the twelve tribes of Israel, including men, women, and children.

Numbers 13—14
The Decisive Rebellion:
The Spy Mission into the Promised Land

More than any other story in Numbers, the spy narrative in chapters 13—14 lays the foundation for the unifying structure and theme of the book. That theme is the death of the old rebellious generation of the wilderness wanderings and the birth of a new generation of hope standing on the threshold of the land of Canaan. As we shall see, the story of the twelve spies who reconnoiter the land of Canaan and come back with their reports is explicitly tied to the first census list in Numbers 1 and to the second census list, that of the new generation, in Numbers 26. These two census lists form the backbone of the structure of the book of Numbers in its present form. The expressly stated reason for the census of the twelve tribes at the beginning of Numbers was to count "everyone in Israel able to go to war" (Num. 1:3). The twelve tribes were then organized into a holy war camp as an army marching toward the land of Canaan (Num. 2). The reader is led to expect some sort of military engagement. After a long series of preparations and initial rebellions, Numbers 13—14 provides the first military action by the Israelites as they arrive at the southern edge of the promised land in "the wilderness of Paran" (12:16). At last Israel has reached the edge of the promised land. Our expectations as readers are high as Israel's trek through the desert is about to reach its goal.

The spy story is one of the most elaborate narratives in the whole of Numbers. Its several scenes and dialogues are carefully constructed. Suspense, irony, and dramatic dialogue give the reader a sense of the heightened importance of this narrative moment. A brief outline of the story may help illustrate the several scenes, confrontations, and movements within the narrative.

Scholars are generally agreed that the present form of Numbers 13—14 is the result of the interweaving of two originally separate literary stories or traditions, one older and the other later. One earlier form of the story appears to confine the area spied out by the Israelites only to the area around Hebron in southern Canaan (13:22–24). The later form of the story widened the area covered by the spies to include the whole territory of Canaan from the wilderness of Zin on the southern edge to Rehob, at the northernmost extremity of Canaan (13:21). Another sign of the possibility that two originally separate forms of the story existed involves the naming of the good spies who trusted God. It seems likely that an earlier tradition named only Caleb from the tribe of Judah as the lone spy who remained faithful to God (13:30; 14:24). This earlier Caleb tradition seems to be part of a series of stories involving Caleb that continue into the books of Joshua and Judges (Josh. 14:6–15; 15:13–19; Judg. 1:10–15). In a later tradition, Joshua (originally called "Hoshea"; cf. Num. 13:8, 16) of the tribe of Ephraim is added alongside Caleb so that the number of faithful spies increases from one to two (14:6, 30).

Given that there may have been an earlier form of the story, how

76

did this more original form differ from the present version? One suggestion is that the original spy story recounted a successful conquest of a part of southern Canaan by a tribe who claimed Caleb as its heroic ancestor. However, the story was transformed from this victorious conquest narrative into a failed attempt to enter the promised land from the south in the present form of the text. This revised story provided the reason for Israel's longer sojourn in the desert and its eventual entrance into the land of Canaan not from the south but from the east, which became the dominant tradition. Israel eventually crossed the Jordan River at the eastern border of Canaan, where twelve tribal chieftains again led Israel's entry into the promised land (Joshua 3—4). Other scholars have argued that the earlier form of the spy story in Numbers functioned as a polemical story told after Israel settled in Canaan. The story of Caleb's great faithfulness was used by people in southern Judah who claimed Caleb as their ancestor. The original story legitimated the religious and political superiority of Judah over the other Israelite tribes of the north, since their ancestor was the only faithful one among the spies. If this is the case, the present form of the story has significantly altered the story's original purpose. The present story has lost any sense of being one tribe's polemical judgment on another tribe. All of the Israelites are implicated in the act of unfaith in the spy story except for the two spies who represent, in a balanced way, the major tribe of the north, Ephraim (Joshua), and the major tribe of the south, Judah (Caleb). The balance here between north and south exhibits once again the evenhanded and inclusive character of Numbers' treatment of all Israel.

Chapters 13—14 begin with Israel on the southern doorstep of Canaan in the "wilderness of Paran" (12:16; 13:3). This becomes the staging area for Israel's first official military foray into the promised land. God directs Moses to send twelve leaders, one from each tribe, to scout out the land. The names of the tribal leaders chosen as spies (Num. 13:4–16) are different from the names of the tribal leaders who supervised the census in Num. 1:5–16 and who brought the gifts from each tribe for the altar in Numbers 7. The physical challenge of a spy mission may have required a younger group of leaders than the more senior leaders who administered the census and presented the gifts. One name of interest among the named spies is Hoshea, son of Nun, of the tribe of Ephraim (13:8). After all the names of the spies are presented, the text adds a note that Moses changed the name of Hoshea to Joshua (13:16). Joshua appeared earlier in Exodus 17:8–13 as a leader of the battle against Amalek, as an assistant to Moses in Exod. 32:17 and 33:11, and as an overly zealous guardian of Moses' prophetic

77

authority in Num. 11:28–29. Joshua will later be designated as Moses' successor (Num. 27:18–23) and eventually will lead Israel into the land of Canaan (see the book of Joshua).

Moses instructs the twelve tribes to survey the land not only to deduce the military might of its inhabitants but also to observe the fertility of the land (13:17–21). The spies reconnoiter the land for forty days and then return to report what they have seen. The initial spy report has some good news and some bad news. The land is indeed fruitful and "flows with milk and honey" (13:27). But the bad news is that the residents of the land are strong and live in large fortified cities (13:28–29, 31–33). The various groups listed (Amalekites, Hittites, Jebusites, Amorites) were historical peoples who lived in or near various parts of the territory of Canaan (13:29). One group especially lifted up by the spies are the descendants of Anak (13:28; cf. 13:22), who were notoriously large warriors. According to later biblical accounts, remnants of these giants remained west of Canaan in the Philistine regions of Gaza, Gath, and Ashdod (Josh. 11:21–22). Four of these giants were killed by David's men (II Sam. 21:18–22), and the giant Goliath of Gath was slain by the young warrior David with a slingshot (I Samuel 17). Up to this point in their report, the spies accurately describe what they have seen (13:21–24), without any evaluation of the Israelites' ability to overcome the enemy.

The suspense builds. Will the Israelites be encouraged by the reports and evidence of the land's fertility? Will the good news about the land overcome their fears about the great strength and size of the residents of Canaan? There is apparently some murmuring and mumbling among the Israelites until Caleb quiets the people. Caleb's exhortation expresses faith in Israel's ability to enter successfully into the land: "Let us go up at once and occupy it, for we are well able to overcome it" (13:30). Caleb stands alone among the spies at this point. He appeals to the strength of the Israelites themselves: "*we* are well able." This confidence in the Israelites' own strength is reasonable in light of the enormous army of over 600,000 warriors who were counted in the first census in Numbers 1. The well-organized and orderly military camp should likewise give the Israelites confidence. But the other spies immediately interject their contradictory and negative assessment, "We are not able to go up against this people, for they are stronger than we" (13:31). How will the people respond now to these two contradictory views? At this point in the story, the dispute is over two varied estimates of the human strength needed to conquer the armies of Canaan. Caleb says "we are able," and the other spies say, "we are not able."

78

The balance is tipped when all the spies except Caleb revise their description of Canaan, mythologizing both the land and the inhabitants into primordial monsters. Canaan is no longer a land flowing with milk and honey but "a land that devours its inhabitants" (13:32). The residents of Canaan include not only the giant historical people called the Anakites. The spies speak as well of semi-divine and mythological giants called the Nephilim to whom they "seemed like grasshoppers" (13:35). The primordial Nephilim (literally "fallen ones") are purported to be the semi-divine offspring of divine beings who had fallen from the heavens and mated with humans (Genesis 6:4). But this mythologizing of the land and its inhabitants does not correspond to what the spies had actually seen. Nowhere does the narrator report any basis for these claims about a devouring land or Nephilim in the actual account of the spies' mission (13:21–24).

The lies of the spies have their intended effect. All the Israelites become afraid and complain against Aaron and Moses, refusing to go into the promised land. The people clamor to choose their own leader and return to Egypt (14:1–4). In a series of a few brief lines, the Israelites repudiate all that God has done for them. They reject all the promises that God has made since first calling Abraham and Sarah to leave their homeland to go the land of Canaan. There God had promised Abraham and Sarah, "To your offspring I will give this land" (Gen. 12:7). How are the gifts and promises of God repudiated? The Israelite rebels yearn for their own deaths: "Would that we had died in the land of Egypt! Or would that we had died in this wilderness" (14:2). The joyous freedom from the suffering of slavery in Egypt, the careful provision of water and manna, the guidance and protection all through the desert—all of these gracious acts and gifts of God are forgotten and renounced. The Israelites fear death by the sword if they enter the promised land. They use their women and children as pretense for their lack of faith: "Our wives and our little ones will become booty; would it not be better for us to go back to Egypt?" Then the Israelites speak words that utterly destroy their covenant relationship with God as they cry, "Let us choose a captain, and go back to Egypt" (13:4).

As soon as the words are spoken, Moses and Aaron fall on their faces, half in anticipation of the divine wrath about to explode upon the people and half in prayerful intercession for God's forgiveness (14:5). Caleb the faithful spy is joined by Joshua as they both tear their clothes in a show of grief and distress over this refusal to enter the promised land. Together they make one more plea to the people to move ahead and conquer the land in obedience to God. Caleb and Joshua counter the majority report of the spies that had mythologized the enemy into

79

larger-than-life opponents. The two faithful spies reemphasize the natural goodness of the land, the human frailty of the inhabitants, and the overwhelming power of God in their midst. The land, they report, is "an exceedingly good land" and the people of the land "are no more than bread for us." They get to the theological heart of what is at stake: "Do not rebel against the LORD; and do not fear the people of the land . . . the LORD is with us; do not fear them" (14:7–9). In the end, the issue is not competing estimates about the human strength of the Israelite army versus the Canaanites. The question is not who is taller or who has larger fortifications or who has more weapons. Ultimately, all such reliance on human power and estimates is irrelevant. The issue is trusting in the power of Israel's God. God is with the Israelites in the midst of their camp; God can be trusted to make good on God's promise to bring the Israelites into the land. God's promise and presence alone are more than adequate basis for their confidence. But the response of the Israelites to Caleb and Joshua is unanimous in its negative verdict: "the whole congregation threatened to stone them" (14:10).

An angry and despairing God appears at the tent of meeting to speak with Moses. Using language reminiscent of the psalms of lament (e.g., Psalm 13), God cries out in agony, "How long will this people despise me? And how long will they refuse to believe in me, in spite of all the signs that I have done among them" (14:11)? God then pronounces an immediate death sentence on all Israel: "I will strike them with pestilence and disinherit them." The last time God "struck with pestilence" was against Pharaoh and the Egyptians in the ten plagues of the exodus (e.g., Exod. 9:15). Like Pharaoh, the rebellious Israelites refuse to believe in the power of God to do what God says. Thus, Israel will suffer the same fate as Pharaoh. Corresponding to their plan to return to Egypt (Num. 14:4), God's punishment will reverse the exodus. Although God had taken Israel out of Egypt as God's "inheritance" (Exod. 34:9), now God will "disinherit them" (Num. 14:12). Moreover, God offers to separate Moses out from the rest of Israel and make of him a great and mighty nation (14:12).

Only one other time before has God decided to abandon Israel and start over again with Moses to form a new nation. When Israel worshiped the golden calf at the foot of Mount Sinai, God told Moses of the plan to annihilate the Israelites: "Now let me alone, so that my wrath may burn hot against them and I may consume them; and of you I will make a great nation" (Exod. 32:10). The golden calf in Exodus 32 and the rebellion in the spy story of Numbers 13—14 form the two great apostasies or rebellions of Israel against God in the Pentateuch.

But in many ways, the rebellion in Numbers 13—14 is the most severe and unprecedented of the two. Three rebellions preceded the spy story, one that affected the fringe of the camp (11:1–3), a second involving the people's complaint about the manna (11:4–35), and a third involving for the first time leaders of the people, Miriam and Aaron (12:1–16). The progression from the fringe to all the people to the leaders builds progressively toward the culminating rebellion in Numbers 13—14. In the spy story, both the leaders in the form of the spies (13:2) and all the people (14:1–2) are involved and implicated. The uniqueness and severity of the spy story rebellion is shown by the people's unprecedented plan to choose their own leader and return to Egypt (14:4). George Coats correctly observes that

> here for the first time, the murmuring is followed by a move to return to Egypt. The murmuring tradition therefore involves not simply an expression of a wish that the Exodus had not occurred or a challenge of Moses' authority in executing the Exodus, but now an overt move to reverse the Exodus. Yahweh is the God "who brought Israel out of Egypt." The murmuring results in a rejection of this deity and a move to elect a new leader to take the people back to Egypt. (Coats, p. 146)

The rejection of the God of the exodus and of God's specially chosen leader Moses who had just been defended by God in chapter 12 leads God to disown the people of Israel.

Moses intercedes, just as he had done after the sin of the golden calf in Exod. 32:11–13, and asks God to forgive the people. Moses advances a remarkable three-pronged argument designed to change God's plans to abandon Israel. Moses makes appeals to God's international reputation (14:13–16), to God's promises made to Israel (14:17–18), and to the consistent character or quality of God's steadfast love (14:19). If God abandons Israel, Moses argues, the news will spread like wildfire among the nations. The Egyptians will hear of it, and they will pass the news on to the Canaanites in the land. They all know that God has been in the midst of Israel's camp guiding their way (14:14). Moses draws the conclusion,

> Now if you kill this people all at one time, then the nations who have heard about you will say, "It is because the LORD was not able to bring this people into the land he swore to give them that he has slaughtered them in the wilderness." (14:15–16)

The nations will conclude that God is weak-kneed and powerless, preferring to kill the Israelites out in the desert rather than stand up to the power of the Canaanites and their gods in the land. Such a conclusion would undo the great acts of power and deliverance in the exodus which were done so that "the Egyptians shall know that I am the LORD, when I stretch out my hand against Egypt and bring the Israelites out from among them" (Exod. 7:5). God is interested in being known by other nations besides Israel. God cannot afford to abandon the Israelites, argues Moses, for the sake of the other nations and their knowledge of Israel's God.

Moses' second appeal to God is to "let the power of the LORD be great in the way that you promised" (14:18). God has an obligation to make good on promises made in the past. The promise to which Moses holds God accountable is an abbreviated form of the important revelation of God's inner character made personally to Moses in Exod. 34:6–7. This important Exodus affirmation of God's character given after the golden calf apostasy is a theologically significant reformulation of a similar affirmation given in the first Sinai covenant in Exod. 20:5–6. It is instructive to compare the two Exodus formulations:

Exodus 20:5–6	*Exodus 34:6–7*
I the LORD your God am a jealous God, punishing children for the iniquity of parents, to the third and fourth generation of those who reject me, but showing steadfast love to the thousandth generation of those who love me and keep my commandments.	The LORD, a God merciful and gracious, slow to anger and abounding in steadfast love and faithfulness, keeping steadfast love for the thousandth generation, forgiving iniquity and transgression and sin, yet by no means clearing the guilty, but visiting the iniquity of the parents upon the children and the children's children to the third and fourth generation.

The definitive golden calf apostasy (Exodus 32) comes between these two proclamations of God's character and creates the crisis which necessitates the second, deeper revelation of God. After the golden calf, the question becomes how a holy God can continue with a sinful people like Israel. The first covenant of Sinai based on Exodus 20 is no longer viable; the tablets are broken (32:19). The new and second covenant made at Sinai is based on a new revelation of God given to Moses, and the shape of that new revelation is made clear by comparing Exodus 20 and Exodus 34 above. Several differences stand out.

1. The sequence of God's jealousy/punishment first and God's steadfast love second in Exodus 20 is reversed; in Exodus 34, God's mercy and love are highlighted first before god's punishment of iniquity.

2. The very brief mention of God's "steadfast love to the thousandth generation" in Exodus 20 is greatly expanded through the addition of several clauses in Exodus 34. What is added is that God is "merciful," "gracious," "slow to anger," "abounding in steadfast love and faithfulness," "forgiving iniquity and transgression and sin."

3. In Exodus 20, God's "steadfast love" is extended to "those who love me and keep my commandments." Exodus 34 contains no such qualifier requiring love and obedience. God simply keeps "steadfast love to the thousandth generation." Period. Instead of the stress on obedience in Exodus 20, Exodus 32 highlights God's forgiving of "iniquity and transgression and sin."

4. Because of the much greater emphasis on God's mercy in Exodus 34, it adds the assurance that consequences remain for the guilty: "yet by no means clearing the guilty." Such an assurance was unnecessary in the stricter formulation of Exodus 20.

In his intercessory prayer in Numbers 14, Moses urges God to let the divine power "be great in the way that you promised," referring to the promise in Exodus 34. Here the greatness of God's power is revealed not first of all in judgment and punishment but rather in God's gracious and steadfast love and forgiveness. Moses holds God accountable to the promise of that abounding and steadfast love made personally to Moses in Exodus 34.

The third appeal Moses makes is to God's past track record of consistently forgiving Israel "from Egypt even until now." Moses exhorts God to be constant in character. God should remain consistent with God's past actions. God has always bent over backward on the side of love and forgiveness.

The three arguments Moses uses with God in Numbers 14 are somewhat parallel to the arguments God used in Exodus 32 when God was ready to destroy Israel for worshiping the golden calf. But the differences are noteworthy. In Exod. 32:12, Moses appeals to God's reputation among the Egyptians only. In Num. 14:13–16, the appeal is to God's reputation among the Egyptians *and* the Canaanites. Exodus 32:13 appeals to the promises God made with the ancestors in Genesis—Abraham, Isaac and Jacob/Israel. Numbers 14:18 appeals to the more recent promise of God's exceptional mercy revealed personally to Moses in Exodus 34. The third appeal to the consistency and regularity of God's acts of forgiveness in the past in Num. 14:19 presumes a past track record that was not in place in the golden calf story in Exodus 32. Thus, the focus of Moses' intercession as we move from the golden calf apostasy to the spy story in Numbers has shifted from Egypt to Canaan, from the promise to the ancestors in Genesis to the

83

definitive revelation given to Moses in Exodus, and from a first-time experience of forgiveness to a longer track record that acts as an ongoing paradigm of God's willingness to forgive Israel's sins.

God's response to Moses' plea follows in Num. 14:20–35. The divine response is in two parts. In verses 20–25, God speaks to Moses and begins, "I do forgive, just as you have asked." Moses' prayerful arguing succeeded in changing God's plans to disinherit the people. But the word of forgiveness is followed by a "nevertheless." True to God's character in 14:18, God by no means simply clears the guilty; consequences ensue from the despising of God and God's gift of the land. Although God did not use an oath when he thought to disinherit Israel in 14:12, God does use a solemn oath formula for the punishment in 14:21: "as I live, and as all the earth shall be filled with the glory of God." The punishment that follows the oath formula is nonnegotiable and cannot be turned away by Moses' intercession. The penalty for despising God's gift of the promised land corresponds to the people's desire to return to Egypt rather than enter Canaan. None of the people who "have *seen*" God's mighty deeds in Egypt and the wilderness "shall *see* the land that I swore to give to their ancestors" (14:23). Caleb alone will enter the promised land "because he has a different spirit." The old wilderness generation is condemned to die in the desert because they "despised" God (14:23).

The second part of God's response follows in 14:26–35. God directs Moses and Aaron to give Israel a message, " 'As I live,' says the LORD, 'I will do to you the very things I heard you say' " (14:28). By an oath, God swears that the punishments of Israel will correspond to fit their rebellious words and actions.

1. The Israelites said, "Would that we had died in this wilderness" (14:2). God grants their wish: "Your dead bodies shall fall in this very wilderness" (14:29).

2. The Israelites did not want to enter the promised land: "Why is the LORD bringing us into this land to fall by the sword?" (14:3). God pledges, "Not one of you shall come into the land in which I swore to settle you, except Caleb . . . and Joshua" (14:30).

3. The Israelites use the well-being of their women and children as a pretext for why they do not want to enter the promised land: "Our wives and our little ones will become booty" (14:3). God promises that the little ones of the next generation will receive the promised land after suffering for their parents' rebellion: "But your little ones, who you said would become booty, I will bring in, and they shall know the land that you have despised. . . . And your children shall be shepherds

in the wilderness for forty years, and shall suffer for your faithlessness, until the last of your dead bodies lies in the wilderness" (14:31–33).

4. The scouting mission of the Israelite spies lasted forty days: "At the end of forty days they returned from spying out the land" (13:25). God's punishment of the wilderness generation will last forty years: "According to the number of the days in which you spied out the land, forty days, for every day a year, you shall bear your iniquity, forty years, and you shall know my displeasure" (14:34).

The reader is left with a sense that God's condemnation of the entire wilderness generation to a gradual forty-year death in the desert is a punishment that fits the crime. In poetic justice, the old generation gets precisely what it asked for and deserved. On the other hand, Israel gets more than it deserves. It receives forgiveness and a second chance with a new generation. God remains committed to Israel. Israel remains God's own inheritance, even though a whole generation will die in the wilderness. Prompted by the earnest intercession of Moses, God in the end cannot let Israel go. The birth and promise of a new generation of God's people will rise phoenix-like out of the ruins of this old rebellious generation. The children of the old generation whom the rebels used as an excuse for not entering the land (14:3) will become the new inheritors of God's promise (14:31). The new census list in Numbers 26 is a sign of the final death of the wilderness generation (vv. 63–65). But at the same time the new census list is tangible evidence that God's promises will be kept. A new generation of Israelites will indeed enter the long-awaited land of Canaan.

Numbers 14 concludes with two brief episodes. In verses 36–38, the ten unfaithful spies who brought the ill report of the land and caused Israel's rebellion die in a plague. Their immediate deaths are a prelude to the upcoming series of rebellions, deaths, and plagues that will eventually fall upon all members of the older wilderness generation. Additional rebellions and deaths will occur in chapters 16, 17, 20, 21, and 25, dispelling any hope for this sinful generation. The tradition of the old generation's "ten" rebellions and subsequent plagues (14:22) mirrors the ten plagues and acts of disobedience by the Egyptians (Exodus 7—12). The old generation is in a sense gradually going back to Egypt, or at least going back to Egypt's sinful and obstinate ways which will lead to their death.

In the second concluding episode in verses 39–45, the Israelites suddenly change their minds. They resolve to rise up and fight the inhabitants of Canaan after all. The story only confirms the people's failure to comprehend the depth of their own sin and lack of understanding. God had sworn with an oath that the old generation would not enter the land (14:20–23). Moses warns the people, "Do not go up, for the LORD is not with you; do not let yourselves be struck down before your enemies" (14:42). Again, the critical issue is not human strength or even human resolve or determination. The key is the presence of God in their midst. The ark of the covenant, the sign of God's presence, remained in the camp and did not go up with the Israelites as they attacked the Canaanites and Amalekites. The result was predictable. The Israelites were soundly defeated in battle (14:45). The death of the old rebellious generation had begun.

The Place of the Spy Story in the Structure of Numbers

The spy story in Numbers 13—14 plays a crucial role within the unifying literary and theological structure of the book of Numbers. The story is closely and directly linked to the two census lists in Numbers 1 and 26 and is recalled in important ways in the second half of the book in chapters 32 and 34. The spy story is explicitly linked to the first census list in Numbers 1 through its use of the specific age formula, "all your number, numbered from twenty years old and upward" (14:29). The same phrase is used repeatedly as a formula throughout the numbering of the twelve tribes in the first chapter of Numbers (Num. 1:3, 18, 20, 22, 24, 26, 28, 30, 32, 34, 36, 38, 40, 42, 45). The spy story is also explicitly tied in with the second census list in chapter 26. A note at the end of the census in 26:63–65 reads:

> These were those enrolled by Moses and Eleazar the priest. . . . Among these there was not one of those enrolled by Moses and Aaron the priest, who had enrolled the Israelites in the wilderness of Sinai. For the LORD had said of them, "They shall die in the wilderness." Not one of them was left, except Caleb son of Jephunneh and Joshua son of Nun.

The note clearly alludes to the spy story of Numbers 13—14 in which the definitive condemnation of the old wilderness generation occurred. The spy story has clear associations with the two pillars of the structure of the book of Numbers; that is, the first census list in chapter 1 and the second census list of the new generation in chapter 26. The theme of the spy story plays a pivotal role as the central narrative in defining the theme of the book of Numbers as a whole—the death of the old generation and the birth of a new generation of hope on the edge of the promised land. We will note other references to the spy

86

story later in chapters 32 and 34, further strengthening the argument for its central place in the theme and structure of Numbers.

Theological Reflections on the Spy Story

The spy story in Number 13—14 gathers together a host of central themes in the theology of the Old and New Testaments. The story explores sin; the interplay of forgiveness and judgment; the death of the old and the birth of the new; trusting in God's power versus trusting in estimates of human power and resolve; and God's power over "giants" versus God's grace on "the little ones." The following are illustrations of ways in which these themes are intertwined in both the spy story in the Old Testament and the New Testament sayings and stories of Jesus as well as early Christian tradition.

1. The nature of the sin in Numbers 13—14 is the despising or spurning of God's free gift of the promised land, which was Israel's for the taking. The the rebels in the spy story fall so low because the sense of expectation and hope that the entire Pentateuchal narrative attaches to this one moment is so high. All the ancestral promises in Genesis and their constant reiteration since Exodus 1 have looked forward to this point when Israel is on the verge of entering the promised land of Canaan. The people refuse to trust God to make good on God's promise.

One New Testament analogy to this moment in the Pentateuchal story is the story of the crucifixion of Jesus. The cross is a sign of the world's despising of God's great gift of salvation in Christ. God's fulfillment of Israel's messianic expectation is met by the people's rejection.

2. A second theme in the spy story is the forgiveness of God through the intercession of Moses. Moses' appeal to God's "steadfast love" (Hebrew *ḥesed*) was an appeal to God's steadfast loyalty and commitment to the promises God made to Israel (Sakenfeld, "The Problem of Divine Forgiveness in Numbers 14"). In the process, Moses denied himself and the possible glory of becoming a great nation. Instead, Moses used his uniquely intimate relationship to God to pray for forgiveness for the people (14:12–19). Similarly, the apostle Paul in Romans 8 assures his readers that nothing in all creation "will be able to separate us from the love of God in Christ Jesus our Lord" (Rom. 8:39). And the basis for that assurance of God's *ḥesed* or steadfast love is in the intercession of Jesus "who died, yes, who was raised, who is at the right hand of God, who indeed intercedes for us" (Rom. 8:34). Like Moses, Jesus denied himself and his own glory for the sake of others through his suffering and death (Phil. 2:1–11).

87

3. The spy story upholds the dialogical tension between God's forgiveness and God's judgment through the paradigm of the death of the old and the birth of the new. Death in the desert was God's just judgment on the old wilderness generation. They would never reach the promised land. But out of death came new life. God promised to raise up a new generation of hope who would enter the land of Canaan. Thus God was above all merciful and faithful to the promises that were made. But God also preserved a sense of responsibility and justice by giving the old wilderness generation the punishment that corresponded to what they had said they wanted (return to Egypt, die in the desert, forty years of wilderness wandering).

In a similar way, the promise of forgiveness and new life arises out of the judgment and death that Jesus bore on the cross. Jesus opens up the way through the death of the old to the birth of the new as he calls his disciples to "take up their cross daily and follow me" (Luke 9:23). The rebels of the spy story wanted to save their lives by refusing to stand up to the enemies of Canaan. Jesus instructs us that the road of faith moves in the opposite direction: "For those who want to save their life will lose it, and those who lose their life for my sake will find it" (Luke 9:24). The way of faith is always through death to new life, through the cross to resurrection. The concrete expression of that movement for the Christian is baptism into Christ signifying the drowning of the old self and the rebirth of a new self: "Therefore we have been buried with him by baptism into death, so that, just as Christ was raised from the dead by the glory of the Father, so we too might walk in newness of life" (Rom. 6:4).

4. The spy story portrays faith as fear and trust in God's power above all else. Martin Luther's explanation of the first of the Ten Commandments, "You shall have no other gods before me," in the *Small Catechism* is simply this: "You shall fear, love and trust God above anything else." The spy story illustrates the two primary ways in which this first commandment is broken. On one hand, the rebellious spies and people feared the inhabitants and the land of Canaan more than they feared God. They exaggerated and mythologized the enemy out of proportion to reality, speaking of a land that devours its inhabitants and of primordial giants called Nephilim (Num. 13:32–33). They despaired of God's power to overcome God's enemies. On the other hand, at the end of the spy story, the Israelites presumed to go up and conquer the land by their own power and resolve. This they did in spite of Moses' warning that God was not with them. In their pride, they trusted in their own efforts and determination to gain for themselves the promises of God. The result was defeat and death (Num. 14:39–45).

88

Whether in pride or despair, the old wilderness generation failed to learn the fundamental lesson of the first commandment—to fear, love, and trust God above anything else.

5. Finally, the spy story affirms both God's mighty power to conquer "giants" and God's loving power to save "the little ones." Caleb and Joshua knew that the giants in Canaan were nothing compared to the power of Israel's God: "The LORD is with us; do not fear them" (Num. 14:9). As God's power defeated the mighty enemies, so God's power will deliver the "little ones:" "But your little ones, who you said would become booty, I will bring in, and they shall know the land that you have despised" (Num. 14:31). The New Testament likewise portrays the power of God to fight the enemies of God. Jesus sends out seventy of his followers to preach and to heal and they come back rejoicing, "Lord, in your name even the demons submit to us!" Jesus responds, "I watched Satan fall from heaven like a flash of lightning" (Luke 10:17–18). The demonic enemies, even the giant Satan, fall before the power of God's holy war weapons of healing and the preaching of the gospel. Ephesians 6:10–12 urges followers of Christ to "be strong in the Lord and in the strength of his power."

In later traditions within the Old Testament, the proper weapons by which God's people conducted holy war against the enemies of God had already begun to be reinterpreted. No longer were God's people to use swords of violence; rather, they were to fight with the weapons of God's word and obedience to God's law, or Torah (Deut. 33:10–11; Josh. 1:7–9; Isa. 2:1–4). This tradition was carried on into the New Testament. Jesus' disciples battled evil not with weapons of violence but with preaching God's word and with a ministry of healing and reconciliation (Luke 22:49–51). And those who received these gifts were often the "little ones" of this world. Jesus called the little ones to his side: "Let the little children come to me, and do not stop them; for it is to such as these that the kingdom of God belongs" (Luke 18:16).

Jesus' parable of the great banquet in Luke 14 is in many ways a commentary on the spy story of Numbers 13—14. A luscious dinner is prepared, not unlike God's preparation of the promised land flowing with milk and honey for the Israelites. The master of the house extends a gracious invitation to many people. However, all those who are invited refuse to come to the banquet and offer excuses as to why they are not able. The master then decides instead to invite "the poor, the crippled, the blind, and the lame" to come and eat a great banquet with him. These "little ones" of the community receive the gracious gift of food. The master vows concerning those first invited: "For I tell you, none of those who were invited will taste my dinner" (Luke

89

14:24). The parable is a metaphor for the kingdom of God and the ministry of Jesus that calls "the little ones" to come and eat at the table of the Lord (Luke 22:24–30). The apostle Paul reminds the Corinthian church that God has chosen the foolish and the weak to shame the wise and the strong: "God chose what is low and despised in the world, things that are not, to reduce to nothing things that are, so that no one might boast in the presence of God" (I Cor. 1:27–29).

As we move on in the book of Numbers from this central and defining narrative of the rebellious spies and the failed attempt to conquer the promised land, these important theological themes of judgment and hope will continue to weave in and out of the laws and narratives that follow. The concluding lines of Anne Killigrew's poem "On Death" express succinctly Israel's failure to trust in God's power and have courage, as is evident in the spy story of Numbers 13—14:

> Thus childish fear did Israel of old
> From plenty and the Promised Land withhold;
> They fancied giants, and refused to go,
> When Canaan did with milk and honey flow.
>
> (Atwan and Wieder, 149)

Numbers 15

A Whisper of Hope: Regulations and Reassurances for Life in the Promised Land

The calm and ordered obedience of the holy camp of Israel in Numbers 1—10 has been broken by wave after wave of rebellion, disobedience, and mutiny in chapters 11—14. It is time to take a break, to go back and review some basics, and to receive some assurances about the future. Numbers 15 functions in this way as a break in the downward slide of Israel's rebellion. The introduction of a series of laws in chapter 15 interrupts the narrative movement of Numbers and mirrors the interrupting effect of the multiple revolts on Israel's progress toward the promised land. The effect of the laws is much like a coach reviewing game strategies and basic fundamentals that have been forgotten following a crushing defeat. It is time to stop and take stock, remember what has been forgotten, and receive encouragement in the face of despair.

Chapter 15 begins with a number of laws concerning sacrifices and offerings that the people are to present to God when they take up residence in the land of Canaan (vv. 1–21). The next section provides regulations for sacrifices that atone for unintentional sins by the community (vv. 22–26) or unintentional sins by an individual (vv. 27–31). The laws on intentional and unintentional sins are followed by a judicial case involving a man gathering wood on the sabbath day (vv. 32–36). This is followed by instructions to the people to wear tassels on their garments as reminders of God's commandments (vv. 37–41).

Is there any internal cohesion or structure to the laws within Numbers 15? And are there any connections between these laws in chapter 15 and the rebellion stories that precede in Numbers 11—14 and the rebellion stories that follow in Numbers 16—17? Many scholars have failed to see any connection between the laws in chapter 15 and the surrounding narratives. Some have even called Numbers "the junk room of the Bible." They assume that later writers haphazardly threw surplus laws and traditions such as chapter 15 into scattered sections of the book of Numbers with little forethought or interconnection, much like throwing scattered odds and ends into a disorganized closet. One commentator, Martin Noth, writes concerning Numbers 15:

> It is not quite clear why this rather unsystematically arranged collection of various cultic-ritual ordinances should have found a place at this particular point in the Pentateuchal narrative. . . . Moreover, the individual parts of this collection have no connection with each other. (Noth, p. 114)

However, a closer look at the internal cohesion of the laws within chapter 15 and their many interconnections with the stories of chapters 11—14 and chapter 16 suggest otherwise. The laws in Numbers 15 contribute significantly to the themes and images of the surrounding material.

The Internal Cohesion of the Series of Laws in Numbers 15

A careful reading of chapter 15 reveals a number of intertwining refrains that are repeated throughout the diverse laws. These refrains include "the alien" or "the alien who resides with you" (15:14, 15, 16, 26, 29, 30); "throughout your generations" (15:15, 21, 23, 37); "when you come into the land you are to inhabit that I am giving you / "after you come into the land to which I am bringing you" (15:2, 18); "all these commandments / everything that the LORD has commanded you" (15:22, 23, 39, 40); "an offering by fire to the LORD" (15:3, 13, 14, 25); "a pleasing odor to the LORD" (15:3, 7, 10, 13, 14, 24); and "the whole congregation" (15:24, 25, 26, 33, 35, 36). These multiple refrains throughout the chapter are one device by which the various sections of laws are effectively linked together.

Another sign of the internal cohesion is the flow of themes from one law into another. This may not be rigidly systematic in our modern eyes, but the laws do follow a sequential logic based on interlocking key words and themes typical of biblical and ancient Near Eastern legal collections. A brief explication of each section of laws will draw out some of the thematic connections and transitions from one law to another.

1. *Numbers 15:1–16* lists a series of burnt offerings or sacrifices of meat that can be made to God—a lamb (v. 5), a ram (v. 6), or a bull (v. 8). Each of these meat sacrifices or offerings are to be accompanied by a grain offering of flour mixed with oil and a drink offering of wine of varying quantities, depending on the size and value of the animal offered. Leviticus 23 specifies that the combination of animal, grain, and drink offerings should be presented at two specific festivals: Offering of Firstfruits (Lev. 23:12–14) and Festival of Weeks (Lev. 23:18). Numbers 6:14–17 requires the combination of animal, grain, and drink offerings together for the consecration of the Nazirite. Numbers 15 takes these specific instructions for the two festivals and the Nazirite consecration and generalizes them to every time "you make an offering by fire to the LORD from the herd or from the flock" (Num. 15:3). What was earlier required only for two specific festivals now applies to all the times when sacrifices and offerings are made.

Numbers 15:13–14 extends this theme of broadening or widening not only to issues of time but also to the groups of persons responsible for obeying the law. The laws on sacrifice conclude with a note that the laws apply to "every native Israelite" (v. 13) and also to "an alien who lives with you" who wishes to make an offering (v. 14). Numbers 15: 15–16 goes on in strong terms to accentuate the welcoming of the sojourner or non-Israelite into the obligations of the assembly or community:

> As for the assembly, there shall be for both you and the resident alien a single statute, a perpetual statute throughout your generations; you and the alien shall be alike before the LORD. You and the alien who resides with you shall have the same law and the same ordinance. (15:15–16)

The concern to include the alien along with the native under the umbrella of God's law was raised in the Passover regulations earlier in Numbers 9:14. But chapter 15 broadens the scope of the alien's participation and obligation to include all sacrifices and offerings. Such offerings are made at the tent of meeting at the heart and center of the camp. Any non-Israelite groups within the holy war camp of Israel were apparently located on the fringes of Israel's camp, since no designated place was assigned to them in the camp's arrangement in Numbers 2. In any case, these non-Israelite groups are welcomed into the center to offer their sacrifices and offerings. In this way, they are given the same status as native Israelites before God: "You and the alien shall be alike before the LORD" (15:15). One hears the echoes of a later affirmation made by the apostle Paul in Gal. 3:28: "There is no longer Jew or Greek, there is no longer slave or free, there is no longer male and female; for all of you are one in Christ Jesus." Of course, some distinctions remained between Israelites and the non-native aliens (e.g., Deut. 14:21). Yet one sees in Numbers 15 a concern to welcome the alien to the central sanctuary of the camp. This conviction is one shared by Solomon's prayer dedicating the First Jerusalem Temple (I Kings 8:41), and by Second Isaiah's vision of the Second Temple. Concerning the "foreigners who join themselves to the LORD," Isaiah writes:

> These I will bring to my holy mountain,
>   and make them joyful in my house of prayer;
> their burnt offerings and their sacrifices
>   will be accepted on my altar;
> for my house will be called a house of prayer
>   for all peoples.
> (Isa. 56:7)

One important refrain is repeated six times throughout this section of 15:1–16: the offering or sacrifice will "make a pleasing odor to the LORD." The image of the pleasing fragrance of sacrifice signifies the desire of the one giving the offering to offer thanks or be reconciled to God. The most dramatic biblical story in which the same image occurs is after the great flood that God sent over the whole world in Genesis 6—9. In the course of God's resolution never to destroy the world in such a way again, Noah offered up burnt offerings to God. Genesis 8:21 gives God's response:

> And when the LORD smelled the pleasing odor, the LORD said in his
> heart, "I will never again curse the ground because of humankind,

93

> for the inclination of the human heart is evil from youth; nor will I
> ever again destroy every living creature as I have done.

The pleasing odor of the burnt offering here becomes associated with God's willingness to continue relating to the world in spite of its inevitable evil inclinations. The image also occurs in the New Testament in Eph. 5:1–6 where the apostle Paul urges his readers,

> Therefore be imitators of God, as beloved children, and live in love,
> as Christ loved us and gave himself up for us, a fragrant offering and
> sacrifice to God.

Again, the theme of the fragrant sacrifice or offering is associated with reconciliation with God and with other human beings.

2. *Numbers 15:17–21* takes the obligation to offer the firstfruits of the harvest in Lev. 23:9–14 and broadens it to include the end products of the human endeavor of baking bread as well. The first batch of dough that a baker makes belongs to the LORD, just as the first grain that a farmer harvests is offered to God (Deut. 26:1–15). As in 15:2, the law applies "after you come into the land to which I am bringing you" (15:18). The law cannot apply to Israel while in the wilderness since its food is only manna; there is no flour or bread dough or settled life that makes baking or processing of food by humans possible. The law assumes settlement in houses, the availability of ovens, wheat grown in fields, and time to engage in baking. Since the wilderness did not provide such opportunities, this is clearly a law for the future when Israel is settled in the land.

Just as the law about offerings and sacrifices in 15:1–16 had widened its regulations in time and in people affected, so the law about offering the first batch of dough extended or broadened the firstfruits law of Leviticus 23. The flour and grain repeatedly mentioned in the first laws in verses 1–16 directs the reader to the law concerning bread dough in verses 17–21. The underlying principle of the first batch of dough law is that products of human manufacture, like products of nature, are gracious gifts from God. To return the first of whatever is grown or made is an acknowledgement that all good things, whether natural or human-made, ultimately have a divine origin and purpose.

3. *Numbers 15:22–26* asks this question: What happens when the Israelite community as a whole unintentionally breaks one of the preceding commandments or any other of those that Moses gave to the people? The remedy brings together several elements of the preceding laws in Numbers 15. Unintentional or inadvertent sins due to a community's ignorance of the law may be forgiven through making a burnt offering of a bull with its accompanying grain and drink offering. This

94

combination of meat, grain, and wine was specified earlier in Num. 15:8–10. A sin offering of a goat should also be given by the community. The priest thus makes atonement for the community's sin due to inadvertent error (15:25). Several of the phrases from earlier in chapter 15 occur again here in verses 22–26: "throughout your generations," "a pleasing odor to the LORD," "an offering by fire to the LORD," "Israelites . . . as well as the aliens."

4. *Numbers 15:27–29* moves from the unintentional sins of the community in verses 22–26 to considering the unintentional sins of an individual. Inadvertent mistakes in obeying the law may be atoned for through the sin offering of one female goat a year old. This law again applies to "both the native among the Israelites and the alien residing among them" (15:29).

5. *Numbers 15:30–31* takes up the opposite case, that of someone who acts "highhandedly" or "blatantly," with full knowledge of the law. Such a highhanded sin that despises the word and commandments of God "affronts the LORD." Such a person should be "cut off from among the people," which may refer either to the death penalty or to banishment from the community (which was considered a kind of death itself).

6. *Numbers 15:32–36* is a case about a man who was found gathering sticks on the sabbath day. He was taken into custody, but the appropriate penalty for what he was doing was unclear. Thus, Moses consults God concerning the case, and the death by stoning is decreed as the penalty. What is the difficulty in deciding the case that leads Moses to consult God about it? Is it whether or not the act of gathering sticks constitutes labor punishable by the law requiring no work on the sabbath day? The law reads in Exod. 35:2:

> Six days shall work be done, but on the seventh day you shall have a holy sabbath of solemn rest to the LORD; whoever does any work on it shall be put to death.

Some scholars argue that if labor on the sabbath were the issue, the punishment is very clear and there would be no need for Moses to consult God. The man was laboring by picking up sticks and thus is subject to the death penalty. Others suggest that the need for the death penalty is clear, but how it was to be carried out, either by stoning or other means, is the debatable issue.

Some have argued that the case of the wood gatherer may have been connected with the law against lighting a fire on the sabbath in Exod. 35:3: "You shall kindle no fire in all your dwellings on the sabbath day." By gathering sticks on the sabbath, the man was starting a

95

process that would eventually lead to building a fire. Was his intention and plan to build a fire sufficient cause to indict him under the specific law of kindling a fire on the sabbath, even though he had not yet built an actual fire on the sabbath?

At any rate, the case of the wood gatherer in its present context seems to function as a concrete illustration of the immediately preceding law about sinning flagrantly or "highhandedly" (Num. 15:30). The man's blatant intention was to build a fire on the sabbath. This highhanded intention formed sufficient grounds to convict him of violating the law against kindling a fire on the sabbath, even though he had not yet actually built the fire. Such bold and defiant sin needs to be punished severely. Thus, this case of the wood gatherer and the laws that precede it share a common theme: the role of a person's intention in determining the degree of guilt and punishment. Sins done unwittingly bear less guilt and so can be atoned for through sacrifice (15:28). On the other hand, an overt and intentional violation of the commandments done "highhandedly" implies a high degree of guilt and the strictest penalty.

7. *Numbers 15:37–40* concludes the series of laws with instructions to the people to wear a blue cord on the corners of their garments as reminders of God's commandments. This section was included in the Jewish liturgy of the postexilic period as part of the prayer known as the "Shema" (Deut. 6:4—"Hear (Hebrew *shema'*) O Israel: the LORD is our God, the LORD alone"). Modern Jews continue to wear the blue cord and fringes on the prayer shawl that is worn during a Jewish worship service. The royal blue cord stands out in color among the white fringes, just as the commandments of God should stand out in the mind of the worshiper. The blue cord and fringes function as a visual aid or sign "so you shall remember and do all my commandments, and you shall be holy to your God" (15:40). The vivid blue of the cord should focus one's eyes just as attention should always be focused on God's will so that one does "not follow the lust of your own heart and your own eyes" (15:39).

8. *Numbers 15:41* concludes the whole series of laws—not with a law but with an important affirmation of the continuing relationship between God and the people of Israel. The affirmation is an emphatic restatement of God's self-description or name that appears first at the head of the Ten Commandments in Exodus 20:2:

> I am the LORD your God, who brought you out of the land of Egypt, to be your God: I am the LORD your God.

The Interconnections between Numbers 15 and the Preceding Stories in Numbers 11–14

The possibility that the laws of Numbers 15 may have a purposeful connection with the stories of rebellion that precede them was suggested already by early Jewish commentators like Ibn Ezra and Nachmanides:

> The incident of the spies is immediately followed by the section containing laws which apply only to the Promised Land. This was intended to give confidence and assurance of the ultimate possession of the land to the next generation, who might have been skeptical about the fulfillment of a forty-year-old promise. (Fisch, p. 870)

That this section of laws for life in Canaan is intended to serve as words of promise for the new generation is confirmed by the concluding verse of the law section. It reaffirms God's relationship to Israel after the trauma of the rebellion stories in Numbers 11—14: "I am the LORD your God, who brought you out of the land of Egypt." The affirmation is important since the major issue in the spy story is Israel's desire to undo the exodus and return to Egypt (14:2–4). The laws in Numbers 15 explicitly apply only when Israel arrives in Canaan, and so the laws carry an implicit promise: it is the land, God promises, that "I am giving you" (15:2) and "to which I am bringing you" (15:18). The reaffirmation of God's relationship and the implicit promise that God will bring Israel into the land is reassurance to the new generation that God will be faithful to the promises made to them (14:31).

Many other connections between the laws in Numbers 15 and the preceding rebellion stories in chapters 11—14 may also be seen. Other refrains in Numbers 15 touch on themes in the revolt narratives.

Numbers 15	*Numbers 11—14*
non-Israelite "alien"	the non-Israelite "rabble" (11:4), the Cushite wife of Moses (12:1)
"throughout your generations"	old generation will die in the desert, but the new generation will live in the land (14:30–31)
"an offering by fire to the LORD"	reversal of "the fire of the LORD burned against" rebels in the camp (11:2–3)
offerings as "a pleasing odor to the LORD"	the anger of the LORD—in Hebrew literally, "the nose of the LORD flares up in anger" (11:1, 10, 33; 12:9)

97

Other associations between the laws in Numbers 15 and the rebellion stories in chapters 11—14 may be mentioned. Examples of "high-handed" intentional sins and "despising" the LORD discussed in Numbers 15:30–36 abound in the rebellion stories: Num. 11:1; 11:4–6; 12:2; 13:32–33; 14:2–4; 14:11. With certain offerings and sacrifices, a priest could atone for unintentional sins (15:25, 28). But in the case of intentional rebellions by individuals or the community as in the spy story, only Moses could seek forgiveness in an extraordinary act of intercession. Even so, the community was severely punished (Num. 14:13–24).

The image of the sacrifices and offerings in the land of Canaan that combine different meats, flour, and wine in 15:1–21 suggests that Canaan is a place of rich food, fertility, and wondrous variety. This portrait confirms the first spy report concerning Canaan that it is "a land flowing with milk and honey" (13:27) as well as Caleb and Joshua's report that it is "an exceedingly good land" (14:7). The delicious variety of foods reflected in the prescribed offerings after Israel arrives in Canaan (15:1–21) provides an answer to the rebels who were tired of the monotony of manna and yearned to go back and eat the variety of foods in Egypt (11:4–6). In effect, the offering laws teach the Israelites how to properly receive and eat the meats God provides—with thanksgiving and the recognition that they are gifts from God (11:32–33; 15:1–16).

The death penalty by stoning in the case of the wood gatherer as commanded by God (15:36) contrasts with the rebellious attempt by the community to use death by stoning against the two faithful spies, Caleb and Joshua, in the spy story in Num. 14:10. The concern with both individual acts of sin and community acts of sin in 15:22–31 reflects the interplay of individuals and the whole community in Numbers 11—14. At times individuals engage in acts of rebellion (the "rabble"—11:4; Miriam and Aaron—12:1–3; the ten unfaithful spies—13:31–33; 14:36–38), and at other times the entire community is implicated as guilty (11:1, 4, 33; 14:1–4, 39–45).

Finally, the blue cords on the fringes of garments remind Israel to be diligent in obeying the commandments so that their eyes do not stray and they do "not follow the lust of your own heart and your own eyes" (15:39). The Hebrew reads literally, "so that you are not spying out [Hebrew *tur*] after your own heart and after your own eyes as you are whoring [Hebrew *zanah*] after them" (15:39, au. trans.). The same pair of Hebrew verbs, "to spy out" and "to whore after," occurs in 14: 33–34. There God condemns the faithless spies and the whole community for their "spying" and "whoring after" or "faithlessness," which led to the punishment of death in the wilderness. The verb "to whore after" is often used as an image for Israel's going after other gods or idols, phantom gods that are not the true God of Israel (e.g., Exod. 34:15–16). The faithless spies had redefined reality by claiming to see things that did not exist: a land that devoured its inhabitants and primordial giants named Nephilim (13:32–33) rather than God's gift of a very good land flowing with milk and honey. The rebellious people redefined reality by claiming to see Egypt as a place of salvation and promise (14:1–4) rather than the land of slavery, suffering, and death (Exod. 1:8–22; 3:7–9). Thus, the blue cord and fringes worn on their garments remind the people of their God and God's commandments, the first of which is that "I am the LORD your God . . . you shall have no other gods before me" (Exod. 20:2–3). Overall, the interconnections between Numbers 15 and the rebellion narratives that precede it are numerous. The laws function in relation to the rebellions as words of encouragement and reassurance to the new generation in spite of the disobedience and death of the old wilderness generation. In this case, the law functions as profound promise for the future.

The Interconnections between Numbers 15 and the Following Story in Numbers 16

The legal material in Numbers 15 also has a role to play in the interpretation of the narrative that follows, namely, the revolts by Korah, Dathan, and Abiram in chapter 16. The incident that causes the rebellion by Korah and his company is not immediately evident within the narrative itself. The rebels' charge against Moses involves his right to be the sole mediator of God's words and laws to the people (Num. 16:3, 13, 28–29). An early Aramaic translation, the Targum Jonathan, suggests that it was Moses' directive about wearing the blue cord and fringes on the people's garments (Num. 15:37–40) that was the specific reason for the rebellion; in this Moses had "gone too far" (Num. 16:3; de Vaulx, p. 189). In fact, the literary juxtaposition of the laws of Numbers 15 and the story of Korah's revolt implies something akin to the Targum's interpretation. The law about the blue cord and tassels may not itself have been the specific cause of the revolt, but it may have been part of the larger issue. Throughout chapter 15, the text notes repeatedly that God speaks only through Moses (15:1, 17, 22, 23, 35, 36, 37). This exclusive use of Moses as God's mouthpiece seems in the present shape of the text to be the necessary background for the otherwise unprovoked and unexplained revolt by Korah. In other words, while the interconnections with the rebellion stories in Numbers 11—14 suggested that the laws in chapter 15 functioned largely as words of promise and reassurance to the new generation, the following story of Korah and his cohorts suggests that these same words of chapter 15 were heard as a burden and threat by other hearers. One kind of hearing brings life to a new generation. Another kind of hearing brings threat and death to an old generation eager to exalt themselves and not accept God's chosen mediator and guide in Moses.

The laws in Numbers 15 also include discussions of intentional sins done "highhandedly" that despise the word of the LORD (15:30–31). Unintentional sins can be atoned for by the priest through an offering, but intentional and flagrant sins require that the person "be utterly cut off and bear the guilt" (15:31). The law about the fringes and blue cord emphasize Israel's need to pay close attention to the careful obedience of God's word. The story of the rebellions of Korah and company clearly presents them as examples of flagrant and intentional despising of God and God's mediator, Moses. The guilt of the rebels is obvious, and their actions require the severest penalty (16:31–35). The thankful offering by fire given to the LORD in a spirit of gratitude in Numbers 15 (vv. 3, 13, 14, 25) contrasts sharply with the rebels' presumptuous desire to take over Aaron's priestly role and to offer fire and incense before God in a spirit of exalting themselves (16:18, 35).

One of the final reminders in the series of laws in Numbers 15 is directed to all the people: "you shall be holy to the LORD your God" (15:40). Those who mount the insurrection in chapter 16 repeat this claim about the holiness of the whole congregation in their attack on Moses and Aaron: "All the congregation are holy, every one of them, and the LORD is among them." The rebels use the holiness of the community members as a basis for arguing that anyone, lay or Levite, can offer incense and sacrifices on the altar; it is not the exclusive right of Aaron and his sons. Their claim is repudiated by God, however, and so Israel learns that the nature of its holiness does not allow everyone in the community to act as a priest in approaching the altar. Numbers 15 portrays an important function of the true priest: "the priest shall make atonement for all the congregation of the Israelites" (15:25, 28). In chapter 16, Aaron confirms his proper status and function as the high priest as he stops the plague, stands between the living and the dead, and makes "atonement for the people" (16:47–48).

Thus, the collection of laws in Numbers 15 is intimately and artfully interwoven in words and themes with the rebellion stories that precede and follow it. The laws are words of promise for a new generation, but they become words of threat and burden for the old defiant generation. Numbers 15 also displays its own internal cohesion and logic of development through its several interlocking refrains and themes. The alleged "junk room" of Numbers is in reality an artfully designed treatise of laws and narrative echoes. The question at the end of Numbers 15 is whether the break in the narrative represented by the new laws and reminders in this chapter will put an end to the series of rebellions that had begun in Numbers 11—14. The answer follows in Numbers 16.

Numbers 16
The Rebellions Continue to Spread: From Levites to Lay Leaders to All the People

Gregory of Nyssa, a fourth-century Christian bishop, wrote a series of reflections on the spiritual life rooted in the biblical story of Moses. Like Moses, Gregory suffered attacks on his leadership by people motivated by envy and jealousy. Thus, Gregory identified with Moses' frustration over the attacks of his Levite brothers in Numbers 16. Gregory wrote these words:

> The envy of his brothers arose against him. Envy is the passion which causes evil, the father of death, the first entrance of sin, the root of wickedness, the birth of sorrow, the mother of misfortune, the basis of disobedience, the beginning of shame. . . . Envy fought against many who lived before Moses, but when it attacked this great man, it was broken like a clay pot being dashed against a rock. (Gregory of Nyssa, pp. 120–21)

If we wondered whether the downward slide into rebellion by the old generation had been effectively stopped by the interruption of laws in chapter 15, we soon find out in Numbers 16 that it has not. As we read through the previous rebellion stories in Numbers 11—14, we notice that the Levites are never mentioned as taking part in any of the uprisings. The reader may wonder about the fate of the Levites. Were the Levites included with the other twelve tribes in the condemnation of the old generation? Or did their separate status as Levites spare them from the rebellion and the sentence of death in the wilderness? Numbers 16 provides an answer. The story of Korah portrays the Levites' pull into the powerful vortex of the whirlpool of rebellion and revolt. The Levites eventually join the old wilderness generation in dying outside the promised land.

101

A number of earlier and later traditions have been brought together in Numbers 16 as the chapter recounts a series of uprisings against Moses and Aaron. The attack against Moses is led by a subordinate Levite named Korah. Joining him are two members of the Reuben tribe, Dathan and Abiram, and 250 other lay leaders of the community (16:1–2). On, another Reubenite, is also named as part of the rebel group in 16:1, but he does not appear again. The earliest form of the story may have focused only on a revolt against Moses by Dathan and Abiram of the tribe of Reuben (vv. 12–15). The narrative was then enlarged to include 250 lay leaders of the community who claimed the right to act as priests and offer incense at the altar in the tent of meeting (16:2, 4–7). They underwent a test to determine whether they were allowed to offer incense at the altar, and they were immediately torched by the fire of the LORD (16:18, 35). One of the last stages in the story's formation was the introduction of a leader from the tribe of Levi named Korah who leads the rebellion (16:1, 8–11, 16–17). These various traditions have been edited and woven together to form the present narrative. The special punishment of Korah, who is a Levite, emphasizes the Levites' role as servants to the true priests, Aaron and his sons. Some scholars have argued that this controversy between the Levites and the sons of Aaron may reflect an actual controversy within the historical priesthood of ancient Israel in the preexilic or postexilic periods. Such a controversy may have been associated with rival claims of priestly groups to supervise priestly duties in the Jerusalem temple. In the present form of the story in Numbers 16, the narrative simply confirms and extends the rebellious character of the old wilderness generation that was already evident in the earlier rebellion stories.

The First Rebellion: The Rebels and Their Charge against Moses and Aaron (16:1–3)

Numbers 16 actually portrays two separate rebellions—one rebellion led by Korah, Dathan, Abiram, and the 250 lay leaders (16:1–40) and a second rebellion by "the whole congregation" (16:41–50). The first rebellion was led initially by Korah, son of Kohath, son of Levi (16:1). The Kohathites were the clan of Levites responsible for the "most holy things" of the ark and tabernacle (Num. 4:4). Therefore, they received special warnings about not touching and not even looking at the holy articles of the tabernacle upon pain of death (Num. 4:15; 17–20). Dathan and Abiram were from the tribe of Reuben, the firstborn son of Jacob whose name was in the place of prominence in the first census list in chapter 1. However, the Reuben tribe was demoted and Judah took over as the lead tribe in the arrangement of the holy war camp (Numbers 2). Moreover, the census totals for the tribe of Reuben diminished somewhat from the first census in Numbers 1:21 (46,500) to the second census list in Numbers 26:7 (43,730), while the respective numbers for Judah increased in similar proportions. The second census list also explicitly mentions the rebellions of Korah, Dathan, and Abiram in 26:9–11. Thus, the demotion of Reuben in the arrangement of the camp and its diminishing numbers from one census list to the other corresponds to the guilt and punishment that the two Reubenite leaders incur in the revolt in Numbers 16. Finally, 250 lay leaders also join Korah, Dathan, and Abiram in confronting Moses and Aaron with the charge that they have exalted themselves over the rest of the holy congregation of Israel; Moses and Aaron "have gone too far" (16:3)!

As we indicated in the study of Numbers 15, the precise cause for this charge is not at all clear within the story of Numbers 16 itself. Presumably, the mediation of all the laws in Numbers 15 through Moses (15:1, 17, 22, 23, 35, 36, 37) and the emphasis on the role of Aaron as priest in receiving sacrifices and making atonement (15:25, 28, 33) provided the immediate context for spurring on the revolt.

Six Responses of Moses to the Attacks against Moses and Aaron (16:4–17)

Moses has six responses to the attack of Korah and his crew. First, Moses falls on his face in a gesture of intercession to God, since he knows this is an attack on God more than an attack on himself and Aaron (16:4). Second, Moses invites "Korah and all his company" to a showdown at the tent of meeting on the morning of the next day. Everyone is to bring their censer or fire pan in which incense is burned to the tabernacle. There they will all light the censers, and then God will choose the holy one who is allowed to bring fire before the LORD (16:5–8). Moses responds to the charge that he has gone too far (16:3) with the counter-charge, "You Levites have gone too far" (16:8)!

The third response by Moses is to Korah alone (16:8–11). Moses reminds Korah that God had separated the Levites out as a special tribe. They were allowed to approach God in taking care of the LORD's tabernacle and to serve the congregation in a place of honor as a buffer between God's presence and the rest of the twelve tribes. Their envy and discontent in not being full priests is equivalent to mutiny, being

103

"gathered together against the LORD" (16:11). After his words with Korah, Moses' fourth response is to send for Dathan and Abiram. They refuse to obey Moses' command to appear before him. Their grievance is less with Aaron's special position as priest and more with Moses' claim as leader. In a dramatic reversal of reality, they charge Moses with taking them out of Egypt, which they claim was "a land flowing with milk and honey;" all Moses has given them is a desolate wilderness. They sarcastically turn Moses' phrase to the Levites in 16:9 against Moses himself in 16:13, "Is it too little that you have brought us out of a land flowing with milk and honey?" In the end, Dathan and Abiram simply refuse Moses' command: "We will not come" (16:12–14)!

The fifth act of response by Moses is to become angry and to speak to God in his own defense against his detractors. He asks God not to pay attention to the offering of the rebels, which would signify the severing of the relationship between them and God. Moses assures God that he has not even taken a donkey from any of them nor has he harmed them in any other way (16:15).

The sixth response by Moses is to turn back to Korah and repeat the instructions for the test on the next day. Korah, the 250 lay leaders, and Aaron will all appear before the tent of meeting with their censers to present fire to the LORD (16:16–17).

The Test: Showdown at the Tent of Meeting (16:18–35)

On the next day, Korah and the 250 lay leaders all stand with Moses and Aaron at the tent of meeting and light their censers with fire. God appears and tells Moses and Aaron to separate themselves from this congregation so that God might "consume them in a moment" (16:21). God had made a similar threat to strike Israel with pestilence and disinherit Israel during the rebellion of the spy story in Numbers 14:11–12. In the Korah rebellion in Numbers 16, however, the issue is not God's total disinheritance of Israel. The issue is the immediate death of the old wilderness generation. The laws in Numbers 15 continue to offer the promise that God would bring the new generation of Israelites to the promised land (15:2, 18). Moses and Aaron fall on their faces in a posture of intercession and pray, "O God . . . shall one person sin and you become angry with the whole congregation" (16:22)? But what does this prayer on behalf of the people mean? The prayer seems to imply that Korah, Dathan, Abiram and

104

the 250 other rebels are the only guilty ones while the rest of the congregation remains innocent. Then the prayer would be somewhat similar to Abraham's bold bargaining with God about the ten righteous people being able to save the whole wicked city of Sodom (Gen. 18:23–33). But is the congregation of Israel really innocent? Why then is the "whole congregation" assembled with Korah in 16:19, apparently on his side? The solution seems to be that clearly the leaders hold the greatest guilt in this "highhanded" rebellion, and the people are relatively less guilty in their intentions at this point. The whole people's moment of rebellion will come later in 16:41–50.

God instructs the congregation to get away from the houses of the rebel leaders—Korah, Dathan, and Abiram. The people obey. Now that they are safely apart from the rest of the Israelites, Moses offers a sign or test to determine whether the charges of Korah and company against Moses and Aaron are true or are acts of rebelling against God. If Korah and company die a natural death, then they are right in their charge that God has not sent Moses as their leader. If God does something new by having the ground open up and swallow them alive into the place of the dead in Sheol, then the people will know that Korah and his crew have despised the LORD.

Immediately, the ground opens up and swallows Korah and his household (16:31–33). Presumably Dathan and Abiram were also swallowed up, although they are not explicitly mentioned at this point. Other Old Testament texts do include them in the earthquake-like swallowing of the rebels (Deut. 11:6; Ps. 106:17). Sheol in the Old Testament is the abode of the dead for both the wicked and the righteous. Sheol is a dark place of silence below the earth where even the righteous can no longer remember or praise God (Pss. 6:5; 18:5). Only much later in the apocalyptic traditions of the Old Testament did notions of resurrection from Sheol emerge (Dan. 12:2–3). Thus, later Christian conceptions of hell as a place of eternal torment only for the wicked and heaven as a place of eternal bliss reflect quite different conceptions from the Old Testament understanding of death and Sheol. The punishment in Numbers 16 is the premature death of the rebels as opposed to their dying a natural death (16:29–30). The destination in both cases is the same, Sheol.

The earth's swallowing of the rebels causes panic among the rest of the congregation as they run and cry out, "The earth will swallow us too" (16:34)! The people reveal some inkling that they may be somewhat implicated in the whole affair as well. Meanwhile, back at the tent of meeting the 250 lay leaders each with a burning censer are suddenly consumed as fire comes out from the LORD (16:35). The bronze

105

censers of the 250 leaders have become holy by being offered to God but "at the cost of their lives" (16:38). The censers are hammered into a covering for the altar as a visual memory aid to remind Israel that only descendants of Aaron should offer incense before the LORD (16:-36–40). Exodus 38:2 also speaks of a bronze overlay for the altar; it may be simply another tradition or the altar covering in Numbers 16 may be a supplemental covering.

The Second Rebellion: All the People and Their Charge against Aaron and Moses (16:41–50)

It was unclear earlier in the story whether "the whole congregation" had been implicated in the guilt of Korah and the other rebels. Numbers 16:19 seemed to indicate that they were standing with Korah in the rebellion, while the prayer in 16:22 suggests that only individual leaders were involved in the rebellion and not "the whole congregation." In verses 41–50, however, it becomes exceedingly clear that "the whole congregation of the Israelites" joins the rebellion against Moses and Aaron. The people accuse them, *"You* [the Hebrew is emphatic] have killed the people of the LORD" (16:41). Moses and Aaron, they claim, are the ones responsible for the death of their leaders.

The response of God is precisely the same as before. God says to Moses, "Get away from this congregation, so that I may consume them in a moment" (17:45). The words are the same, but the context is somewhat different. Before in 16:21 when God spoke the same words, Korah and the individual leaders were the guilty ones, and yet their individual actions endangered the whole community, which was largely innocent. Now in 16:45, the community as a whole is clearly guilty and thus Moses cannot use his earlier argument of appealing to God to spare the innocent. Instead, Moses sends Aaron to take fire out from the altar in his censer and carry it into the midst of the congregation "and make atonement for them" (16:46). God's wrath had already begun as a plague, but Aaron's act of atonement stopped the plague so that Aaron "stood between the dead and the living" (16:48). Over 14,700 people died as a result of the plague and rebellion, a tragic step along the way of the wilderness generation's gradual dying off during its forty years of desert sojourn to nowhere.

To stand between the dead and the living is the place and vocation of the priest. As we have seen in the earlier discussions of the ark and the arrangement of the camp (Numbers 2—4), the priests and the Levites formed a buffer zone between the sinful people of Israel and the fiery holiness of God's presence in the midst of the camp. Aaron's success in stopping the plague with his censer is further demonstration of his unique and proper status as the high priest of Israel who makes atonement for Israel's sin.

Echoes Elsewhere in Numbers

The story of Korah, Dathan, and Abiram resonates in several ways with other texts throughout the book of Numbers. Our discussion of the laws in Numbers 15 already noted several connections with Korah's rebellion in chapter 16 (highhanded sin, priest as making atonement, commandments only through Moses as cause of Korah's complaint). Korah's status as a Levite and a Kohathite leads us back to the picture of total obedience and careful order in the arrangement of the camp and the assignment of duties surrounding the tabernacle in Numbers 2—4. The Levites' special status as the tribe closest to the tabernacle should have brought satisfaction and fulfillment to them, but in chapter 16 Korah wants the full privilege and responsibility of the high priest (16:3, 8–11). This envious revolt signals the further unraveling of the meticulous ordering of the holy war camp which had begun in earnest in the spy story in Numbers 13—14. In the spy story, the rebels claimed that the land of Canaan "devours its inhabitants" (13:32), a mythic image that caused the people to rebel against going into the land. Now in Numbers 16, what Israel feared in Canaan becomes reality in the desert as God opens up the ground, which swallows Korah and his cohorts alive (16:31–33).

The 250 lay leaders sought to usurp the role of Aaron the priest by offering fire and incense before the LORD. Ironically, they suffer the same fate as Aaron's two sons, Nadab and Abihu: "fire came out from the LORD and consumed" them (16:35). Numbers 3:4 earlier reported, "Nadab and Abihu died before the LORD when they offered illicit fire before the LORD."

Conflicts over authority and jealousy have appeared earlier in Numbers. Aaron himself along with Miriam had challenged Moses' authority with a question quite similar to Korah's: "Has the LORD spoken only through Moses? Has he not spoken through us also" (12:2)? Aaron found himself on the other end of that same question when Korah and his company asked Moses and Aaron, "All the congregation are holy, every one of them. . . . So why then do you exalt yourselves above the assembly of the LORD" (16:3)? The message of the Korah story is that certain functions associated with the holy tabernacle and leadership of the community should be performed only by those leaders and priests whom God has chosen and commissioned. Yet these leaders are not perfect; Aaron in his rebellion against Moses is one example. Moreover, Moses at times had welcomed guidance from outside divinely chosen channels. Examples include Hobab the Midianite (10:29–32) and the prophesying in the camp by Eldad and Medad (11:26–30). Thus, the total witness of Numbers suggests communities of faith ought to honor their leaders and respect certain divisions of functions between lay people and ordained clergy. But community leaders also need to be open to their own sinfulness and to listen to voices of potential wisdom and guidance. Problems in either case, whether among leaders or followers, arise when envy, self-exaltation and personal attack take over from a genuine concern for obedience to God's will and the well-being of the entire community.

The story of Korah's rebellion raises the large issue of the role of ordination and clergy within the Christian church. Among Protestants, the notion of "the priesthood of all believers" sounds strikingly similar to Korah's words, "All the congregation are holy, every one of them, and the LORD is among them." Martin Luther built his notion of all Christians as priests on the foundation of the text in I Peter 2:5, 9:

> Like living stones, let yourselves be built into a spiritual house, to be a holy priesthood, to offer spiritual sacrifices acceptable to God through Jesus Christ. . . . You are a chosen race, a royal priesthood, a holy nation, God's own people.

This New Testament text in turn has its roots in the Old Testament narrative of God's transformation of the slave people of Israel in Egypt to their new status as God's holy and exalted nation: "You shall be for me a priestly kingdom and a holy nation" (Exod. 19:6). Korah and his followers seem to have some biblical basis for their position!

However, the Exodus and I Peter texts are speaking of the community or people as a whole functioning as God's priestly people, set apart as a holy instrument of God "in order that you might proclaim the mighty acts of him who called you out of darkness into his marvelous light" (I Peter 2:9). The texts do not speak to issues of individual leaders or priests within the community. Other biblical texts deal with such issues of church order more directly (e.g., I Peter 4—5; Nelson, pp. 166–68).

Christians have varied widely on the question of ordained clergy. Some traditions reject any notion of a special clerical office. Others have clearly defined offices for preaching and administering the sacraments. Requirements for ordination vary from the need for apostolic succession through bishops to a call from a larger church body to the call of any single congregation. Some traditions call their ordained ministers priests, and others carefully avoid such a designation. One significant New Testament text in this regard is the letter to the Hebrews, in which Jesus is named the "great high priest" who "holds his priesthood permanently, because he continues forever" (Heb. 4:14; 7:24). Like Aaron who made atonement and interceded for Israel as he stood between the dead and the living, Jesus as priest "is able for all time to save those who approach God through him, since he always lives to make intercession for them" (Heb. 7:25). Hebrews argues that the sacrificial role of human priests has been taken over by Christ's one-time sacrifice on the cross:

> Unlike the other high priests, he has no need to offer sacrifices day after day, first for his own sins, and then for those of the people; this he did once for all when he offered himself. (Heb. 7:27)

Some Christian traditions have seen the priestly office as entirely taken over by the sacrificial act of Jesus and so prefer other titles for their clergy or leaders. Other traditions continue to use the term priest for clergy, as the office encompasses a variety of functions beyond only the offering of sacrifices.

As we return to the context of the narratives and development of the book of Numbers, the rebellion of Korah, Dathan, Abiram, the 250 lay leaders, and finally the whole congregation suggests a spreading out and extension of the spirit of rebellion among the members of the old wilderness generation. In spite of the interruption of the additional laws in Numbers 15, the old generation has continued its downward spiral into ongoing rebellion, disintegration as a community, and despising God and God's gifts of the land, God's commandments, and God's chosen leaders. Are there ways by which Aaron's prerogatives as priest can be visually hammered home into the minds of the Israelites? Does Israel need a review of the rights and responsibilities of the priesthood and the role of the Levites? These questions form the basis for the next two chapters, Numbers 17 and 18, in which the issue of Aaron's claim to the priesthood and the functions of priests and Levites will be given more detailed and sustained attention. This may help preserve the lives of the old wilderness generation for a time longer, although their eventual sentence of death in the wilderness is irrevocable since God swore it with an oath (Num. 14:28–30). But equally irrevocable are God's longstanding promises to Israel that God would bring them to the promised land, promises which now are given to the new generation of "little ones" who are growing up in the wilderness even as their parents are dying in the desert (Num. 14:31; 15:2, 18, 41).

Numbers 17—18
Aaron's Flowering Staff and the Priests' Duties and Support

The rebellions of Korah, Dathan, Abiram, and the 250 lay leaders in Numbers 16 had challenged the exclusive role of Aaron as the high priest of Israel. The challenge to Aaron came from two directions, one from a fellow Levite and the other from the non-Levite lay leaders. Korah was a member of the tribe of Levi, the same tribe to which Aaron belonged (Exod. 6:16–20). Korah's major concern was to expand the priesthood beyond Aaron and his sons to include all Levites (Num. 16:8–10). Dathan and Abiram and the 250 other lay leaders, on the other hand, defied the authority of Moses and Aaron because they wanted to extend the privileges of priesthood not just to other Levites but to all Israelites from any of the twelve tribes (Num. 16:3, 12–14, 41–50).

The rebellions of chapter 16 clearly display some of the people's lingering resistance to the importance of a separate and designated priesthood among them. The story of Aaron's rod in chapter 17 addresses this lingering opposition. The story of the flowering rod of Aaron confirms once and for all God's appointment of Aaron and his sons to the priesthood. In the end, the people finally assent to their need for priests to represent them before the altar of the LORD (17:12–13). Numbers 18 follows with laws that spell out the duties of the Aaronic priests and Levites. The chapter also outlines the means of supporting the material needs of the priests and Levites from the sacrifices, offerings, and tithes brought to the altar by the people.

Aaron's Budding Almond Rod (17:1–12)

In Numbers 16, Moses had set up a dangerous test for the rebels as they brought censers with fire before the altar of the LORD. They were literally playing with fire, and the explosive holiness of God's presence erupted in fire, earthquake, and plague upon those who dared to encroach upon the tabernacle. The leaders of the revolt were

110

dead. Thousands more died in the plague. These dramatic events should have been sufficient proof to the Israelites of Aaron's special status as high priest. But one more sign was required as an ongoing reminder or visual aid that Aaron and his sons alone could mediate between God and the people at the altar of the sanctuary.

God instructs Moses to set up one final test in order to persuade the people of God's selection of Aaron as priest. This time the test is less dangerous and less dramatic. The leaders of the twelve ancestral tribes bring their tribal "staffs" to the tent of meeting and set them before the ark of the covenant. The leaders write their individual names upon their own tribal staffs. Aaron also takes the staff of the tribe of Levi and writes his name upon it (17:1–7). It is unclear in verse 6 whether 12 or 13 staffs are set up; the narrative seems to assume that there are 12 tribal staffs plus one Levite tribal staff. A word play is at work in this test; the Hebrew word for "staff" or "rod" is *matteh,* which also means "tribe."

Moses then deposits the tribal staffs overnight in the tent of meeting. God decrees that the tribe and the person whose rod sprouts on the following day is the one chosen by God to officiate at the altar. God assumes that this will provide definitive proof, "thus I will put a stop to the complaints of the Israelites" (17:5). Moses enters the tent of meeting and finds that the tribal staff of the Levites with Aaron's name on it has sprouted buds, flowers, and ripe almonds. The dead stick has come to life as a sign of God's special choosing of Aaron and the Levites to care for and administer the sanctuary cult. Moses then brings out all the tribal staffs so the whole congregation will see that only Aaron's had sprouted. God instructs Moses to place the sprouted staff of Aaron before the ark of the covenant for the future "as a warning to rebels, so that you may make an end of their complaints against me, or else they will die" (17:8).

The test apparently works too well. The people have seen the awesome power and danger of God's holy presence in their midst. The dead bodies of rebels are all around. The amazing budding of Aaron's staff suggests a power at work in their midst that far exceeds their comprehension. The people are thrown into a frenzied panic and fear for their lives. They cry to Moses: "We are perishing; we are lost, all of us are lost! Every one who approaches the tabernacle of the LORD will die. Are we all to perish?" The pendulum has swung from one extreme to the other. Earlier the leaders of the people had confidently approached the altar with fire under the mistaken conviction that all members of the community could take on the role of priest. Then the people run away from the tabernacle in terror, afraid for their lives.

111

At this point the people have reached a teachable moment. It is time to re-learn what had been taught earlier but apparently forgotten. The separate priesthood exists for the sake of protecting the community. The priests and Levites serve as a buffer of protection against the people encroaching upon the holy sanctuary (Num. 3:10, 38). The priests also provide a channel by which the powerful blessing of God is mediated to the community (Num. 6:22–27). Thus, the people are ready to accept the division of labor and responsibility assigned to the priests and the distinctive means of supporting the priests and Levites through sacrifices, offerings, and tithes, all of which will be outlined in some detail in the next chapter, Numbers 18.

The community of Israel has discovered that God's power in their midst is experienced either as threat or promise, death or life. Two visual aids are set up in the sanctuary for future remembrance by succeeding generations of the danger and the blessing associated with approaching God's presence. One visual aid is the bronze covering of the altar made from the charred censers or fire pans. The rebels had used the bronze censers to offer fire to God without priestly mediation, and they had died in a fiery holocaust. The altar covering of bronze is a cold, metallic, and lifeless reminder of death (16:39–40). The second visual aid displayed in the sanctuary is the budding, blossoming, fruit-bearing staff of Aaron. It signifies the blessing power of God's holy presence as conveyed through the Aaronic priesthood that gives life and bears fruit among God's sinful people. These two visual signs capture both the potential power of death and the power of life that flow from God's presence in the midst of God's people.

The story of Aaron's budding staff caught the imagination of ancient Christian commentators who saw it as a type of the resurrected Christ who blossomed to life after being dead on the cross. Aaron's flowering staff was also joined with the image of the budding stump of Jesse, father of King David. Thus, Aaron's rod was a witness to the coming of God's Messiah in Isa. 11:1–2: "A shoot shall come out of the stump of Jesse, and a branch shall grow out of his roots." The story of the blooming staff of Aaron distinguished between true and false priests and so recalled for early Christian commentators the words of Jesus regarding true and false prophets:

> Beware of false prophets, who come to you in sheep's clothing but inwardly are ravenous wolves. . . . Every good tree bears good fruit, but the bad tree bears bad fruit. . . . Thus you will know them by their fruit. (Matt. 7:15–20)

Like Aaron, Jesus proved to be the true high priest not by exalting himself but by being truly called by God. In its discussion of Jesus as the great high priest, the letter to the Hebrews observes that

> one does not presume to take this honor, but takes it only when called by God, just as Aaron was. So also Christ did not glorify himself in becoming a high priest, but was appointed by the one who said to him, "You are my Son, today I have begotten you." (Heb. 5:4–5; de Vaulx, pp. 202–3)

The poet Howard Nemerov draws together the whole complex of biblical images of trees and staffs and wood, and he uses them to trace the biblical story of human salvation. In Nemerov's poem, one hears allusions to the tree of life standing between the rivers in the Garden of Eden (Gen. 2:9–10), Aaron's rod that turned into a serpent before Pharaoh and swallowed the other serpents (Exod. 7:8–13), the flowering staff of Aaron (Num. 17:1–8), the Messianic stump of Jesse (Isa. 11:1–2), and the three crosses of the Gospels' crucifixion scene that appear like the masts of a sailing ship with Jesus and the two robbers hanging from the crossbeams. The poem concludes with the wooden crown of thorns, a wooden lance or spear, and the wooden ladder the soldier used to climb up and pierce the side of Jesus from which came the blood that gives life and salvation (John 19:31–37). In the eleventh stanza of his poem "Runes" Nemerov writes:

> A holy man said to me, "Split the stick
> And there is Jesus." When I split the stick
> To the dark marrow and the splintery grain
> I saw nothing that was not wood, nothing
> That was not God, and I began to dream
> How from the tree that stood between the rivers
> Came Aaron's rod that crawled in front of Pharaoh,
> And came the rod of Jesse flowering
> In all the generations of the Kings,
> And came the timbers of the second tree,
> The sticks and yardarms of the holy three-
> Masted vessel whereon the Son of Man
> Hung between thieves, and came the crown of thorns,
> The lance and ladder, when was shed that blood
> Streamed in the grain of Adam's tainted seed.
> (Jeffrey, 3–4)

Aaron, the high priest of Israel, stands in a long line of God's chosen deliverers who have brought life and blessing to God's sinful people.

Mutual Obligations: The Responsibilities of Priests and Levites, the Responsibilities of the Community, and the Responsibility of God

The atmosphere of these chapters in Numbers has gradually shifted. We began in Numbers 16 with a dangerous test of offering fire to the LORD that ended in earth-shattering and fire-blazing death. The test of the tribal staffs in Numbers 17 was much calmer and ended in a positive affirmation of Aaron's priesthood rather than the rejection and death of rebels. As we move into Numbers 18, the narrative action stops for a time as first Aaron and then Moses receive God's further instructions in regard to the priesthood. The instructions include the obligations of the Aaronic priests and Levites toward God and the community. The instructions also include the reciprocal obligations of the community toward the priests and Levites. The community is well prepared to receive the instructions insofar as they realize more than ever the necessity and the well-being that a truly faithful priesthood brings to the congregation of God's people.

Chapter 18 begins with the words, "The LORD said to Aaron" (18:1). The phrase occurs again twice in 18:8 and 18:20. In every other case in the Pentateuch except one (Lev. 10:8), God never speaks to Aaron directly but always through Moses (e.g., Num. 8:1–2). In this case, God gives Aaron the benefit of a personal and direct word as a further sign of his special relationship to God. This and the other events of the preceding chapters confirm Aaron's status of high priest, a status that may have been under some question since Aaron and Miriam's challenge to Moses and affront to God in chapter 12 and the challenges of the community in chapter 16.

God's words to Aaron stress the responsibility of the inner circle of Aaronic priests to be on the front lines of bearing the sin of the community. The priests are to protect the community from drawing near to the holy vessels and furnishings of the inner sanctuary. Failure to do so will result in the death of those who approach as well as the death of the priest responsible for guarding the altar (18:3). The Levites form a second line of protection around the tent of meeting. Together the priests and Levites guard the Israelite camp from encroaching upon the holiness of God's presence in their midst in the tent of meeting. In this way, they protect the community from the wrath of God and the death that it brings (18:1–5). This service that the priests and Levites

114

offer to the community is a gift from God designed for their own well-being. Therefore, support of the priests and the Levites should be generous and done from a sense of gratitude and not mere obligation (17:6–7).

Numbers 18:8 begins an extended summary of the sacrifices, the firstfruit offerings of crops, the firstborn animals, and the devoted items captured in holy war conquests that the priests are to receive as their due. The basic understanding is stated by God to the priests in this way: "I have given you charge of the offerings made to me . . . ; I have given them to you and your sons as a priestly portion due you in perpetuity" (8:8). In other words, people make offerings to God, and God in turn passes these gifts on to the priests. Many of these same laws concerning sacrifices and offerings are found in other texts in the Pentateuch (e.g., Lev. 6—7; 27). Their role here is to review the obligations the community bears to support the priests as they make their offerings and sacrifices in thanksgiving and repentance before God.

God pledges in a "covenant of salt forever" that "all the holy offerings that the Israelites present to the LORD I have given to you, together with your sons and daughters, as a perpetual due." Salt is a preservative, and it often formed a significant part of covenant meals and agreements in the ancient Near East (Milgrom, p. 154). Thus, the chapter deals with obligations and responsibilities on the part of the priests and Levites as well as the community and God. The system of support is extended to future generations "as a perpetual due." This reminder pushes our gaze for a moment to the future of a new generation in the promised land. Like the laws on sacrifices and offerings in Numbers 15, the laws here in chapter 18 concerning the sacrifices and offerings and devoted spoils of holy war all pertain only to the time when Israel has arrived and settled in the land of Canaan. The long list of various sacrifices and offerings conjures up a picture of a lush and fertile land, settled and secure communities, productive agriculture, and herds and flocks on all the hills. This specific note about the sons and daughters of Aaron also points ahead to the death of Aaron in Numbers 20 and the succession of the priesthood to his sons. These laws ensure that material support for the priests will continue even after Aaron is gone.

The primary rationale for the priests receiving the offerings made to God is noted in Num. 18:20. God says to Aaron, "You shall have no allotment in their land, nor shall you have any share among them; I am your share and your possession among the Israelites." The priests lived in total dependence on God, with no property base of their own in the land of Canaan. The priests were a constant reminder of what was ultimately true of all the Israelites; they all lived in dependence on God's gifts and blessing.

Numbers 18:21–29 turns its attention from the priests of Aaron to the Levites. Although the Levites had been implicated in the previous revolts of Korah and company (Num. 16:1, 7), God reassures the Levites that their role in providing service to the sons of Aaron will continue. God also assures the Levites that they will receive the tithe (or tenth part) offering of the people. God's provision for the support of the Levites through the tithe offering reinforces in no uncertain terms their important role into future generations. The Levites, like the priests, will have no allotment or tribal territory of their own in Canaan. The Levites will be dependent on God and the tithe offerings of the people (18:24).

In the final section, God turns from speaking to Aaron and speaks instead to Moses (18:25). The change in addressee occurs because God is instructing the Levites about their need to give an offering to the priestly sons of Aaron from the offerings they receive. It would appear unseemly for Aaron himself to command the Levites to give an offering to Aaron and his sons, and so God turns to Moses for this part of the instructions. The Levites receive the tithe or one-tenth offering to help support their life and work in the tent of meeting. In turn, the Levites are to give a tithe (one-tenth) of the tithe they receive to the Aaronic priests. The tithe they give is to be the best part of what they receive (18:25–31). In this way, the important but subordinate role of the Levites is built into the very structure of their ongoing support and work. The words to the Levites end in 18:32 with a final warning that any further revolts or misuses of the holy gifts of the Israelites as in the case of Korah will end only in death.

The New Testament also deals with the need to support the leaders and preachers in their work of spreading the gospel. The apostle Paul in I Corinthians 9 defends the need of the community to share its material benefits with the apostle and other congregational leaders. Paul makes reference to the priests and Levites and asks,

> Do you not know that those who are employed in the temple service get their food from the temple, and those who serve at the altar share in what is sacrificed on the altar? In the same way, the Lord commanded that those who proclaim the gospel should get their living by the gospel. (I Cor. 9:13–14)

116

Paul's reference to what "the Lord commanded" may be a saying of Jesus embedded in the account of his sending out the disciples on a mission to proclaim the gospel. Jesus sends them out without any money so that they might be dependent on the offering of hospitality from the towns they visit, "for laborers deserve their food" (Matt. 10: 10; Luke 10:7). First Timothy 5:17–18 takes up the same saying in urging the support of the church's elders.

The special calling of the priests and Levites in Numbers 18 included having no tribal territory of their own in the land in Canaan. Jesus called his followers to a similar life of trust and dependence on God without excessive worry over material needs: "Strive first for the kingdom of God and his righteousness, and all these things will be given to you as well" (Matt. 6:33). The disciples of Jesus had left everything to follow him, and Jesus responds, "Everyone who has left houses or brothers or sisters or father or mother or children or fields, for my name's sake, will receive a hundredfold, and will inherit eternal life" (Matt. 19:27–29). The special calling of priests and proclaimers of the gospel entails living in profound trust in God's providential care and working in diligent obedience to the call and will of God. The community of faith, in turn, is likewise called to diligent support of those who lead and guide the community in its life of worship and service.

Pro-Priestly Texts and a Healthy Hermeneutics of Suspicion

Before leaving this section on the priests and Levites, we need to make one additional point. The texts of Numbers 16—18 have been heavily pro-priestly in their outlook. They have emphasized the community's obligation to support the Aaronic priests and Levites in their work of protecting the people and ministering in the sanctuary at the center of the camp. As we have noted, historical conflicts and rivalries among various priestly and Levitical groups in the actual life of ancient Israel and its cult may well lie behind some of these texts. Readers infected with a healthy dose of a hermeneutics of suspicion may look at this material rather cynically. They may conclude that these stories are simply pro-Aaronic propaganda pieces designed to ensure unquestioning loyalty and support to the one surviving priestly group who had the final word in giving these stories their present shape.

The stories, however, show some evidence of having been shaped and edited over a considerable length of time and through various contexts in Israel's history, whether before, during, or after Judah's exile to Babylon. They have continued to function in communities of faith on through the life of the Jewish synagogue, the New Testament and early

117

church, and up to the present day. We have seen analogies to their perspectives and themes in the New Testament that ring true to the experience of communities of faith. Moreover, the Old Testament itself contains an ample dose of a hermeneutics of suspicion in regard to the potential for abuse and misconduct among priests and other leaders of the community.

This long experience with priests and other leaders is one distinctive contribution that the Old Testament makes to a full biblical understanding of the offices of priests and others who hold special authority or functions within the community of faith. Israel's long history included numerous incidents of clergy misconduct, misappropriation of offerings, and general abuse of authority. God condemned the priestly sons of Eli to death for abusing their office, mishandling the temple sacrifices, treating the offerings of the LORD with contempt, and engaging in sexual misconduct outside the tent of meeting at the sanctuary at Shiloh (I Sam. 2:12–36). The prophets, too, frequently passed judgment on the abuses of clergy. Hosea 4:8 and 5:1 aimed words of judgment at the priests in northern Israel. The prophet Amos challenged the King's priest named Amaziah, who tried but failed to silence Amos's words of judgment against him and the nation as a whole. Jeremiah was called to prophesy against the rulers and priests of Judah (Jer. 1:18). His so-called Temple speech delivered in Jerusalem was a biting critique of the priests and worship life of the Jerusalem temple (Jeremiah 7; 26). The priests joined other leaders in a failed attempt to kill Jeremiah and thus silence his criticism (Jer. 26:7–24). Late in the Old Testament period, the prophet Malachi detailed the extensive abuse of the priests who served in the Second Temple in Jerusalem (Mal. 1:6—2:9).

The Old Testament's recognition of the potential sinfulness of the priesthood was built into its account of the inauguration of the Israelite priesthood. The high priest Aaron included among the sacrifices at the altar a sin offering to make atonement for the sins of Aaron himself (Lev. 9:7–8). The narrative of the death of Aaron's two sons, Nadab and Abihu, in Lev. 10:1–7 is also a dramatic reminder at the very start of the Israelite priesthood that priests were capable of grave sin and subject to the judgment of God. This incident is recalled in Num. 3:4, and again in Num. 26:61 in the course of the second census list of the new generation. The rebellion of Korah the Levite also testifies to the potential for disobedience among those who serve in the worship life of the sanctuary (Numbers 16). Thus, the Old Testament has a built-in critique of the priesthood that guards against an idealizing of the Aaronic, Levitical, or any other priestly group. Any exercise in the hermeneutics of suspicion aimed at biblical texts will be most faithful if it is rooted in the Bible's own inner critique of human abuse of power and sin against God.

Numbers 19
Staying Clean in the Midst of Death: The Ashes of the Red Cow and the Purification of the Unclean

The first half of the book of Numbers has progressed from the organization of the holy war camp of Israel in Numbers 1—10 through a series of rebellions beginning in Numbers 11. The rebellions and subsequent punishments for thousands of Israelites saturate the stories in chapters 11—18 with death. Some on the fringes of the Israelite community were consumed by the fire of the LORD in 11:1. A "very great plague" associated with eating quail caused the death of many in 11:33. The ten rebellious spies died of a divine plague in 14:37. Other Israelites were killed in a failed military venture into the promised land in 14:45. The households of Korah, Dathan, Abiram, and 250 other insurrectionists were destroyed by earthquake and fire. The latest plague up to this point had killed 14,700 Israelites before Aaron's act of atonement stopped any further death (16:49). From Num. 5:2 we know that contact with dead bodies renders a person unclean and endangers the purity of the whole community unless it is cleansed. With so much death and the pollution of corpses in their midst, how are Israelites to be rendered clean and pure? It is this pressing question that Numbers 19 seeks to address by means of its ritual of purification involving the ashes of the red heifer or red cow.

The immediately preceding texts about Korah in chapter 16, Aaron's almond staff in chapter 17, and the duties and support of the clergy in chapter 18 placed the spotlight on reaffirming the structure and service of priests and Levites within the community of Israel. The circles of holiness emanating out from the central sanctuary affirmed the place of the priests in the inner circle, the Levites as a secondary circle, and the twelve tribes in the outer rim of the Israelite camp. The ritual of the red cow changes the focus from the inner circles of the clergy to the lay members of the community. The red cow ritual for purifying those who had touched a corpse could be performed by lay

119

people and did not require priests. Matters of purity and ritual were not entirely the concern of religious professionals; the red cow ritual involves all Israelites in keeping the camp ritually pure and clean. Thus, we move from a focus on priests in chapter 17 to priests and Levites in chapter 18 to lay people in chapter 19.

Contact with a dead body was considered a severe form of contamination in ancient Israel and throughout much of the ancient Near East. The mixing of the ashes of a red cow with water and other elements to make a solution with which to purify oneself after touching a dead body probably had roots in a very ancient practice associated with beliefs in the spirits and power of the dead to affect the living. But in its present form in the book of Numbers, the ritual of purification is necessary because of the holiness of God's presence in the middle of the community of sinful people (see the Excursus on "Purity in the Bible" in the discussion of Numbers 5—6). The prevalence of death and the necessary concern for its polluting effects on the camp stem in large part from the sinful rebellions of the people against the God of Israel.

Although lay people could apply the purifying water mixed with the ashes of the red cow, the priest supervised the production of the ashes. The details of the priest's preparation of the special cleansing agent are given in verses 1–10. The Israelites bring to the priest a red cow. The NRSV translates the Hebrew word as red "heifer," (i.e., a female bovine that has not yet had a calf). However, the Hebrew word does not necessarily mean only a heifer and should better be translated as a red "cow." The cow is to be without defect, unblemished, and never used for work. The red cow is slaughtered before the priest "outside the camp." The priest takes some of the blood and sprinkles it seven times toward the front of the tent of meeting. This signals that the primary concern of the red cow ritual is preserving order within the camp for the sake of the tabernacle in its midst. Then all of the cow is burned—its skin, flesh, blood, and even its dung. No other biblical ritual has such strict requirements for burning the whole animal. The priest adds cedarwood, hyssop (or marjoram), and crimson material or yarn to the fire as additional cleansing agents that become part of the ingredients of the resulting ashes (v. 6). These same elements are used in other biblical purification rituals as well (e.g., Lev. 14:6; cf. Ps. 51:7).

The priest assigned to oversee the making of the ashes from the red cow is Eleazar, the son of Aaron (19:4). The reason for Eleazar rather than Aaron as overseer may be that the ritual was liable to make the priest himself ritually impure for a time, a condition that the high priest Aaron would seek to avoid if possible (Lev. 21:10–24). Eleazar is also beginning to take over more of a priestly role as the narrative anticipates the approaching death of Aaron and Eleazar's investiture as the new high priest (Num. 20:22–29).

The redness of the cow, the unusual burning of the blood of the animal (v. 5), and the crimson or red material added to the fire (v. 6) all appear to signify blood and its powerful ability to draw out impurity and lead one from the realm of death (contact with a corpse) to the realm of life (a state of cleanness and return to the camp). In the biblical understanding, blood is connected with both death and life. The spilling of blood is a sign of death. But blood is also the primary carrier of life: "the life of the flesh is in the blood" (Gen. 9:4; Lev. 17:11, 14). Because of its dual association with both life and death, blood is seen as a powerful and effective agent for ritually leading someone from the realm of death to the realm of life.

The ashes from the burning are swept together and stored until they are mixed with water for cleansing. The red cow is burned "outside the camp" (v. 3), and its ashes are stored "outside the camp" (v. 9). This concern to keep the slaughter of the red cow and the storage of the ashes outside the boundaries of the camp is evidence of the power and danger associated with the red cow ashes and the contamination from contact with the dead. When mixed together, the ashes and water become a purifying agent to make clean those who are ritually impure (v. 9). The purified person is led from the realm of death to the realm of life. The priest oversees the making of the ashes, but the purifying ash and water mixture can be applied by any lay member of the community.

Throughout the first part of the instructions in 19:1–10, there is no mention of the specific use of the ashes for making clean those who have touched a dead body. This mixture of the ashes of the red cow with water may have originally been a more general purifying agent. The linking together of the ashes of the red cow with the specific act of purifying those who touch a dead body was established with the addition of the ritual regulations about corpse contamination in 19:11–19. Allusions to the red cow ashes and the water are made in verses 11–19 in reference to contact with the dead in verse 12 ("water") and verse 17 ("ashes of the burnt purification offering, and running water"). The refrain repeated in verses 13 and 20 emphasizes the importance of the purifying ritual for those who have had contact with a dead body. Its importance derives not from fear about the spirits or the power of the dead but rather fear and reverence for the presence of the living and holy God in Israel's midst, and for God's commandments about the impurity of contact with the dead. Those who fail to be purified "defile the tabernacle/sanctuary of the LORD" (19:13, 20) through their

121

disobedience of God's commands. The ritual of the ashes of the red cow provides a way by which ordinary members of the community can participate in maintaining God's holy presence in their midst in spite of the continuing deaths of the old wilderness generation (Num. 14:28–35; 26:64–65).

The actual purification ritual is fairly simple and available to both native Israelites and aliens living in the land (19:10). A person who is ritually clean (not necessarily a priest) mixes some of the ashes of the burnt purification offering (the red cow ashes) with running water from a stream or spring. The person then takes a sprig of hyssop, dips it in the water, and sprinkles the cleansing water and ash mixture on objects or individuals that are impure from contact with the dead. Hyssop is a plant with a hairy surface that retains liquid, and so it functions well in sprinkling. The Israelites in Egypt used hyssop to sprinkle the blood of the Passover lamb on their doorposts (Exod. 12:22). Here the sprinkling is done on the third and seventh days after the contamination. On the evening of the seventh day after washing one's clothes and bathing, one becomes pure (19:17–19).

The chapter concludes with a note about the person who does the sprinkling. The sprinkler becomes unclean for a day since the water mixed with the ashes of the red cow, blood, crimson material, hyssop, and cedarwood acts as a kind of sponge, drawing the impurity out of objects and persons and absorbing it into itself. Thus, the cleansing water becomes unclean along with the one sprinkling the water (19:20–21).

The ritual of purification for those who have had contact with the dead plays an important role at this juncture in the book of Numbers. The provisions given by God allow all members of the community to act as purifiers in the face of widespread ritual impurity due to the deaths of thousands of members of the old generation. The ritual is simple, available to natives and foreigners, not restricted to priests, and as mobile as a sprig of hyssop and a bowl of water. Preserving the life and purity of the camp in the face of one of the most severe pollutants, contact with the dead, is a community-wide responsibility. Like the Nazirite vow that was a way of involving lay people in special tasks in service to God (Numbers 6), so the purification ritual of the red cow involves the lay members of the community in maintaining the holiness of the camp.

One New Testament text makes allusion to Numbers 19 in its comparison of the purifying effects of the blood of the red heifer and the purifying effects of the blood of Jesus:

122

> For if the blood of goats and bulls, with the sprinkling of the ashes of a heifer, sanctifies those who have been defiled so that their flesh is purified, how much more will the blood of Christ, who through the eternal Spirit offered himself without blemish to God, purify our conscience from dead works to worship the living God! (Heb. 9:13–14)

Blood and no blemish. Holiness and purity. Death and life. This is the complex of themes through which Israel wrestled to understand how a holy God could remain present among a sinful people. The letter of Hebrews moves in the same thought-world to explore the significance of Christ's death as God's holy presence in a sinful world.

As we move to the next chapter in Numbers, death and water form an interlocking set of themes that bind together chapters 19 and 20. The cleansing water of Numbers 19 renders the most unholy and impure members of the community (those contaminated by death) pure and clean so that they can continue the journey to the promised land. The drinking water of Meribah in Numbers 20 renders the most holy and important members of the community (Moses and Aaron) sinful and condemned to die outside the promised land.

Numbers 20
The Deaths of Israel's Leaders:
The Ultimate Rebellion by Moses and Aaron against God

The narrative in chapter 20 returns the reader to a forward movement of Israel's camp after the interruption of laws and revolts and more laws in Numbers 15—19. Numbers 20:1 reports that the whole congregation of Israelites "came into the wilderness of Zin in the first month, and the people stayed in Kadesh." The people have traveled from Egypt in a southeasterly direction through the Sinai peninsula to Mount Sinai. From there, they have moved north to the southern edge of the promised land (Numbers 13—14), but they then have turned back into the wilderness to wander for forty years. Numbers 20:1 places them at Kadesh in the wilderness of Zin, located in the northeastern part of the Sinai Peninsula. At this point in the narrative, the people are moving closer again to the promised land. Many in the old wilderness generation have already died, but the new generation of Israelites is growing toward adulthood.

However, just as chapter 20 gets the march of Israel's camp underway, it recounts a series of dramatic events that rock Israel to the core: the death of the leader Miriam; the rebellion against God by Moses and Aaron; God's command that Moses and Aaron would not lead Israel to the promised land; the refusal of the brother nation of Edom to allow Israel safe passage through its territory; and the death of Aaron the high priest. This series of tragic blows again interrupts the reader's sense of a moving narrative and a moving Israelite camp. After the spy story, every time Israel gets up and recovers from one of its rebellions, it is interrupted again by enumerations of laws, by revolts, and by death. Progress for the old wilderness generation is slow, painful, and ultimately futile, for they will all end by dying outside the promised land.

The Death of Miriam (20:1)

Chapter 20 opens with a one-sentence account of the death and burial of Miriam at Kadesh. Miriam had last appeared on stage in chapter 12 alongside Aaron in a revolt against the authority and leadership of Moses. Miriam, Moses, and Aaron were sister and brothers (Exod. 6:20; 15:20), and they were co-leaders in the wilderness journey from Egypt to Canaan (Micah 6:4). Numbers 12 recounted the jealous challenge of Aaron and Miriam to Moses' authority, and described the skin disease that Miriam alone suffered as punishment. She was healed by the intercession of Moses but then banished from the camp for seven days as a result of the shame of her revolt. Although Aaron was equally guilty, only Miriam was punished. The end of Numbers 12 noted that all the people waited the seven days for Miriam before setting off again on the march. Her leadership clearly was honored by the people, and that honor is extended to her again according to the death and burial notice in 20:1. The text does not imply that Miriam's death outside the promised land was a result of her rebellion; it simply reports that she died and was buried in Kadesh. The same will not be true for the upcoming deaths of Aaron and Moses; as we shall see, they die outside the land of Canaan because of their sin.

The Rebellion of Moses and Aaron (20:2–13)

124

Verse 2 begins, "Now there was no water for the congregation; so they gathered together against Moses and against Aaron." The story appears to be a reworking of a similar story in Exod. 17:1–7 about the people complaining of a lack of water in the wilderness. Both stories contain a lament over a shortage of water and mention the rod used by Moses and the name for the place, Meribah, meaning "Quarrel." The version in Exodus 17 presents the request for water by a refugee slave people in the desert as a legitimate need. But at this point in the narrative of Numbers, readers are conditioned to assume that any complaint here by the people is a sign of sinful rebellion—not only against Moses and Aaron but also against God. We are primed to believe the people are deserving of divine judgment whenever they complain.

The cycle of complaints and rebellions in Numbers has been consistent and unrelenting. The people complained about their misfortunes, and the anger of the LORD burned the edges of the camp (11:1–4). The Israelites tired of manna and yearned for meat, and God sent a plague in connection with eating quail meat (11:4–6, 33). A jealous Aaron and Miriam challenged the authority of their brother Moses, and God struck Miriam with a skin disease and banished her from the camp for seven days (12:2, 10, 15). The whole people heard the spy report of Canaan and refused to enter the promised land, planning instead to choose a new leader and return to Egypt (14:2–4). God responded in anger by condemning the old wilderness generation to die in the desert (14:20–24). Korah, Dathan, and Abiram and 250 other lay leaders challenged Moses and Aaron in their roles as leader and priest, and God caused the earth to swallow some of them while others were burned with divine fire (16:3, 31–35). The whole congregation accused Moses and Aaron of killing their leaders, and God sent a plague (16:41, 44–50). Every time we hear the first hint of whining from the people in Numbers, we automatically assume that the people's complaint is illegitimate, that the attack on Moses and Aaron is unjustified, and that God's anger and righteous judgment on the people will follow like clockwork. This narrative background is crucial in understanding the dynamics of the enigmatic story in Numbers 20 about water from the rock.

The narrator tells the reader at the beginning that "there was no water" for the people, which causes them to complain to Moses and Aaron (v. 2). This is a somewhat jarring note because lack of water in the desert seems a very legitimate complaint. Yet we have been conditioned to assume every complaint in Numbers is unreasonable and self-serving (monotonous food, desire for power, envy, self-protection). This is the first hint to the reader that something different is going on in this story. The people begin the stock complaints of wishing they were dead or back in Egypt instead of wandering in the

125

wretched wilderness. Moreover, "there is no water to drink" (v. 5). The people's own description of what they experience matches the narrator's report of the "facts" ("there was no water," v. 1).

The complaint against Moses and Aaron sets in motion the same sequence of actions that Moses and Aaron have performed in other complaint stories. They go to the front of the tent of meeting, fall on their faces to prepare to hear God's angry word of judgment, and wait as the glory of God appears (v. 6). When God arrives, we expect to hear of God's anger and the announcement of some great plague or fire. But surprisingly, we hear nothing of God's wrath. God simply instructs Moses to "take the staff, and assemble the congregation, you and your brother Aaron, and command [literally, "speak to"] the rock before their eyes to yield its water. Thus you shall bring water out of the rock for them" (v. 8). God's directives to Moses and Aaron suggest that the people's need for water is legitimate and God intends to satisfy their need. But the reader cannot be sure; in an earlier request for meat, God had responded with abundant quail, but a plague also accompanied it (11:33).

Moses takes the "staff from before the LORD." This staff may be Moses' own staff (Exod. 4:1–4; 7:20; 17:5–6; Num. 20:11) or it may be the staff of Aaron that had sprouted in Numbers 17 that was placed "before the covenant" in the tabernacle (Num. 17:10). Moses is proceeding as God "had commanded him" by taking the staff and with Aaron gathering the assembly before the rock (vv. 9–10a). However, usually such notices about Moses' obedience of God's commands appear at the end of a sequence of actions rather than in the middle of the action, as here. This may indicate that what preceded was done according to God's directives; what follows, as we shall see, is open to interpretation.

At this point, Moses deviates from God's instructions and says, "Listen, you rebels, shall we bring water for you out of this rock?" (v. 10b). This vague question in its Hebrew form could communicate at least five possible meanings, depending on the tone of the speaker and the reaction of the hearers:

1. It could be a rhetorical question that assumes a positive answer. "Listen, you rebels, are you ready for us to bring water for you out of this rock? Of course you are!" One hears affirmative cheers from the crowd. This would imply that Moses and Aaron are proceeding with God's command to provide the water in response to their legitimate need. But Moses' accusation in addressing the people as "rebels" throws a dissonant chord into this otherwise positive reading.

2. It could be a rhetorical question that emphasizes Moses and

Aaron as the ones responsible for producing the water, rather than God. "Listen, you rebels, shall *we* [not God] bring water for you out of this rock?" In this case, Moses and Aaron are stealing God's thunder and taking the credit for providing the water themselves.

3. It could be a real question directed to the Israelites. "Listen, you rebels, do you really want us to bring water for you out of this rock? Don't you remember the quail you asked for and the plague that came with it (Numbers 11)? This could be equally as dangerous. So what will it be? Should we go ahead and produce the water or not?" The sense here is that Moses and Aaron are toying with the Israelites. As representatives of God to the people, they present God as willfully malicious, playing a game of chicken with the Israelites. If they say yes, they risk death through possibly poisonous water. If they say no, they risk death through dehydration.

4. A fourth possibility is that the question implies that Moses and Aaron (and thus God) are not able to produce the water out of the rock. "Listen, you rebels, do you really think we can bring water for you out of this rock?" The implied answer is "No, of course not!" This would indicate the failure of Moses and Aaron to trust in God's power to do what God promises, and it would diminish the respect of God's power among the congregation.

5. The question may imply that Aaron and Moses (and thus God) simply do not want to produce the water out of the rock, even though they may be able to. "Listen, you rebels, we could produce water out of this rock, but do you think we will? No way!" In the face of what appears to be a legitimate need for water (20:2), this form of the question would imply a God who is unresponsive to the real needs of God's own people.

Of the five possible meanings of Moses' questions, the first one seems least probable. The accusatory label of "rebels" used by Moses for the people seems to rule out the positive possibility of the first meaning. But the other meanings remain possible readings. Meanings 2–5 implicate Moses and Aaron in various acts of unfaith, either as taking credit for the miracle for themselves and away from God or portraying God as malicious, weak, or unresponsive to legitimate needs. Given the entire context of the story, the second meaning may be the most probable. In any case, Moses and Aaron have departed from God's commands by speaking to the assembly, whatever the exact nuances of their words were.

Moses next lifts up his hand and strikes "the rock twice with his staff; water came out abundantly, and the congregation and their livestock drank" (20:11). The act of Moses striking the rock not once but

127

twice appears to be presented in deliberate contradiction to God's instructions to Moses to "command [speak to] the rock;" God did not say anything about striking the rock once, much less twice (20:8). The successful miracle is unexpectedly followed by God's severe judgment on Moses and Aaron. They will not bring the Israelites into the promised land "because you did not trust in me, to show my holiness before the eyes of the Israelites" (20:12). The punishment is clear, but what Moses and Aaron did wrong to deserve such a severe punishment is not entirely evident. The reason for the punishment has historically been one of the great puzzles of biblical interpretation; a large number of possible solutions have been proposed from ancient times to the present (Milgrom, pp. 448–56).

A host of anomalies surround this episode. Were the people really "rebels" and acting improperly? Their need for water seemed reasonable, and God in the end provided it (20:11). Moses calls the people "rebels" (20:10). In 20:24, God ironically turns this accusation around onto Aaron and by implication Moses. Were Aaron and Moses the real "rebels," not the people? The scene concludes with the narrator's note that "the people quarreled with the LORD" (20:13). But quarreling with God is not necessarily rebellion, as the other version of the same story of water from the rock demonstrates (Exod. 17:1–7). Thus, the people overall are portrayed favorably, and it is Moses' conclusion that they are rebels that appears misguided.

What caused the punishment of Moses and Aaron? What was their sin? Was it the question Moses asked? If so, which of the many possible meanings was the cause? Or was the cause striking the rock with the staff, an action God never commanded? In my judgment, the text is intentionally ambiguous and does not demand that the sin of Moses and Aaron be pinpointed to only one action or word. The multiple possibilities simply increase the magnitude and complexity of the two leaders' rebellion. It involves disobedience of God's commands (Num. 27:14), arrogating to themselves God's power and honor, and not trusting in God's power to fulfill God's promises. This latter sin of not trusting in God is explicitly stated in 20:12. The same Hebrew phrase characterized the sin of the Israelites in the spy story in Numbers 14:11; the Israelites did not trust in God's power to do what God promised, namely, to bring them into the promised land. Not only is the verb the same, "did not trust [believe in]," but the punishment in both Numbers 14 and 20 is the same: the Israelites and now also their leaders, Moses and Aaron, will die outside the promised land. Thus, the sin involved in both cases is likely to be similar—a public failure to trust God to fulfill God's word.

128

Another anomaly in the story is that Moses does nearly all the speaking and acting throughout the story. The only action that Aaron takes is to help Moses gather the assembly together (20:10). Yet Aaron is punished as severely as Moses (20:12, 24). The sense of unfairness concerning Aaron's punishment can be meaningfully joined with the first verse in Numbers 20, in which Miriam's death is noted. The unfairness that Miriam experienced by her punishment in the rebellion of Aaron and Miriam in Numbers 12 is answered with Aaron's own experience of unfairness in Numbers 20. In their mutual deaths outside the promised land, Miriam and Aaron are joined in that ultimate equality that finally binds all humanity together: "You are dust, and to dust you shall return" (Gen. 3:19).

Numbers 20 clearly indicates that Moses will also join Miriam and Aaron in a death outside the promised land because of his own sin (20: 12; 27:12–14; cf. Deut. 32:48–52). But the book of Deuteronomy contains an alternate tradition that ascribes the reason for Moses' death not to his own sin but to the sin of the people (Deut. 1:37; 3:26; 4:21). Moses' death is recorded in Deuteronomy 34 as he is united with the other great leaders of the Exodus and the wilderness journey who had died, Miriam and Aaron (Olson, *Deuteronomy and the Death of Moses*, pp. 165–71). The dominant characterization of Moses throughout Numbers has been as an obedient servant of God of heroic proportions, interceding for the people, turning down a chance to become a great nation on his own, welcoming the guidance and help of others, working selflessly for the good of the people. But under the surface of this dominant portrait, some fissures in the heroic veneer have appeared. Moses requested God to put him to death because of his annoyance with the people (11:11–15). Moses seems to take the revolt of Korah and company personally, asking God not to accept their offerings and defending himself to God against them (16:15). And in Numbers 20, it appears that Moses is not at all sensitive to the genuine needs of his people. Instead, he calls them "rebels" when in fact it is he and Aaron who are the true rebels and are punished. In the end, Moses is human, fallible, and conflicted within himself and with God. He goes the way of the old wilderness generation, with his siblings dying outside the boundaries of the promised land.

The story of the rock in the wilderness and its life-giving water provided images for New Testament and early Christian reflections—on Jesus, the waters of baptism, and new life through the hearing of the gospel. In I Cor. 10:4, Paul allegorizes the rock into an image of Christ: "all ate the same spiritual food, and all drank the same spiritual drink. For they drank from the spiritual rock that

129

followed them, and the rock was Christ." The same image of the rock and its water stands behind Jesus' words in John 7:37–38, "Let anyone who is thirsty come to me, and let the one who believes in me drink." Jesus' discussion with the Samaritan woman concerning "living water" is an echo of the Old Testament rock and its water of life (John 4). Finally, after the disciple Peter's confession that Jesus was the Messiah, Jesus tells Peter (whose name means "Rock") that "on this rock I will build my church" (Matt. 16:18). Jesus then tells his disciples of his coming suffering and death, but Peter pledges that this must never happen to Jesus. Jesus delivers a surprisingly strong rebuke to Peter: "Get behind me, Satan! You are a stumbling block to me; for you are setting your mind not on divine things but on human things" (Matt. 16:23). The severity of the rebuke of Peter, the leader among the twelve disciples, echoes God's stern rebuke and judgment against Moses and Aaron, the leaders of the twelve tribes. Both Old and New Testaments share a healthy realism about the frailty of human leadership and the capacity of even the most trusted leaders to fail to discern God's will and to fall into disobedience.

Israel's Passage through Edom Refused (20:14–21)

Israel is moving closer to its goal of entering the promised land. The most direct route from Kadesh to their destination on the eastern boundary of Canaan is through the land of Edom. Thus, Moses sends messengers to the king of Edom with a message couched in the form common to ancient Near Eastern communication among kings and leaders (addressee, sender, body of message). The message begins, "Thus says your brother Israel" (20:14). The reference to "brother Israel" is typical diplomatic language for someone considered an equal and an ally. But "brother" has a double meaning in that it alludes to the ancestral relationship of the brothers Jacob/Israel and Esau/Edom (Gen. 25:21–26; 35:9–15; 36). Jacob and Esau were twin brothers, and they are portrayed as the ancestors of the Israelites and the Edomites. Jacob was notorious for having stolen his brother Esau's birthright and blessing as the eldest son (Gen. 25:29–34; 27:45); their sibling rivalry no doubt reflects the conflicts of the two nations.

Moses' message to the Edomite king is an exercise in rhetorical persuasion, arguing that the king should allow safe passage for the Israelites through the territory of Edom. They are "brothers" in more than one sense of the term. The message recounts Israel's great "adversity" and dramatic rescue from Egypt in order to rouse sympathy from the Edomites (20:14–17). Israel is now poised "on the edge of your territory," so there is some urgency in this request (20:16). The message pledges that no economic cost to Edom will be involved; the Israelites "will not pass through any field or vineyard, or drink water from any well" as they march through the land on the King's Highway, the main road through Edom (20:17).

The Edomites respond negatively and threaten to attack the Israelites if they try to march through Edom. The Israelites begin to negotiate, promising to stay on the highway and to pay for any water they might happen to use (20:19). The king of Edom again refuses passage, sends out a large and well-equipped army of soldiers, and "Israel turned away from them" (20:20–21).

The encounter between Edom and Israel is a reverse replay of the last time Jacob and Esau encountered each other in Genesis 32—33. In that encounter, Jacob/Israel is also coming back home to Canaan after living as an alien in a foreign land. Jacob sends a message to Esau asking for safe passage for himself and his family and livestock. Esau comes with an army of four hundred men to meet him (Gen. 32:3–8). When the two brothers finally meet, Jacob and Esau embrace. But when Esau offers to join forces with Jacob, Jacob refuses and insists that the brothers should go their separate ways (33:4–17). This was the last encounter between Jacob and Esau before the meeting of Israel and Edom in Numbers 20. With memories of Jacob negotiating Esau out of his birthright and blessing and refusing to join with Esau in their last meeting, the past comes home to roost. Edom refuses to negotiate with Jacob for anything and insists that they go their separate ways.

Edom's rejection of Israel's request may form the background for Amos 1:11, in which the prophet announces judgment on Edom "because he pursued his brother with the sword and cast off all pity." Like many siblings, the relationship between Israel and Edom throughout the Bible is complex and varied, running the gamut between intense hateful competition and friendship (Num. 24:18; II Sam. 8:13–14; I Kings 11:14–17; II Kings 3:4–27; Isa. 34:5–7; Obadiah). An alternate tradition of the story that is in Numbers 20:14–21 tells of Israel's safe passage through the land of Edom on its journey from the wilderness to Canaan (Deut. 2:1–8).

The effect of this incident with Edom in Numbers 20 is to force further delay in Israel's progress toward the land. But it also provides another example of Israel's leadership going its own way without consulting God. There is no command from God that Israel ought to approach Edom. Moses seems to be acting on his own, and it leads to failure (20:14). Earlier in Numbers 20, we noted parallels between Moses' and Aaron's sin at Meribah and the spy mission in Numbers

13—14 both in the nature of the sin (not trusting God) and the punishment (dying outside the promised land). Another parallel is that both rebellions are followed by failed missions due to the lack of God's involvement. Israel had tried to invade Canaan without God in 14:39–45; Moses tried to pass through Edom without conferring with God in 20:14–21.

The Death of Aaron (20:22–29)

The stripping of priestly vestments and the death of Israel's first high priest, Aaron, occurs on top of Mount Hor "in the sight of the whole congregation" (20:27). The mountaintop scene is a somber outcome of Aaron's rebellion against God's command at Meribah (20:24). The public shame Aaron experiences at the end of his life mirrors the shame of Miriam, who was banished from the community for seven days because of her rebellion with Aaron (Num. 12:14–15). Moses escorts Aaron and Aaron's son Eleazar to the top of the mountain. There Aaron's priestly garments are stripped and placed on Eleazar, who takes over the role of Israel's high priest. For Moses, this is a rehearsal in preparation for his own climb up to another mountain and his death outside the promised land (Deut. 34:1–12). Aaron's death and Eleazar's succession to the position of high priest signal the approaching end of the first generation and the beginning of a new generation of hope and promise. The continuing of the priesthood through Eleazar demonstrates God's continuing commitment to Israel and the institutions through which God works for the well-being of God's people.

The circles of holiness within Israel's camp had been carefully organized in Numbers 1—10, but they have since been slowly undone. The twelve tribes in the outer circle of the camp engaged in their definitive rebellion in Numbers 13—14 in the spy story. The Levites who care for and guard the tent of meeting in the midst of the camp revolted in Numbers 16—17. Even the leaders closest to God who stand at the very center of the camp, the high priest Aaron and the leader Moses, have been infected with a rebellious lack of faith in Numbers 20. This spreading of sin and rebellion throughout the camp of Israel suggests that sin has some elements of a contagious condition not unlike that of contact with impurity or uncleanness (chapter 19). The destiny of the entire generation of Israelites who first came out of Egypt is sealed. Except for Joshua and Caleb (14:30), no one in the old wilderness generation, not even Moses, will enter the land of Canaan. Beginning in Numbers 26, the holy camp

of Israel will need to be reorganized in conjunction with the rise of a
new generation of God's people.

III. Hitting Bottom: The End
of the First Generation—Signs of Hope
in the Midst of Death

NUMBERS 21—25

A major break in the narrative of Numbers occurs with chapter 21.
For the first time in this predominantly negative portion of the book, a
positive tone is struck with the account of Israel's first military victory
over the Canaanite king of Arad. Ever since chapter 11, Israel has repeatedly rebelled and resisted God's commands, with the result that
God has punished Israel with numerous plagues and military defeats.
This negative portrait is abruptly interrupted by the positive conquest
story in 21:1-3. This hopeful story is followed quickly by another rebellion in 21:4-9 and then another positive conquest account of military
triumphs over two kings, Sihon and Og, in 21:10-35. An extended
cycle involving King Balak of Moab and the foreign prophet Balaam
follows in Num. 22:1—24:25. The centerpieces of the Balaam cycle are
a series of climactic promise oracles directed to Israel. A final rebellion
narrative in 25:1-8 recounts the death of the remaining members of
the old wilderness generation who continue to rebel despite God's
faithfulness and promises. This section concludes the first half of
Numbers (chaps. 1—25) by weaving together stories of ultimate death
and failure by a generation past and anticipation of profound promise
for a generation of the future.

Numbers 21
God-Given Victories, People-Driven Rebellions

Hormah Revisited:
God Gives Victory over Arad (21:1–3)

The narrative of Israel's victory over Arad takes place at a site called "Hormah," which means in Hebrew, "Destruction." We have encountered Hormah before in the book of Numbers at Israel's first military engagement against the Canaanites in the spy story of Numbers 13—14. After initially refusing to accept God's invitation to move forward into Canaan, the Israelites changed their mind and mounted an attack on Canaan. But Moses warned them against doing so since God was not with them. The Israelites proceeded in spite of the warning and were soundly defeated, the Canaanite army "pursuing them as far as Hormah" (14:39–45).

Israel's victory against the Canaanite king at Hormah in 21:1–3 provides a glimpse of what should have happened in Israel's first foray into Canaan back in chapters 13—14. The Canaanite king of Arad attacks Israel in an aggressive move, taking some of the Israelites captive. Israel is placed in a posture of self-defense (21:1). Instead of proceeding without God's presence or counsel as in Numbers 14 or as Moses had done against Edom in Numbers 20, Israel consults with God. Israel vows to follow standard holy war procedure and dedicate all the towns they capture to God by utterly destroying them; this they pledge to God "if you will indeed give this people into our hands" (21:2). God accepts the vow, hands over the Canaanites to Israel, and Israel completely razes all their towns so that the place is called Hormah, or "Destruction" (21:3).

The long series of Israel's revolts in Numbers had begun with a brief, almost paradigmatic rebellion story in 11:1–3. Within three verses, all the basic elements of a rebellion story were present: the people's complaint, God's angry punishment, the people's cry, Moses' prayer of intercession, and the end of the punishment. In Numbers 20, at the end of the old generation and as a model for the new generation, we are provided with a similar but positive paradigm of how the new

134

generation should proceed with its conquest of Canaan. Again, all the basic elements of a proper holy war engagement are present: encounter with the enemy (who is often the aggressor), Israel's vow to dedicate any booty to God if God will give them victory, God's acceptance of the vow, God's handing over of the enemy, and Israel's dedication of all that is captured to God either by destroying it or giving it to the priests (cf. Num. 18:14, "devoted thing"). One might hope that perhaps the old generation has finally begun to develop a sense of trust and obedience in God, but the story that follows about the bronze serpent quickly dashes those hopes.

The Bronze Serpent (21:4–9)

The Israelites set out from Mount Hor where Aaron was buried to go to the Red Sea and thus detour around the land of Edom (Num. 20:21, 25). Detours and delays often frustrate people, and the old generation of Israelites is no exception. They "become impatient along the way" and begin to complain "against God and against Moses" (21:4–5). This is the last of the complaint stories in Numbers, and it is one of the worst. Typically, the people complained against Moses and sometimes Aaron, but rarely do they complain directly against God as they do here. The people drag out the same old laundry list of complaints about dying in the wilderness, yearning to go back to Egypt, the lack of food and water, and the monotony of the manna. If the preceding story of the conquest of the Canaanite king was a hopeful glimpse of what Israel's obedience could be (21:1–3), then this complaint story is a tired old snapshot of what Israel's disobedience has been all along (11:1, 4–6; 14:2–4; 16:13–14; 20:3–5).

God sends "poisonous" snakes as a judgment against the people, which bite and kill many of them. The Hebrew word for "poisonous" literally means "fiery," likely referring to the burning sensation of a snake bite upon human skin—an apt metaphor for the fiery anger of God (11:1). The people come before Moses and confess, "We have sinned," and they ask Moses to pray to God to take away the serpents. Israel had confessed its sin after a rebellion only one other time in Numbers—in the spy story in Numbers 13—14. Here, after God had condemned the old generation to die in the wilderness, the Israelites confessed their sin (14:40). But then they promptly set out to attack the Canaanites against Moses' stern warning that God was not with them and they would be defeated (14:39–45). Their confession of sin was shallow; they believed they could fulfill the promises of God through their own efforts, without God's help. They failed to understand the

135

deeper source of their sin, their unwillingness to trust God to deliver them and to fulfill God's commitments to bring them into the land.

The background of Israel's earlier confession of its sin in Numbers 14 helps to explain why God does not simply get rid of the serpents immediately. Each individual Israelite needs to take the confession of sin and the need for God's deliverance to heart. Thus, God instructs Moses to make a poisonous serpent out of bronze and to set it on a pole. "Everyone who is bitten shall look at it and live" (21:9). Confession of sin and forgiveness are thus both a community and an individual responsibility. The plague of the serpents remained an ongoing threat to the community, and the raised bronze serpent remained an ongoing reminder to each individual of the need to turn to the healing power of God.

The phrase in 21:9, "a serpent of bronze," is a wordplay since the words "serpent" and "bronze" are closely related in Hebrew, *nehash nehoshet*. Several hundred years later in Israel's history, King Hezekiah tore down and destroyed what was alleged to be Moses' bronze serpent, called "Nehustan." The bronze serpent had been kept in the Jerusalem temple as a sacred object, but people had begun making offerings to it as if it were an idol or image of God. This clearly violated the first of the Ten Commandments, which prohibits idolatry and making images (Exod. 20:3–4). As part of his attempt to reform Judah's worship practices, King Hezekiah destroyed the bronze serpent in the temple (II Kings 18:4). Scholars have debated the nature of the relationship between the Mosaic bronze serpent and Hezekiah's Nehustan, but the tradition clearly links the two.

The symbol of the snake or serpent played important roles in the religious and cultural life of ancient Egypt, Canaan, Mesopotamia, and Greece. The serpent was a symbol of evil power and chaos from the underworld as well as a symbol of fertility, life, and healing. The bronze serpent in Numbers 21 bears some relationship to a healing ritual known as sympathetic magic, common in the ancient Near East. If an individual suffered from the poison of some plant or animal, then gazing upon an image of that same poisonous animal or plant was thought to heal or guard the person from further attack. Such a view does not fit well with the biblical understanding that often resists such magical manipulation. Thus, the deuterocanonical book of the Wisdom of Solomon recalls the story of the bronze serpent in the form of a prayer spoken to God, speaking of the Israelites who

> received a symbol of deliverance to remind them of your law's command. For the one who turned toward it was saved, not by the thing

that was beheld, but by you, the Savior of all. . . . For you have power
over life and death; you lead mortals down to the gates of Hades and
back again. (Wisd. Sol. 16:6–7, 13)

In *Serpent Symbolism in the Old Testament,* Karen Randolph
Joines summarizes the human fascination with the snake:

> Antipathy and fear for the serpent have equalled respect for it. Its
> slender fangs can puncture the flesh of a strong man, and he is no
> more. Conversely, the serpent represented life. It glides from the
> earth—it is the living essence of the soil; it annually sloughs its old
> skin cells, an image of its former self—it represents recurring youth-
> fulness; its penetrating eyes sparkle with unusual lustre—it signifies
> superhuman wisdom. This is the serpent—a strange synthesis of life
> and death, an object of both intense animosity and reverence.
> (Joines, p. vi)

The serpent is a potent symbol of both life and death. The high priest
Aaron had "stood between the dead and the living" and stopped the
plague in Num. 16:48. Similarly, the pole with the bronze serpent
stood between the dead who were not willing to look to God's chosen
instrument of healing and the living who were willing and were healed
(21:9). The story stands at a strategic place in the book of Numbers
between death and life, between the end of the old wilderness generation whose last remnants will die in the apostasy of Numbers 25 and
the beginning of a new generation of hope whose numbers will be
counted in the second census of Numbers 26 as they stand on the edge
of the promised land, ready to enter Canaan (26:63–65).

The bronze serpent in Numbers 21 is one of the best-known images of the book of Numbers for Christians because of its use by Jesus
in the Gospel of John. Jesus discusses his destiny with a Jewish teacher
named Nicodemus, using the Hebrew Bible or Old Testament, which
is their common Scripture: "And just as Moses lifted up the serpent in
the wilderness, so must the Son of Man be lifted up, that whoever believes in him may have eternal life" (John 3:14–15). Then follows what
is for Christians perhaps the best-known New Testament text, John
3:16 ("For God so loved the world that he gave his only Son . . ."). The
words of Jesus emphasize God's desire to give eternal life to all those
who look to and believe in Jesus. The image of the "lifting up" of the
bronze serpent is associated elsewhere in John with images of Jesus
being "lifted up" and dying on the cross (John 8:28; 12:32). But this
lifting up of Jesus appears to point both to Jesus' crucifixion and to his
resurrection from the dead ("rise from the dead," John 20:9; "as-
cended to the Father," John 20:17). Thus, the cross in John's Gospel,
like the pole with the bronze serpent, signifies both the poison of death

137

as well as the life-giving power of God for all those who believe and look to God for healing and new life.

Israel's Victories over King Sihon and King Og (21:10–35)

Israel begins to move more rapidly toward its destination the Transjordan, the area located east of the Jordan River and opposite the eastern boundary of Canaan. The Transjordan will be the staging area and entry point for the new generation of Israelites as they prepare to come into the promised land. The text presents a brief summary of places Israel traveled, including Arnon and the boundary of the nation of Moab (21:10–13). The mention of the latter two place names provides an occasion to include a brief poetic snippet from an otherwise unknown document called the "Book of the Wars of the LORD" (21: 15–16). Israel continues to a place called "Beer," which in Hebrew means "Well," and the Israelites stop for a round of drinks and a drinking song (21:16–18). Several other stopping places along the way are mentioned before Israel finally comes to the territory of King Sihon of the Amorites.

Suddenly the tempo of the march has picked up, Israel is on the march, poetry is recited, songs are sung, and progress is being made. We will soon have a longer poem in the next section, and two major kings will be defeated in the Transjordan area, Sihon and Og. There is a sense of something building, some heightened expectations, some glorious good news around the corner. That will come with the great oracles of blessing and promise spoken by the pagan prophet Balaam in Numbers 22—24. But before we get there, we will witness two more victories for Israel—over the king of the Amorites and the king of Bashan.

Israel sends messengers to King Sihon of the Amorites asking for safe passage through their land. The message sounds very much like the one given to Edom in Num. 20:14–21. Like Edom, King Sihon refuses Israel passage. Sihon gathers his army and goes out against Israel and fights against Israel (21:21–23). Sihon appears much more the aggressor, and so Israel defends itself, defeats Sihon, and captures his territory, which includes land captured from the former king of Moab (21:26). The song in 21:27–30 celebrates King Sihon's defeat of the nation of Moab, otherwise known as the "people of Chemosh" (Chemosh was a Moabite god). Scholars have wondered why Israel would preserve a victory song celebrating one foreign nation's defeat of an-

other. Israel did have a strong anti-Moabite tradition that may account
in part for the inclusion of the song here (Numbers 25; Judg. 3:12–30;
II Kings 3; Isaiah 15—16; Jeremiah 48). Jeremiah 48:45–46 contains a
slightly different form of the same song as in Num. 21:27–30. The song
celebrating Sihon's victory over Moab also serves in the present literary
context to set up the reason why King Balak of Moab is so desperately
afraid of Israel that he seeks a professional cursing service in the form
of Balaam (22:2–6). If a strong Sihon has defeated a weak Moab and if
Sihon has in turn been defeated by even stronger Israel, then Moab
surely has reason to take desperate measures to defeat Israel in chapters 22—24.

The note in 21:31–32 about Israel settling in the land of the Amorites serves as background to a future controversy in Numbers. In chapter 32, the Israelite tribes of Reuben and Gad negotiate with Moses
over their desire to settle in this captured Transjordan area rather than
enter the promised land.

In a second military encounter in 21:33–35, Israel is attacked by
and defeats King Og of Bashan. Israel obediently follows the holy war
procedure with the assurance that God has given the enemy into Israel's hand. No survivors are left, and Israel takes possession of the
land. When Israel is faithful and obedient, God demonstrates faithfulness by granting success against those who attack Israel.

Deuteronomy 2:26–37 and 3:1–7 provide parallel accounts of Israel's military victories over Sihon and Og. Scholars have raised a number of issues in terms of the historical background of these events and
whether the two versions in Numbers and Deuteronomy might be dependent on one another or independent but parallel forms of the same
tradition. In any case, the function of Num. 21:21–35 in the present
shape of the text is to show God's faithfulness as Israel moves toward
the promised land. God provides Israel a foretaste of the conquest of
the land. For the first time in the book of Numbers, Israel successfully
captures towns and land, although it remains east of the Jordan River
and not yet in the promised land. But Israel is getting very close. For
the first time since the spy story in Numbers 13—14, Israel is once
again at the boundary of the promised land "in the plains of Moab"
(22:1). This hopeful setting provides the backdrop for the climactic
promise oracles spoken by the prophet Balaam to the Israelites in the
three chapters which follow.

Numbers 22—24
A Crescendo of Hope: Balak, Balaam, and the Blessing of Israel

On the eve of the final death of the old wilderness generation in Numbers 25 and the beginning of a new generation in Numbers 26, God confirms the divine commitment to bless Israel through some of the most lavish words of blessing and promise in the entire Pentateuch. Moreover, God speaks these words of blessing and promise not through an Israelite but through a foreign prophet. As Hobab the Midianite had joined God in guiding Israel (10:29–32), so Balaam the prophet joins God in blessing Israel.

Four main characters are at work in this enigmatic story in Numbers 22—24. The first character is Balaam, a professional seer or prophet who travels about and curses military enemies for money. He is a kind of unattached hired gun, a mercenary, but his only weapons are words that have the power to curse or to bless. In the history of biblical interpretation, the character of Balaam has received mixed reviews. Some commentators view Balaam as a true and faithful prophet of God. Others have labeled him an evil and false prophet. The variation in interpretation is due in part to the complexity of the biblical witness itself. The figure of Balaam emerges out of chapters 22—24 in an essentially positive light. Although Balaam is lampooned in the donkey episode in 22:22–35, he ends up faithfully speaking God's words of blessing rather than curse. Micah 6:5 puts Balaam in a favorable light: "O my people, remember now what King Balak of Moab devised, what Balaam son of Beor answered him." According to Micah, Balaam turned back the evil scheme of King Balak. On the other hand, Deuteronomy 23:3–6 portrays Balaam negatively and uses his association with Moab as a reason for prohibiting the Moabites and Ammonites from ever entering the assembly of God's people. Later in Numbers itself, Balaam is killed for having counseled the Midianite women to lead Israel astray in the apostasy of chapter 25 (Num. 31:8, 16).

This ambivalence toward the character of Balaam probably extends back into the oral tradition, when stories about the legendary prophet named Balaam circulated among Israel and its Near Eastern neighbors. Archaeologists have discovered plaster panels in a non-

140

Israelite temple at Deir 'Allah near the Jordan River that name a famed professional prophet named Balaam. In the inscription dated to the eighth century B.C.E., Balaam has a vision from the gods at night. The vision includes a message from the council of gods, the so-called *shaddayin* (cf. Num. 24:16, "the Almighty," Hebrew *Shaddai*). The message tells of a drought to come on the land and the overturning of the order of nature, whereupon Balaam intercedes (Milgrom, pp. 473–76). Thus, the character of Balaam portrayed in Numbers 22—24 is probably built upon a legendary seer or prophet who was known in the Transjordan area near Moab where the Balaam story is set.

The second main character is Balak, king of Moab. Moab is the nation that shares a boundary with Canaan on the eastern edge of the promised land. Moab is also the country that was defeated by and lost territory to King Sihon, an event celebrated in Sihon's victory song in Num. 21:26–30. Thus, a weakened Moab fears that the large Israelite fighting force that rolled over the Amorite King Sihon (21:23–24) will even more quickly roll over Moab: "Now Balak son of Zippor saw all that Israel had done to the Amorites" (22:2). King Balak of Moab has no faith in his own army and so decides to turn to a non-military means of attacking Israel. He hires Balaam the prophet to curse God's people, but the weapon of curse in the end turns back upon King Balak and his country of Moab.

The third main character in the story is God, who has several different names in this text, a reflection of various early and later traditions that were brought together to form the story. God is called "God," (in Hebrew, *Elohim;* 22:9), "the LORD" (in Hebrew, *Yahweh;* 22:13), the "Most High" (in Hebrew, *Elyon;* 24:16), the "Almighty" (in Hebrew, *Shaddai;* 24:16). While King Balak thinks he has found a way to curse Israel and thus shape the course of Israel's history, God emerges as the one character who truly has the power and will to ensure Israel's ultimate destiny. God determines that destiny to be one of blessing rather than curse.

The fourth main character in the story is one who has no active role at all in the drama. Throughout the Balaam cycle, the people of Israel are passively "camped in the plains of Moab across the Jordan from Jericho" (22:1). Israel is oblivious to the intense life and death struggle going on between Balak's desire to curse Israel and God's commitment to bless them. A fifth character, Balaam's donkey, has a brief speaking part (22:28–30).

The Balaam cycle of Numbers 22—24 falls into three large sections: (1) Numbers 22:1–40—Balaam's three encounters with God as King Balak calls Balaam to curse Israel; (2) Numbers 22:41–23:12—

141

Balak's three attempts to curse Israel foiled by the three blessings of Balaam, who can only speak "what the LORD puts in my mouth"; (3) Numbers 24:14–25—Balaam's fourth and climactic oracle of blessing for a distant future beyond the present generation of Israelites. The Balaam cycle is a carefully crafted story with recurring cycles of three scenes or episodes built into its narrative structure. The repeated theme of "seeing" or "not seeing" appears throughout both the narrative scenes and the oracles of Balaam as another means of binding the cycle into an artfully constructed unity (Alter, pp. 104–7).

Balaam's Three Encounters with God as Balak Calls Balaam to Curse Israel (22:1–40)

Numbers 22:1–4 sets the stage. King Balak of Moab is in "great dread" of the Israelites because he "saw all that Israel had done to the Amorites" (as recorded in 21:21–35) and "because they were so numerous" (as confirmed by the census list in Numbers 1). Moab tells the elders of Midian that "this horde" of Israelites will lick them up like "an ox licks up the grass of the field." The Moabites and Midianites will eventually learn that the devouring and mighty ox is not Israel itself but the God who stands behind Israel: "God who brings him out of Egypt, is like the horns of a wild ox for him; he shall devour the nations that are his foes and break their bones" (Num. 24:8). The mention of Moab and Midian together in 22:4 and again in 22:7 suggests that the two groups are identified as allies, although Moab is a nation with territory and Midian appears more often as a wandering group of tribes. The alliance of Moab and Midian in the Balaam story prepares us for the involvement of both in the story of apostasy that follows in chapter 25. As we shall see, this will be one of several ways by which the Balaam cycle is linked to the crucial story of the old generation's last act of rebellion and apostasy through Israel's worship of Baal of Peor (Numbers 25; cf. Num. 31:7–8, 16).

Convinced of Moab's military weakness before Israel, King Balak resorts to unconventional warfare. He sends messengers to Balaam, son of Beor, asking him to come and curse Israel "since they are stronger than me." As the story unfolds, the irony of the king's final statement in his message will come back to haunt Balak: "for I know that whomever you bless is blessed, and whomever you curse is cursed" (22:6). Leaders from Moab and Midian are sent with "the fees for divination" in hand to hire the professional seer or prophet Balaam to come and to curse Israel. They assume that paying Balaam for his

142

services will guarantee that he will speak only what they want him to speak, namely, curses against their enemy Israel. The practice was common in the ancient Near East. Kings often hired royal prophets to advise them, and these messengers of the divine word were under pressure to give the king what he wanted to hear or else lose their financial support or their lives. The struggle between prophets and royal leaders is evident in the stories of Jeremiah's near-death experience (Jer. 26:20–23) and the prophet Micaiah's conflict with the king of Israel (I Kings 22).

The prophet Balaam asks the money-toting messengers to spend the night and promises a response in the morning "just as the LORD speaks to me" (22:8). In the first of three encounters between Balaam and God, God tells Balaam not to go with the messengers back to King Balak: "You shall not curse the people, for they are blessed" (22:12). Here at the end of the old generation, God affirms what God had instructed the priests to do at the beginning of the book of Numbers: "Thus you shall bless the Israelites" (Num. 6:22–27). The next day Balaam reports to Balak's messengers that "the LORD has refused to let me go." When the messengers report to King Balak, they mention nothing about the LORD's refusal. They say only that "Balaam refuses to come" (22:13–14).

King Balak assumes anyone can be bought for a price. Balak believes he has the power to change Balaam's mind simply by sending a second cadre of more numerous and higher level officials with payment in the form of a blank check: "whatever you say to me, I will do" (22:17). But Balaam replies to this second group that even Balak's own house of silver and gold could not dissuade him from speaking only what God commands. Balaam again instructs the messengers of Balak to stay the night while the prophet consults with the deity. In this second encounter between God and Balaam, God tells Balaam to go with the messengers. But God warns Balaam, "do only what I tell you to do" (22:20). In the morning, Balaam saddles his donkey and starts out with the messengers from Moab. At this point, the reader will begin to wonder why God had suddenly changed God's mind and allowed Balaam to go after first saying no. The mystery grows even deeper as we move to the third encounter between Balaam and God, who here appears in the form of an angel.

Numbers 22:22 introduces a jarring note immediately after we hear that God commanded Balaam to go to Balak: "God's anger was kindled because he was going, and the angel of the LORD took his stand in the road as his adversary." The startling eruption of God's anger against an apparently obedient Balaam recalls in some ways God's

143

unexpected judgment against Moses and Aaron in 20:12. As readers, we scurry about for reasons to explain this sudden and inexplicable turnabout. Why does the angel of God with drawn sword suddenly put up a roadblock before a prophet who is obeying God's command to go forth on a mission? The motif is actually not unique in the Bible. God commanded Jacob to return home to Canaan after a long exile (Gen. 31:3). Jacob obeyed, and he was promptly attacked and permanently disabled by God's angel in a night of wrestling (Gen. 32:22–32). As Moses was on his way to lead the Israelites out of Egypt in obedience to God's call, "the LORD met him and tried to kill him" (Exod. 4:24). Joshua was obediently leading the Israelites into the promised land when he was stopped by an angelic commander of the LORD's army "standing before him with a drawn sword in his hand" (Josh. 5:13). What is the function of these strange texts? They all possess an aura of mystery, of human encounter with divine forces incomprehensible to the human mind. These enigmatic encounters suggest that an individual called to be an instrument of God's working in the world remains under God's vigilance, control, and judgment. God's favor cannot simply be assumed; God retains the right to fight against even those appointed by God if God so wills. Thus, Balaam joins an illustrious crew of great Israelite leaders, Jacob, Moses, and Joshua, in his encounter with a divine angel with drawn sword standing in his way.

The plot of this angelic encounter thickens in a folkloric manner as Balaam's donkey begins to see things and to talk. The theme of "seeing" and "not seeing" becomes prominent in this episode as Balaam's donkey twice sees the angel of the LORD when Balaam does not (22:23, 25). In the third encounter, Balaam finally sees what the donkey sees— the angel of God standing in his way (22:27, 31). The irony, of course, is that an ass is able to see divine matters more clearly than this professional "seer," Balaam. The first time the donkey sees the angel with the drawn sword, the donkey swerves off the road. Balaam strikes the animal to bring it back on the way (22:23). The donkey sees the angel in a second encounter. This time the angel does not stand in a wide road but "in a narrow path" with a wall on either side. The donkey squeaks past the angel by hugging close to one of the walls, scraping Balaam's foot. Balaam again strikes the donkey, oblivious to the angelic threat from which the donkey is saving him.

Finally, the donkey sees the angel a third time. The angel stands "in a narrow place, where there was no way to turn either to the right or to the left." This time the donkey simply lies down under Balaam, "and Balaam's anger was kindled" (22:27). The latter phrase points back to Numbers 22:22 when "God's anger was kindled." Balaam's ex-

144

perience with the donkey is in some way parallel to God's experience with Balaam. Balaam will be reminded that the life of a prophet of God is like riding a donkey. Balaam's own personal ability to steer the course of history and see what lies ahead is minimal, less than the animal on which he rides. Lest Balaam have any thought that he can make an end run around God, the angel teaches Balaam that he must lay down his own initiative in cursing or blessing Israel and allow God to use him as God sees fit. Balaam confesses his sin and offers to turn around and go back home. But the angel changes commands once again, telling Balaam to go with the men of Moab but to "speak only what I tell you to speak" (22:35). Balaam eventually reaches Moab where he finds King Balak anxiously waiting at the border. Balaam repeats what he has surely learned even more emphatically along his journey, "The word God puts in my mouth, that is what I must say." King Balak sends sacrifices to Balaam in preparation for the divination that Balak hopes will end in Israel being cursed (22:36–40).

King Balak's Three Attempts to Curse Israel Foiled by Balaam's Three Blessings of Israel (22:41—24:13)

The sequence of actions in Balak's three attempts to curse Israel are virtually identical. Each of the three episodes contains the same six elements.

a. In each of the three episodes, King Balak brings Balaam to a high point or mountain overlooking the people of Israel, who are encamped on the plains of Moab. The names of the three high places or mountains are Bamoth-baal ("High Places of Baal," 22:41), Mount Pisgah (23:14), and Mount Peor (23:28). When one place fails to result in Israel being cursed, the anxious king moves Balaam to another location that he hopes will work. In the end, none of them do.

b. Balak builds seven altars and sacrifices a bull and ram on each altar (23:1–2, 14, 29–30). These sacrifices may be intended to bribe the deity to give Balak the curse on Israel that the king desired. Just as Balak sought to buy Balaam, so the king seeks to buy God. The sacrificed animals may also provide livers or other entrails that Near Eastern diviners often used to discover information about the future or to discern the will of the gods, something akin to reading tea leaves. Certain kinds of divination and attempts to manipulate the deity were rejected in the biblical traditions (Lev. 19:31; Deut. 18:9–14).

c. Balaam tells Balak to stay at the altars while he goes elsewhere

145

to consult with God. God puts a word in Balaam's mouth and instructs Balaam on what to say in the first two scenes (23:3–5; 15–16). In the third scene, Balaam does not "look for omens" to mechanically read an oracle. Rather, the third poem seems to come from Balaam's own heart as well as from God. Balaam "looked up and saw Israel camping tribe by tribe" and "the spirit of God came upon" him (24:1–2). Balaam begins to appear as a true prophet who personally embodies the divine word. He no longer only mechanically spouts oracles like a robot.

d. Balaam pronounces an extended poetic oracle of blessing on Israel. The contents of the first two oracles are dependent on and closely intertwined with the narrative (23:7–10, 18–24). In contrast, the third oracle seems less dependent on the immediate narrative context and may originally not have been attached to the Balaam story. Many scholars date the poem from quite early in Israel's history, perhaps the time of King Saul or David or later in the preexilic period. The present literary context, however, places the poem in Balaam's mouth as his third oracle of blessing.

e. King Balak reacts negatively to the oracle of blessing, his sense of frustration increasing in each of the three scenes. In the first scene, a puzzled Balak asks Balaam, "What have you done to me? I brought you to curse my enemies, but now you have done nothing but bless them" (23:11). After the second oracle, a somewhat frustrated Balak tells Balaam to say nothing: "Do not curse them at all, and do not bless them at all" (23:25). After the third oracle, Balak's frustration builds into the same intense anger that Balaam (22:27) had earlier experienced when he struck his donkey:

> Then Balak's anger was kindled against Balaam, and he struck his hands together. Balak said to Balaam, "I summoned you to curse my enemies, but instead you have blessed them these three times. Now be off with you! Go home! I said, 'I will reward you richly,' but the LORD has denied you any reward. (24:10–11)

Balak's reactions gradually intensify from a question to a mild rebuke to an angry accusation of breach of contract and a firing without severance pay!

f. In varied words, Balaam makes the same final response to King Balak at the end of each scene: "Must I not take care to say what the LORD puts into my mouth" (23:12)? "Did I not tell you, 'Whatever the LORD says, that is what I must do'?" (23:26). "Did I not tell your messengers, . . . 'what the LORD says, that is what I will say'?" (24:12–13).

146

Balaam's rhetorical questions all imply that he has no other option than to speak the words of God, which are words of blessing, not curse.

The structure of each of the three scenes containing the three oracles of Balaam is built out of an almost mechanical repetition of the six elements in each scene. In this way, the repetitive character of the three scenes mimics Balaam's almost mechanical and repetitive speaking of God's words of blessing. The repetition breaks down in the third oracle when Balaam appears to invest more of himself into the pronouncement of blessing, no longer relying on manipulative omens but speaking as the spirit of the LORD comes upon him.

The experience of King Balak and Balaam and the three oracles is a mirror image of the story of the three encounters of Balaam and his donkey with the angel of God. The donkey was caught three times between the angel's sword and Balaam's stick. In his three meetings with Balak, Balaam is likewise caught each time between Balak's demands to curse Israel and God's command to bless Israel. In the three episodes with Balaam and his donkey, Balaam becomes increasingly frustrated and angry with the donkey. Similarly, the angry response of King Balak increases each time Balaam blesses rather than curses Israel. In both cases, God demonstrates God's ability to accomplish what God desires through the actions and the words of the prophet.

The Climactic Fourth Oracle: A Star out of Jacob, a Curse on Moab (24:14–25)

The final oracle of Balaam's four pronouncements stands alone and outside the repetitive structure of the three scenes in which the other three oracles are embedded. The fourth oracle is thereby marked off as a special and climactic oracle. The fourth oracle is also not preceded by the building of altars and sacrifices nor by the search for omens nor even by the spirit of the LORD coming upon Balaam. This fourth oracle is Balaam's departing word to King Balak, and it becomes clear that Balaam no longer needs the crutch of omens or sacrifices or even the special rush of God's Spirit. Balaam fully embodies a true prophet of God, and the words flow out of Balaam with no outside assistance, no prompting, and no mechanical manipulation. After Balaam speaks the oracle, King Balak and the prophet Balaam exchange no further words and both go their separate ways.

What is the role and meaning of the fourth oracle within the Balaam cycle as a whole? That question may be answered by tracing the

147

progression of (1) Balaam's role in the introductions to each of the four oracles; (2) what Balaam sees throughout the four oracles; and (3) the interplay of overlapping themes and images of rising, falling, kingship, and several metaphors for Israel and God drawn from the natural and animal world.

1. Balaam's role as portrayed in the introductory verses of each oracle progresses toward an increasingly positive and active role as a prophet of God. The first two oracles define Balaam's role primarily in negative terms: Balaam cannot curse what God has not cursed (23:8) and Balaam cannot revoke a blessing on Israel that God has already given (23:20). Much of the content of the first two oracles is simply descriptive rather than a real speech act of blessing. In the third oracle, Balaam takes on more of the true prophetic role as a conveyer of God's word and vision: "the oracle of one who hears the words of God, who sees the vision of the Almighty" (24:3–4). The fourth and final oracle extends Balaam's role as not only one who hears God's words and sees the vision of the Almighty; Balaam also "knows the knowledge of the Most High" (24:15–16). The content of the third and fourth oracles is oriented more to the future and to specific words of blessing. Balaam appears to grow into his role as a true prophet of God over the course of the four oracles.

2. Verbs of "seeing" and "looking" run throughout both the poetic oracles and the prose story of Balaam. What Balaam "sees" in the oracles moves from the vague vision of a solitary Israel as an innumerable dust cloud in the first oracle (23:9–10) to Israel as a rising lioness that "does not lie down until it has eaten its prey" (23:24). In the third oracle's vision, Balaam begins to see Israel in more vivid and colorful detail than the dry dust cloud of 23:10; the beauty of Israel is painted with images of water, trees, rivers, and gardens (24:5–7). Balaam's gaze ends in the fourth oracle by focusing in detail on one specific star or scepter that rises out of Israel (24:17).

3. The four oracles display a meaningful progression in the play of metaphors and imaginative images, especially around the topic of kingship, both human and divine. The theme of "rising" and "falling down" also plays a role in the movement of the oracles. The first oracle makes no mention of a king, only Israel in general as a people alone among the nations. The prophet Balaam begins in the first oracle as the one who is high up on a hill, looking down on Israel camped below on the plains of Moab (23:9). In the second oracle, it is the people of Israel who are "rising up like a lioness, and rousing itself like a lion" (23:24). Kingship is mentioned for the first time in the second oracle, but it is a

148

divine kingship: "The LORD their God is with them, acclaimed as a king among them" (23:21). The second oracle also introduces the simile of God who is "like the horns of a wild ox," but the image receives no further explication.

Balaam had risen and stood high above Israel in the first poem (23:9), but in the third oracle Balaam "falls down" before the vision of the Almighty. The image of God as "like the horns of a wild ox" is repeated and developed in more detail: God "shall devour the nations that are his foes and break their bones" (24:8). While Israel was the lion in the second oracle (23:24), God is now portrayed as the crouching lion or lioness, lying down and ready to be roused up (24:8). Kingship is mentioned again in the third oracle: Israel's "king shall be higher than Agag, and his kingdom shall be exalted" (24:7). Agag is the human king of the Amalekites (I Samuel 15; Num. 24:20). The referent for Israel's "king" is ambiguous here in the third oracle. Is Israel's exalted king to be identified with God, as in the second oracle? Or is Israel's king the human counterpart to King Agag of the Amalekites, one of Israel's human monarchs like Saul or David? Those questions will be addressed only in the fourth oracle.

Thus, the images of the third oracle leave us with a beautiful Israel blessed with images of fertility and life, a crouching divine lion ready to pounce, an unspecified king waiting to be defined, and an image of God as the horns of a wild ox who devours the enemy nations. The density of metaphors and imaginative images reaches a dramatic crescendo in the third oracle. The images of nature and kingship beg to be interpreted and translated into historical and political reality. It is helpful at this point to recall the narrative context in which the poems are set. King Balak has grown increasingly frustrated and angry at Balaam for his oracles that move more and more toward positive blessing for Israel. The oracles also contain increasingly ominous but as yet unspecified warnings about lions eating their prey and a wild ox devouring its enemies. At the end of the third oracle, Balak tries to put an end to this building series of blessings on Israel and vague curses on Israel's enemies by sending Balaam home without pay (24:10–11). Balak does not want Balaam to take the next crucial step and turn the obscure metaphors of the preceding oracles into historical specifics. In the ancient Near Eastern understanding of blessing and curse, such direct and powerful words from a prophet aimed at specific nations would set in motion the events they define. In spite of Balak's protestations, Balaam feels compelled to let fly with one last climactic oracle in which nations are named and the metaphors and images of the preceding

149

oracles are translated into concrete historical realities. Balaam tells Balak, "Let me advise you what this people [Israel] will do to your people [Moab] in days to come" (24:14).

In this way, the fourth oracle unleashes all the power of the preceding heavenly visions onto the stage of earthly history. Balaam sees in this last vision a human king rising out of Israel sometime in the distant future: "I see him, but not now; I behold him, but not near—a star shall come out of Jacob, and a scepter shall rise out of Israel" (24:17). The image of a star could be used as a metaphor for a king (Isa. 14:12). The image of a scepter or royal staff symbolized royal authority, much like the staffs of Moses and Aaron represented their authority as leader and priest of Israel. As Balaam speaks to King Balak, Balaam warns Balak of the rise in some future time of a royal rival to Moab's kingship. This Israelite king "shall crush the borderlands of Moab" (24:17) and Moab's neighbors to the south: Edom (24:18), the Amalekites (whose king Agag had been mentioned in the preceding oracle in 24:7) (24:20), and the Kenites (24:21), who were a subgroup of the Midianites and indirectly related to Israel (Num. 10:29; Judg. 4:11). Behind this human king of Israel will be the power of Israel's God: "Alas, who shall live when God does this" (24:23)? The final verse is somewhat obscure: Kittim is usually another name for Cyprus; Asshur is often the biblical name for the empire of Assyria; and Eber is uncertain. What is certain is that these empires and nations "also shall perish forever" (24:24). Balaam's oracle sets in motion the historical forces that will lead to the rising of Israel's power and king and the fall of Moab and its neighbors in some distant future time. Many scholars see the future royal figure as pointing to King David and his victories over Moab and Edom (II Sam. 8:2, 11–14). The blessing of Jacob in Genesis 49 uses the image of the crouching lion and lioness waiting to be roused for Judah (King David's tribe). The blessing promises that "the scepter shall not depart from Judah" (Gen. 49:9–10); this blessing clearly points to the line of King David and uses imagery similar to Balaam's blessing. In the history of Israel, the promise of a new king or messiah was extended beyond King David to a future hope for a messiah who would usher in God's kingdom in a new apocalyptic age (e.g., Daniel 7; Rev. 2:26–28). The image of the star and its association with the coming messiah is associated with the star over Bethlehem, a sign that the messiah had been born (Matt. 2:1–10).

In its present context in Numbers, however, the fourth oracle is a final vision of Israel's future exaltation over its enemies as it becomes established as a nation in the promised land of Canaan. Together, the four oracles build into a rising crescendo of hope and promise for a new generation poised on the brink of entering Canaan. The oracles of Balaam reaffirm God's promises first made to Abraham and Sarah in Genesis 12:1–3 and repeated throughout the Pentateuch, namely, promises of land, descendants, and blessing. Balaam's first oracle affirms Israel's positive relationship with God as well as its innumerable population (Num. 23:10; cf. Gen. 13:16). The second oracle concentrates on God's faithfulness to the promises of the past and the irreversibility of God's blessing of Israel (23:19–20). The third and fourth vision describe Israel's future victory over its enemies and the peace and prosperity that Israel will enjoy in the land of Canaan (24:3–9, 15–24).

The Balaam Cycle in the Book of Numbers

Numbers 22—24 plays an important role in the overall theme of the book: the death of the old sinful generation of the wilderness and the birth of a new generation of hope on the edge of the promised land. The story of Balaam occupies a strategic position at the end of the first generation (chapter 25) and the genesis of a new generation (chapter 26). Through the mouth of a foreign prophet, God blesses Israel with accolades and promises that are unsurpassed in the rest of the Pentateuch. The oracles point to a future time of well-being, strength, victory, and hope. But this lofty and exalted vision comes crashing down for the old generation as in the next chapter it immediately returns to the way of rebellion and disobedience. The sin that follows the Balaam oracles in Numbers 25 is the old generation's final rebellion, and it is also one of its worst. The resulting plague kills the last members of the generation that was counted in Numbers 1. In the midst of the dismal end of the old desert generation, a new generation of hope is about to rise up. These children of the wilderness will be propelled into a more hopeful future by the powerful words of blessing that God has resolved to speak through Balaam in the face of all outside pressures to the contrary.

Numbers 25
The Final Rebellion:
The Death of the Remainder
of the Old Wilderness Generation

Numbers 25 tells the tale of the Israelite worship of a god named Baal Peor at a place called Shittim in the plains of Moab. Along with the apostasy of worshipping other gods, the men of Israel have sexual relations with the women of Moab (25:1) and the women of Midian (25:6, 14–16). This last episode in the first half of Numbers brings the story of the generation of the exodus and Sinai to a tragic conclusion. The faithfulness of God to promises and commitments made to Israel had been amply demonstrated in the narrative of Balaam in chapters 22—24. Throughout this conflict over blessings and curses, Israel remained passively encamped in its tents. Israel had been entirely unaware of God's struggle to ensure Israel's future against the threat from the Moabite king. In stark contrast to that divine devotion to Israel, the narrative in chapter 25 displays the fickle faith and shallow commitment of the old generation.

Poised on the threshold of the land of Canaan, the Israelites have every reason to be confident and hopeful. The visions of Balaam reveal a glorious future ahead for Israel. Their numbers are large, virtually innumerable (23:10). God is with them and will fight for them like a wild ox with horns (23:21–22). The setting is a replay of the same scenario as in the spy story of Numbers 13—14 when Israel had also been perched on the boundary of the promised land. Israel had everything going for it then as well—God in its midst, a huge army, a carefully structured military camp. But Israel had lost faith in God then, and now once again in Numbers 25 the Israelites disobey and turn from God.

The story of apostasy in chapter 25 is bound together in a number of ways with the Balaam-Balak story in chapters 22—24. The Balaam cycle featured a recurring theme of "seeing" and "looking" in both its prose and poetry sections. The Balaam story narrated how even a donkey was able to see and recognize an angel of God. Even a pagan prophet like Balaam could see God and obey God's commands. Balaam sees glorious visions of Israel's grand future. "Seeing" also plays an important role in Numbers 25, but what is seen is not God but idols, not obedience but apostasy. In chapter 25, the Israelites see only themselves engaging in prostitution with the foreign women of Midian and Moab and being drawn into the worship of alien gods. An Israelite leader brings a Midianite woman into the camp "in the sight of Moses and in the sight of the whole congregation" (25:6). The priest Phinehas also "saw" this threat to the integrity of the holy camp and takes action to stop it by piercing the Israelite man and the Midianite woman with a spear (25:7).

The two texts of Numbers 22—24 and Numbers 25 are united in other ways as well. Moabites and Midianites play a role in both the Balaam cycle and the incident with the god Baal Peor (Num. 22:4, 7; 25:1, 6, 17). The figure of Balaam is also tied to both stories. Balaam is obviously a central character in Numbers 22—24. However, Balaam is also linked to the story of Numbers 25. In Numbers 31 the narrator reports that Balaam was the one who secretly encouraged the Midianite women mentioned in Numbers 25 to entice the Israelites into apostasy (31:8, 16). Thus, the Balaam cycle and the final rebellion and apostasy of the old generation are joined together in a dramatic contrast. As God is struggling on the mountaintops surrounding the camp of Israel to bless God's people, the Israelites are down in the plains of Moab reveling in idolatry and disobedience.

Only one other Pentateuchal narrative contains this same contrast between God working to ensure a relationship with Israel while in the meantime Israel rebels by worshiping another god. That narrative is the story of the golden calf in Exodus 32. On top of Mount Sinai, Moses and God established a relationship and a covenant between God and the people. But down below the mountain, the Israelites were worshiping a golden calf as their god. The golden calf and the apostasy with Baal Peor are the only two explicit instances of Israel worshiping another god in all the events of the exodus and wilderness sojourn. In Numbers, there have been many complaint stories about the lack of food and water or the special authority given to Moses or Aaron. But never before in Numbers have the Israelites actually bowed down and worshiped other gods until chapter 25. A number of striking similarities between the Baal Peor apostasy and the golden calf story suggest that these two stories are intended to function as bookends for the experience of the old generation from Mount Sinai to the edge of the promised land:

a. In both stories, the people worship and make sacrifices to another god (Exod. 32:6; Num. 25:2).

b. Both stories involve foreigners, either the gold from the

153

Egyptians for the calf idol (Exod. 12:35; 32:2–4) or the women of Moab and Midian (Num. 25:1–2, 6).

c. In the aftermath of the golden calf story in Exodus 34:15–16, God commands Moses and the Israelites to avoid exactly what happens in Numbers 25:

> You shall not make a covenant with the inhabitants of the land, for when they prostitute themselves (Hebrew *zanah*) to their gods and sacrifice to their gods, someone among them will invite you, and you will eat of the sacrifice. And you will take wives from among their daughters for your sons and their daughters who prostitute themselves to their gods will make your sons also prostitute themselves to their gods.

Numbers 25 displays this intermingling of sexual intercourse and the worship of foreign gods, using the Hebrew word, *zanah*, in 25:1.

d. The Levites kill 3,000 of those guilty of apostasy in worshiping the golden calf (Exod. 32:28). The "judges" or leaders of Israel are instructed to kill "any of your people who have yoked themselves to the Baal of Peor" (Num. 25:5).

e. Because of their obedience in carrying out God's punishment against the idolaters, the Levites are ordained as priests to God: "Today you have ordained yourselves for the service of the LORD" (Exod. 32:25, 29). In Numbers 25, the priest Phinehas executes God's punishment on the sinners, and a special covenant with Phinehas is established: "It shall be for him and for his descendants after him a covenant of perpetual priesthood, because he was zealous for his God" (Num. 25:6–13).

f. After the golden calf incident, Moses "makes atonement" for Israel (Exod. 32:30). The priest Phinehas "makes atonement" for Israel in the Baal Peor episode (Num. 25:13).

g. A plague is sent as punishment in both the golden calf story (Exod. 32:35) and the Baal Peor story (Num. 25:9).

The significant parallels between the golden calf and the Baal Peor stories suggest that the old generation of Israelites have made little or no progress in their commitment to God's covenant. They end up where they began—worshiping other gods and breaking the first and most fundamental of the Ten Commandments: "You shall have no other gods before me" (Exod. 20:2). The one glimmer of hope in the Baal Peor story is the priest Phinehas, the grandson of the old high priest Aaron. While Aaron had been a leader in leading the Israelites astray in the worship of the golden calf (Exod. 32:1–5, 25, 35), his grandson Phinehas is a leader in upholding God's commands and in stopping the disobedience among the Israelites (Num. 25:6–13). Per-

154

haps there is hope for the new generation of Israelites who are about to continue the journey to the promised land, beginning in Numbers 26.

Scholars generally agree that Num. 25:1–5 contains an earlier form of the story that involves the women of Moab, the punishment of the chiefs of the Israelites, and the role of the judges in executing the punishment against these leaders. This earlier version was then augmented by the account in 25:6–18, which brought in the women of Midian, the judgment on all the people (25:9), the zealous character of the priest Phinehas in executing a specific punishment, and God's pledge of a perpetual priesthood to Phinehas and his descendants. Some of these elements are found in Ps. 106:28–31, which may have been one of the sources used by the writers of Numbers.

The inclusion of the women of Midian in enticing the Israelites into the worship of an alien god became the reason that justified the later assault against Midian in Numbers 31. At the end of the Baal Peor story, God commands Moses, "Harass the Midianites and defeat them, for they have harassed you by the trickery with which they deceived you in the affair of Peor" (25:16). The plague that runs through the camp of Israel as a sign of God's anger is a common motif in the other rebellion stories in Numbers (11:33; 14:37; 16:46). The role of the priest Phinehas in killing Zimri, the son of an Israelite leader from the tribe of Simeon, and Cozbi, a daughter of a Midianite clan leader, led to a covenant with Phinehas and his line of an eternal priesthood. Some scholars understand this portion of the story as written at a time when the priestly line of Phinehas's descendants was being challenged. The notes about Phinehas in Ezra 8:2 and I Chron. 9:20 may be reflexes of this same concern to legitimate the priestly line of Phinehas in the postexilic period of Israel's history.

A number of oddities emerge as one reads through the narrative of Numbers 25. God tells Moses to impale the chiefs of the people as punishment for their sin (25:4), but the text never reports that this was done. Moses instructs the judges of the people to "kill any of your people who have yoked themselves to the Baal of Peor" (25:5). Again, the text never indicates that Moses' command was followed. Moses does not seem to obey God. The chiefs are to be impaled in the sun for their sin. The judges do not carry out Moses' orders. Moses had been the one in previous rebellions who had turned back the wrath of God, but that task now falls to young Phinehas, the priest. Moses has a strangely passive role in this story. Some of these disjunctions within the narrative may have resulted from the combining of earlier and later traditions into one story. But the disjunctions create for the reader a sense of the breakdown and disintegration of the carefully ordered holy war camp and the chain of authority and command running from God to Moses and on to the leaders and the people. Numbers 1—10 had repeatedly noted how the commands of God or Moses were carefully obeyed as the Israelite camp was organized. Numbers 25 portrays the final disintegration of that carefully arranged structure within which the wilderness generation was obedient to God. The new generation will begin again with an entirely new census (Num. 26) and new challenges as it prepares to move ahead and enter the land of Canaan. Will the new generation repeat the rebellions and disobedience of the past? Or will they learn from the past and move ahead in their life-journey toward trust and faith in God?

Most of Israel's rebellions in the book of Numbers have involved all Israelites of all the tribes. This appears to be the case in Numbers 25:1–5 as well. But one Israelite named Zimri is singled out as committing a particularly shameful and public act of disobedience in bringing the Midianite woman into the camp. Zimri was the son of an ancestral clan leader in the tribe of Simeon (Num. 25:14). One other rebellion story in Numbers had singled out particular tribal members as leaders in the revolt, namely, Korah of the tribe of Levi, and Dathan and Abiram of the tribe of Reuben, in chapter 16. Thus Levi, Reuben, and Simeon are tribes that receive a special censure in the book of Numbers, even while the entire old generation of Israelites is also counted as responsible for its many rebellions. Mary Douglas understands the special punishment of Levi, Reuben, and Simeon in Numbers as a reflection of the curses these three sons received in Jacob's deathbed "blessing" of his twelve sons in Genesis 49:1–7 (Douglas, pp. 194–95). Jacob condemns his first three sons, Reuben, Simeon, and Levi, for their violence and disobedience. As Balaam's blessing of future generations of Israelites is proclaimed in Numbers 22—24, Numbers 25 closes the book on the curses pronounced on an earlier generation in Jacob's blessing of Genesis 49. The slate is clean, and a new generation can now begin again with the warnings of the past and the promises of the future as their guide into the land of promise.

The story of Israel's worship of an alien god in Numbers 25 brings to an end the life of the first generation of Israelites who came out of Egypt. The twenty-four thousand Israelites who died in the plague in 25:9 are presumably the last remnants of the old generation. They have left the stage to make room for a new generation who will again stand on the edge of the promised land. The advent of this new generation of hope is marked by the second census list of Israel's twelve tribes in Numbers 26.

PART TWO

The Rise of a New Generation on the Edge of the Promised Land

NUMBERS 26—36

The second half of Numbers and the emergence of a whole new generation of Israelites is inaugurated by the second census list in Numbers 26. The first census list of the twelve tribes in Numbers 1 marked the beginning of Israel's march from Mount Sinai through the wilderness and on to the promised land. The overriding question in the first half of Numbers has been this: How was a holy and powerful God of life to dwell in the midst of a sinful people? The structure of the camp and the concentric circles of holiness around the tabernacle and the presence of God in Israel's midst were designed to protect the Israelites so that the journey could continue. But the constant rebellions of the people, of the leaders, and even of Aaron and Moses themselves led to the death of the entire wilderness generation and God's denying them entry into Canaan. The second census list in Numbers 26 signals the reconstitution of the twelve-tribe camp of Israel by the sons and daughters of the wilderness generation. Now the overriding question in the second half of Numbers is this: Will this second generation find a way to be faithful and enter the promised land, or will they rebel and fail as the first generation had done? What can the second generation do differently to avoid the rebellions and disasters of the first generation? And is God willing to continue to guide Israel into the land and to be faithful to the promises God has made? This latter question has already been addressed quite dramatically in the Balaam oracles of

157

blessing in chapters 22—24, in God's promise in 14:31 that God would bring "the little ones" into Canaan, in the laws like those in chapter 15 that were aimed at life in the promised land, and in the preliminary military victories God had given at the end of the first generation in chapter 21. Here at the beginning of the second generation, God's commitment and devotion to Israel remains strong and unchanging. The spotlight will be on the new Israelites as they ready themselves to enter the land of Canaan.

The large number of parallels between Numbers 1—25 and Numbers 26—36 suggests that the new generation will be given challenges and opportunities that are similar to those of their parents. The parallels begin with the census list itself in chapter 26. The same formula for God's command in 1:2–3 is used again in 26:2. The lists of the twelve tribes in chapter 1 and chapter 26 are exactly the same, except for a minor reversal in the order of the two Joseph tribes, Ephraim and Manasseh. A census of the Levites comes immediately after the twelve-tribe head count in both halves of the book (chapters 3—4 and chapter 26). A legal discourse concerning women and the referral of judgment from humans to God in chapter 5 finds a counterpart in the legal discourse involving women and the referral of judgment to God in the case of Zelophehad's daughters in chapter 27. Laws involving vows in chapter 6 parallel laws concerning vows in chapter 30. Provisions for the material support of the Levites in 18:21–32 find an analogue in the provisions for cities for the Levites in chapter 35. The list of tribal offerings at the dedication of the altar for the tabernacle in chapter 7 and the laws concerning sacrifices and offerings in chapter 15 are echoed by the list of offerings to be given at appointed festival and holy days in chapters 28 and 29. The celebration of the festival of Passover in chapter 9 is complemented by the instructions for future celebrations of Passover in 28:16–25.

Other parallels include the list of tribal leaders who acted as spies in Numbers 13 and the list of tribal leaders chosen to supervise the allotment of land in Canaan in Numbers 34. The itinerary of all the places visited by Israel in the wilderness in the course of its travels in chapters 1—25 is summarized by the wilderness itinerary in chapter 33. The story of the spies and the people's lack of trust in chapters 13—14 is recalled as a history lesson for the new generation in 32:6–15. The first generation victories over King Sihon and King Og in the Transjordan region on the east side of the Jordan River boundary prepare for the second generation of the tribes of Reuben, Gad, and the half-tribe of Manasseh to settle in the Transjordan area in Numbers 32 (cf. 32:33). As we saw in Numbers 25, the last narrative of the old generation and its worship of an alien god in connection with the Midianite women provides the occasion in chapter 31 for an act of holy war against the Midianites by the new generation of Israelites.

These numerous parallels between the two halves of Numbers, the first generation in Numbers 1—25 and the second generation in Numbers 26—36, suggest that the new generation will work through many of the same kinds of narratives, laws, and issues as their parents did in the wilderness. The reader is invited to identify with this new generation, to learn from the past, and to follow the new generation in its struggles to find a better way as it moves out of the wilderness and into Canaan. This new generation becomes in effect a paradigm for each succeeding generation of God's people, a model of the struggles and the strategies that may offer hope of moving into the land of promise. If the new generation of God's people is indeed the implied audience for the book of Numbers, then the social location of this audience is a new generation who grew up in a time of disaster, social and religious disintegration, and perhaps exile from the land of Canaan itself. The Babylonian exile from Judah may have been such a time, but other times both before and after the exile would have seen new generations struggling to learn from past eras of failure and looking forward to new visions of a renewed life in the homeland of Israel or Judah.

As it struggled to live as God's holy people, the fate of the first generation ended in failure, rebellion, and death (11:1—25:18). Failure and death were not inevitable, however. Because of their faith and trust in God, Caleb of the tribe of Judah and Joshua of the tribe of Ephraim were two members of the old generation whom God allowed to continue on into the promised land (14:30). The presence of Caleb and Joshua in the midst of the new generation gave hope to the new Israelites that faithfulness was possible and death outside the land was not an inevitability. Thus, the fate of the second generation remains open as we move toward the end of the book of Numbers. Will the new generation be faithful or not?

There are signs of hope that emerge in the course of the final chapters of Numbers. Major disputes are resolved through peaceful negotiation rather than open rebellion and death (27:1–11; 32:1–42; 36:1–13). Laws are issued that can apply only when Israel is safely settled in the land of Canaan (Numbers 27; 34—36). Such laws imply the hope that this new generation may implement them in the land. In the course of its many rebellions, thousands upon thousands of the old generation died in the wilderness. A special purity ritual using the ashes of a red cow was required for many who became impure through contact with dead bodies (Numbers 19). In profound contrast to the

159

predominance of death throughout the first half of Numbers, not a single Israelite is recorded as dying throughout the whole second half of Numbers. And while the first military engagement for Israel (in the spy story of Numbers 13—14) ended in judgment and death, the first military encounter against the Midianites results in a God-given victory over those who had earlier seduced the old generation into apostasy. These signs of hope open the door to a whole new beginning, the ultimate end of which remains undecided as the book of Numbers comes to a close. That open door stands as an invitation to each new generation of God's people to walk through it and join the journey toward God's good land of promise and hope.

Numbers 26
A Second Census:
The Rise of a New Generation
of Hope

Numbers 26:1 begins with a significant opening phrase, "After the plague the LORD said to Moses and to Eleazar son of Aaron the priest . . .". The plague in question is the one in Numbers 25 that had put to death the last of the old rebellious generation. Although condemned to join the old generation in death outside the land of Canaan, Moses remains for an interim time as a teacher and guide to the new generation until his death in Deuteronomy 34. Moses' leadership in the last half of Numbers (chaps. 26—36) and the book of Deuteronomy that follows function as Moses' enduring legacy to the new generation. Finally, Eleazar, the son of Aaron and one of the new generation, has taken over his father's role as high priest for Israel. Thus, in these first few words of Numbers 26, we have summarized the end of the old generation, the transitional leadership of Moses, and the new generation of leadership represented by Aaron's son, Eleazar the priest.

God instructs Moses and Eleazar to "take a census of the whole congregation of Israel, from twenty years old and upward, by their ancestral houses, everyone in Israel able to go to war" (26:2). This command and the second census list of Israel's twelve tribes that follows is very similar in form to the census of the tribes in Numbers 1. God's commands to take the census use the same formulas, and the sequence in the list of the twelve tribes is identical except for the minor reversal in the order of Ephraim and Manasseh. A census of the Levites follows the twelve-tribe census in 26:57–62, just as it does in Numbers 3—4. As we have argued, this symmetrical construction of the two census lists suggests that they are intended to function together as the primary structural pillars of the book of Numbers.

One important difference between the two census lists is that Numbers 26 adds one more level of names of clans for each of the twelve tribes. An example is the tribe of Gad. In Num. 1:24–25, we read simply, "The descendants of Gad, their lineage, in their clans, by their ancestral houses . . . those enrolled were forty-five thousand six hundred fifty." The only information given is the name of the whole tribe and its number. In the second census list in 26:15–18, the tribal name Gad is listed. But a number of clans within the tribe are also named: "The children of Gad by their clans: of Zephon, the clan of the Zephonites; of Haggi, the clan of the Haggites; of Shuni, the clan of the Shunites . . . These are the clans of the Gadites: the number of those enrolled was forty thousand five hundred." The effect of adding a list of named clans to each tribe in the second census list is to reinforce the sense that another new generation has been added in this second tribal census.

The names for these clans appear to be related to the list of the children of each of the twelve sons of Jacob in Gen. 46:8–27. Thus, in reference to the tribe of Gad, one sees clearly the relationship of Numbers 26 and Genesis 46 when they are placed side by side:

Genesis 46	**Numbers 26**
Gad	Gad
sons of Gad:	sons of Gad:
Ziphion	Zephon—Zephonites
Haggi	Haggi—Haggites
Shuni	Shuni—Shunites
Ezbon	Ozni—Oznites
Eri	Eri—Erites
Arodi	Arod—Arodites
Areli	Areli—Arelites

There are deviations from this pattern in moving from Genesis 46 to Numbers 26, some of which derive from textual corruptions, previous narratives in Numbers that have an effect on the genealogical progression within a given tribe (e.g., the death of Dathan and Abiram in Numbers 16 for the tribe of Reuben), or other factors that are not immediately apparent. One important deviation occurs with the tribe of Joseph through Manasseh in Num. 26:28–34. The enumeration of clans in the Manasseh tribe extends to a depth of seven generations; most others in Numbers 26 extend only to two or three generations. The reason for this detailed family tree is to trace the line all the way to the daughters of Zelophehad who belong to Manasseh and are explicitly named in Num. 26:33. The five daughters, Mahlah, Noah, Hoglah, Milcah, and Tirzah, will be featured in the episode after the census in an important judicial case (27:1–11). This branching out of the tribe into the next levels of family groups or clans in chapter 26 leaves the distinct impression of another generation that has been added since the first census in chapter 1. Moreover, none of the names among these new clan groups in chapter 26 appear in any of the other previous lists of clan leaders in Numbers. The second census list represents an entirely new generation.

It is interesting to compare the numbers counted in the two census lists in Numbers 1 and 26. The total number for all twelve tribes decreases only slightly from the first to the second census list: a total of 603,550 in Num. 1:46, and a total of 601,730 in Num. 26:51. The difference is less than two thousand people. God had faithfully brought the "little ones" to the edge of the promised land, in spite of the fears of the old rebellious generation that their "little ones" would only die in the wilderness or in the conquest of Canaan (14:3). One tribe among the twelve experiences a dramatic decrease in its numbers, the tribe of Simeon. There were 59,300 Simeonites in Numbers 1, and only 22,200 in Numbers 26. The dramatic act of faithlessness and disobedience of Zimri the Simeonite in Numbers 25 may be reflected in this diminishing of the Simeon tribe, an example of God "visiting the iniquity of the parents upon the children to the third and fourth generation" (Num. 14:18). The overall effect of the total numbers remaining relatively the same in spite of all the rebellions of the preceding generation and all the rigors of life in the wilderness is to affirm God as "abounding in steadfast love, forgiving iniquity and transgression, but by no means clearing the guilty" (14:18).

Two important passages in Numbers 26 guide the interpretation of this second census. First of all, 26:52–56 indicates that this second head count of all the tribes is primarily for the purpose of distributing fair amounts of land to the tribes based on their relative sizes. The larger the tribe, the larger will be their allotment of territory in Canaan. The location of the land, however, will be determined by lot. This land distribution function of the census is a shift from the purpose of the first census list in Numbers, which focused on military preparation for war. The formula, "all those who were able to go forth to war," was repeated fourteen times in the census list of Numbers 1, but it does not appear at all in the second census in chapter 26, except once in 26:2. The census in chapter 26 is no longer for estimating available military strength and numbers of warriors as a means of gaining the land. The goal of the second census is more to ensure that each tribe receives its fair share of God's gift of the land according to the needs of its particular population size.

The second text of note is Num. 26:63–65. These verses explicitly sound the theme of the whole book—the death of the old generation and the rise of a new generation of God's people. This theme had been formulated in a definitive way in the story of the unfaithful spies in chapters 13—14. God had declared then for the first time that the old generation would die in the course of forty years of wilderness wandering. But God would bring their "little ones" of the next generation into the land of promise (14:26–35). The concluding note to the second census list recalls God's words as it describes those who were not included among those counted in this second census:

> Among these there was not one of those enrolled by Moses and Aaron the priest, who had enrolled the Israelites in the wilderness of Sinai. For the LORD had said of them, "They shall die in the wilderness." Not one of them was left, except Caleb son of Jephunneh and Joshua son of Nun. (Num. 26:64–65)

This text provides a programmatic summary of the structure of Numbers. The second census list is both a sign of completed judgment on the first generation and a sign of God's promise for a new generation.

Numbers 27:1–11
The Daughters of Zelophehad and the Inheritance of the Land: A Legal Dispute Resolved

The census list in Numbers 26 was intended primarily as an aid in calculating allotments of land for each of the twelve tribes of Israel. Tribes with larger populations would require large tracts of land; tribes with smaller population numbers would need smaller allotments of territory (26:52–54). The precise location of the land was to be decided by lot, lest any one tribe complain about getting land that was less desirable or more vulnerable than others (26:55–56). This care in deciding the distribution of the land in Canaan reflects a basic concern that

163

each tribal and family unit have a sufficient and fairly distributed land base for its economic well-being. Ancient Israel had a patrilineal inheritance system whereby the land was passed from father to son and so kept within the family and tribe. This ensured that the land originally apportioned to a given tribe stayed with that tribe.

But what if a father has no sons and only daughters? The question is implicitly raised already in the census list in 26:33–34. An extended family tree traces the genealogy of Manasseh for seven generations, more than any other tribe in the census list. At the end of the family tree, the father Zelophehad had five daughters and no sons. Their names were Mahlah, Noah, Hoglah, Milcah, and Tirzah. In Num. 27:1–11, these five bold women appear before Moses the judge and argue their case. The women begin by reminding Moses that their father did not participate in the revolt against God by Korah and his company and thus did not forfeit his claim to land in Canaan. Their father died in the wilderness "for his own sin" and thus should be treated as fairly as any other Israelite. The women claim that they should inherit their father's land so as to preserve their father's name on the land: "Why should the name of our father be taken away from his clan because he had no son?" (27:4).

Two competing customs or laws are at work in this dispute. One custom in ancient Israel in its patrilineal system was that only males could inherit property. On the other hand, there is the high priority of keeping land with the original clans and tribes. The tradition sought to prevent any one tribe from accumulating too much territory of its own at the expense of other tribes. In the laws of the Pentateuch, tribal lands could be bought and sold among the tribes. But every fifty years was to be a year of Jubilee when all tribal lands that may have been bought or sold in the period since the last Jubilee year reverted back to their original families and tribes (Lev. 25:8–55; 27:16–25). The value placed on maintaining the fair distribution of the land among the twelve tribes was high in the tradition out of which the book of Numbers was written. But did that value of fairness and equity override the custom of only males inheriting property?

Faced with this dilemma, Moses turns to God for guidance in this unprecedented case. As in the case of the jealous husband and the woman accused of adultery (chap. 5), the determination is seen as beyond human competence; the decision is left in the hands of God. God agrees with the five women that the land must remain in the family's possession, even if it means contradicting the custom that only men can inherit land (27:5–7). But what happens to the land if and when these daughters of Zelophehad marry someone outside their

164

tribe? Does the land then leave the tribe with the women? This additional complication will be taken up at the end of the book of Numbers when the five daughters of Zelophehad will again appear (36:1–12). In the case of Numbers 27, God clearly affirms the priority of maintaining the system of equal distribution of the economic base for each family and tribe. Other rules can be broken and other precedents can be overridden in favor of justice in the economic life of Israel.

The important function of this case in chapter 27 and its counterpart in chapter 36 in the larger structure of the book of Numbers should not be overlooked. We have already noted that this case about male and female inheritance is linked with the preceding census list in Numbers 26 in two ways. They both have to do with issues of the distribution of land once Israel is settled in Canaan, and the extended genealogy of Manasseh in the census had highlighted the five daughters of Zelophehad in anticipation of this legal dispute (26:33). Moreover, Numbers 27 and 36 form an *inclusio* or frame around all the material related to the new generation. The writers of Numbers appear to place a spotlight on these five women and the issue of the land. Three major themes emerge from the story of Zelophehad's daughters in relation to the larger book of Numbers: (1) a reaffirmation of God's promise of the land; (2) a concern for the inclusiveness of all the tribes; and (3) a model of critical and creative affirmation of tradition.

1. Earlier in the commentary, our study of the laws in Numbers 15 indicated that they served to keep the promise of the land for the new generation in view after the debacle of the spy story in Numbers 13—14. In a similar way, the laws about land distribution in the case of the five daughters of Zelophehad provide reassurance that entry into Canaan is imminent. God's promise is well on its way toward fulfillment. Moreover, the chapters that fall in between the two texts involving the daughters of Zelophehad (chaps. 28—35) either deal directly with the inheritance of the land of Canaan (boundaries of the land, supervision of the land's allocation) or presuppose a settled life in Canaan (cultic and sacrificial regulations, towns for the Levites, and cities of refuge). The reaffirmation of the promise of the land for the new generation of God's people is made strongly, repeatedly, and consistently throughout this second half of the book, in chapters 26—36.

2. A second theme of Numbers 27 and 36 is the concern to maintain the inclusiveness of the promised inheritance to all twelve tribes of Israel. The reason given in chapter 27 for allowing the daughters to inherit their father's land is to ensure that each tribe retains its full inheritance and integrity as a tribe. No one tribe is to benefit from situations that threaten to deprive another tribe of its land. The same

reason is given for the decision in chapter 36. As we have noted at other points in our study of Numbers, this insistence on including all the twelve tribes in the promises of God is a theme running throughout the book. It occurs in the construction of the census lists and in other lists of the leaders of the twelve tribes (supervisors of the census, tribal offerings at the dedication of the altar, the spy story, supervisors of the division of the land of Canaan). No one tribe escapes the judgment or the promise of God.

3. A third theme arising out of the legal material in chapters 27 and 36 is the affirmation of the flexibility of the tradition and the warrant for reinterpreting the past for the sake of the new. The very nature of the legal dispute in Numbers 27 and 36 suggests that no precedent was available in past traditions by which to decide the issue. New situations may arise that will not find direct answers in the tradition. The case of the wood gatherer breaking the sabbath in chapter 15 also involved an unprecedented case, but here in the second half of Numbers the theme is much stronger. Much of the material in Numbers 28—35 that lies between the two daughters of Zelophehad texts exhibits a similar movement of reinterpreting the past for the sake of the new generation. The most obvious example is Numbers 32, in which the lesson of the spy story in Numbers 13—14 is explicitly recalled as a warning to the new generation of what might happen again.

At the beginning of the book of Numbers, an important transition occurred. Israel moved from the immovable setting of Mount Sinai where the definitive revelation of God's will for Israel was revealed (Exodus, Leviticus) to the portable tent of meeting, or tabernacle. God promised to continue to reveal the divine will from the tent of meeting as new circumstances and questions arose (7:89). The people of Israel in Numbers are a people on the move, and God and God's law moves with them. The tent of meeting stands as a symbol of the openness of revelation, the dynamic flexibility of Israel's tradition, and the invitation for ongoing dialogue between God and God's people. God's word is not a sterile and entrenched legalism but a robust and living tradition that leans toward the future in hope and anticipation.

The five bold women who bring their case before Moses in Numbers 27 provide a model for the new generation. The women challenge their tradition of male only inheritance by appealing to what they see as the tradition's own more foundational values, namely, the just distribution of land and maintaining the integrity of all the tribes. The five daughters of Zelophehad provide a constructive example of how the second generation may move forward in its journey with God while honoring the traditions of past generations. The old generation had

166

sought change through a number of inappropriate avenues: complaining about its own selfish and often unreasonable wants and desires for better food or for more power in the community, abandoning the tradition entirely by rejecting the God who brought them out of Egypt (in the spy story of Numbers 13—14), or worshiping other gods and following their ways. The daughters of Zelophehad remain faithful to the living God of the exodus and respectful of their dynamic tradition. They seek change by appealing to the basic values of the tradition that may override other less important customs of that same tradition. The motivation of the five women is not selfishness but advocacy on behalf of others. They act not so much for themselves as for the good of their whole community—family, tribe, nation, and the whole tradition of God's people.

Finally, the case of the five women in 27:1–11 raises issues of equity and gender. The decision in favor of Mahlah, Noah, Hoglah, Milcah, and Tirzah may be seen as one small step toward enhancing the status of women in the world of the biblical narrative. But the underlying system of patrilineal inheritance remains essentially intact even in this case. The land will revert to a male husband when one of the daughters marries, a point that will be raised in chapter 36. It is also not clear to what extent this case represents actual practice in ancient Israelite society (Sakenfeld, "In the Wilderness, Awaiting the Land"). However, these five sisters are able to take one small step toward greater justice for women by appealing to the core values of their shared Israelite tradition. They may provide encouragement and direction for those in our own time concerned about issues of justice and gender. These five women teach us to dig deeply and argue persuasively from within a shared biblical tradition if we would overturn old customs and create new possibilities in the social and economic relationships between women and men. These women are models of boldness fueled by hope, models of advocacy fueled by a concern for the larger community, and models of faithfulness fueled by a dynamic relationship with their tradition and with their God.

Numbers 27:12–23
The Succession of Leadership from Moses to Joshua: A New Generation of Leadership

The medieval Jewish commentator Rashi wondered why this section about the impending death of Moses and the succession of leadership from Moses to Joshua should follow immediately after the case of Zelophehad's daughters. One possible explanation he offers is that Moses' hopes had perhaps been raised when God commanded him, *"You* shall indeed let them possess an inheritance among their father's brothers" (27:7). Having heard this divine decree, Rashi reports what some interpreters imagined Moses might have said to himself:

> Moses thought to himself: "God commanded *me* to give them their portion in the land; perhaps then the decree concerning me has been relaxed and I will be permitted to enter the land?" Hence, God immediately stated, "My decree stands." (Rashi, p. 179)

Rashi raises this interpretation as only one possible explanation for the close literary juxtaposition of Zelophehad's daughters and the reminder of Moses' imminent death, both in Numbers 27. But the interpretation does get at the issue of the new generation's urgent need for leadership. The dispute over land inheritance reminds us that entry into the land is coming soon, and Moses knows he cannot set foot on Canaan's soil with the new generation of Israelites because of his sin at the waters of Meribah (Num. 27:14; cf. 20:1–13). Moses will see the land at a distance from a mountain, but he will die outside the land like his brother Aaron. As we observed in chapter 20, the nature of the sin committed by Aaron and Moses was not entirely clear, but it was sufficient to deny them entry into Canaan. The book of Deuteronomy includes an alternate tradition about why Moses had to die outside the land; Moses died not for his own sin but on account of the sin of the people (Deut. 1:37; 3:26; 4:21).

God's reminder of his fast-approaching death prompts Moses to ask God to appoint a new leader for this new generation of Israelites. The new high priest is already in place, with Aaron's appointment of his son, Eleazar, just prior to Aaron's death on Mount Hor (20:22–29).

168

Numbers 27:12–23 recounts only the transfer of leadership from Moses to Joshua, not the actual death of Moses, since that will come later at the end of the book of Deuteronomy, in chapter 34. Joshua had joined Caleb as one of the two faithful spies in Numbers 13—14 who brought back a favorable report of the land. Joshua had been a close assistant and advisor to Moses for some time (Exod. 17:8–13; 32:17; Num. 11:28).

Joshua, however, does not simply step into the shoes of leadership as a new Moses. Moses gives only some or a portion of his authority to Joshua (27:20). God spoke to Moses "face to face" in a direct and unmediated way (12:6–8). Joshua, on the other hand, will rely on more indirect divine guidance through the priest and his casting of lots using the Urim and Thummim (cf. Exod. 28:30; I Sam. 28:6; Ezra 2:63). The epoch of Moses and his revelation of God's words to Israel was drawing to a close and would never be repeated in Israel's history. For a brief interim period, Joshua and Moses will lead the Israelites together until Moses' death, which occurs in Deuteronomy 34. Joshua will then take over full leadership of Israel as they move into the promised land of Canaan, but his leadership will be guided by the written book of the Torah of Moses (Josh. 1:7–8).

Although Joshua is not simply a carbon copy of Moses, an essential continuity of leadership exists between them. This continuity is expressed through the laying on of hands by Moses on the new leader, Joshua. The ceremony of placing the hands upon another signified the transfer of the power of authority, blessing, or sin from one to another. The one upon whose head hands are placed becomes a representative or substitute for the other. Jacob placed his hands on his grandsons and blessed them (Gen. 48:14). People could ritually transfer their guilt or sin to another person or sacrificial animal by placing their hands on the head of the person or animal (Lev. 1:4; 24:14). God instructed the Levites to act as substitutes for all the firstborn of Israel; this role was enacted through the laying on of hands by the people of Israel (Num. 8:10–12). Thus, the imposition of Moses' hands upon the head of Joshua was a public acknowledgement that Joshua was now to be the leader of the new generation of Israelites. Although Joshua, as a new leader, would receive God's guidance in less direct ways than Moses, he and the new generation would benefit from the Mosaic legacy of stories, laws, warnings, and promises of the past—guides into an uncharted future in the land of Canaan.

Numbers 28—30
Appointed Offerings and Voluntary Vows:
Preserving Order and Holiness
in the Promised Land for a New Generation

Appointed Offerings, Cycles of Time, and God's Order in Creation (Numbers 28—29)

A central issue at the beginning of the book of Numbers was the arrangement of Israel's camp structure, which allowed God's powerful and holy presence to dwell in the midst of the people (Numbers 2—4). The design of the holy war camp with the central tabernacle and its surrounding concentric circles of priests and Levites functioned as a buffer zone between a holy God and a sinful people. The order of the camp was an attempt to create a space or zone of safety and mediated blessing in the volatile interaction between the holiness of God and the sinful people.

Thus, the introductory chapters of Numbers focused on creating spatial order within the camp of Israel. Such order helped to keep at bay the forces of sin, chaos, and disintegration that threatened the fragile community in the wilderness. The wilderness remains a potent metaphor for the threatening forces of evil, chaos, and death even after Israel's occupation of the land of Canaan. Israel's community remains under threat and temptation from forces both inside and outside the boundaries of Canaan (Judg. 2:1–5). For the second generation of Israelites who stand poised to enter the land of Canaan, the focus moves from creating order in space to creating order in time. Numbers 28—29 depicts a systematic program of offerings and sacrifices that mark boundaries of time through the cycle of days, weeks, and the year. The quantities of required offerings and their assigned dates are given for daily morning and evening sacrifices (28:3–6), the sabbath offerings (28:9–10), the offerings on the first of the month (28:11–15), and offerings for various festivals (28:16—29:40).

The sacrifices at these appointed times function as markers of points of crossing, boundaries, and transitions that are deemed dangerous but manageable through proper ritual observance and sacrifice. These observances of time and its boundaries provide the people with a way of participating in God's ongoing creation of order in the cosmos. Behind the sacrifices and appointed times of Numbers 28—29 stands the story of God's creation of the world in Genesis 1. The story of creation in Genesis is a story of God's dividing and ordering the cosmos into day and night, into a week of six days of profane work and a seventh day of holy sabbath rest, and into an ongoing cycle of months and seasons within a year marked by the sun and the moon. Any crossing of a boundary, any point of transition from one state to another, is a point of special vigilance where chaos threatens to undo the order of the cosmos and of the community (Gorman, pp. 215–27).

We may summarize the interaction between the creation story in Genesis 1 and the appointed times for offerings in Numbers 28—29 in the following manner:

1. Genesis 1 begins the first day of creation with the creation of day and night: "God saw that the light was good; and God separated the light from the darkness. God called the light Day, and the darkness he called Night" (Gen. 1:4–5). Daily sacrifices are to be offered, one in the morning in the transition from night to day and one in the evening in the transition from day into night (Num. 28:3–8).

2. God finished work on the seventh day of creation: "So God blessed the seventh day and hallowed it, because on it God rested from all the work that he had done in creation" (Gen. 2:3). Special offerings mark off each sabbath day as set apart and holy from the rest of the week (Num. 28:9–10).

3. The interplay of the lunar calendar that used the phases of the moon to calculate time was used for certain festivals. On the other hand, the rhythm of the seasons of the year was influenced by the sun's position in the sky, and so some festivals were linked more to seasons of planting and harvest and the spring and autumn equinox. On the fourth day of creation, we read:

> And God said, "Let there be lights in the dome of the sky to separate the day from the night: and let them be for signs and for seasons and for days and for years. . . . God made the two great lights—the greater light to rule the day and the lesser light to rule the night—and the stars. (Gen. 1:14–16)

Thus, the offerings for the beginning of each month and for the various festivals of the year mark significant boundaries and transition points from one month to another, from one season to another, from a non-ritual or non-festival period to a ritual or festival time. These are all related to the ordering of time marked by the sun's varying positions within the heavens and by the phases of the moon.

171

INTERPRETATION

The year is divided into twelve months. The year is also divided into two major halves. Just as the day is divided into two halves of day and night and the week into six days of work and one day of sabbath rest, so the year has a bipartite structure. Significant festivals in the first month mark the first half of the year, and another set of significant festivals occur in the seventh month to mark the second half of the year.

First Half of the Year
First month
  1st day of the month—monthly offerings (28:11–15)
  14th day of the month—offerings for Passover (28:16)
  15th–21st days of the month—offerings for the Festival of Unleavened Bread (28:17–25)—a seven-day festival; day 1 and 2—"a holy convocation"—no work
  [Offerings for Day of the Firstfruits/Festival of Weeks—beginning of wheat harvest—a sabbath day plus 7 times 7 days after the Festival of Unleavened Bread (28:26–31; cf. Lev. 23:15–21)]

Second Half of the Year
Seventh month
  1st day of the month—offerings for the Festival of Trumpets (29:1–6)—"a holy convocation"—no work
  10th day of the month—offerings on the Day of Atonement—"holy convocation," "deny yourselves"
  15th–21st days of the month—offerings for Festival of Booths (29:12–34)—seven-day festival (harvest thanksgiving festival)
  22nd day—offerings for "solemn assembly" (29:35–38)

The regular sequence of offerings throughout these special moments of the yearly cycle maintained a sense of order in time. Through its offerings, the community sought to align itself with the rhythms and seasons of time embedded in creation by God at the very beginning of the cosmos. Much more detail about the individual festivals may be found elsewhere in the Bible, especially in Exodus, Leviticus and Deuteronomy (Exodus 12—13; 23; Leviticus 16; 23; Deuteronomy 16). But the focus of Numbers 28—29 on the structure of offerings at each of the important boundaries of time provides a summary of a theology of time whereby Israel aligns itself with an embedded cosmic order created by God at the beginning of time.

This rhythm of marking the boundaries and transitions of morning and evening, the sabbath day and other days of the week, the new month, and the festivals in the year sets the community apart as a holy people dedicated to a distinctive order of time as commanded by God. In Israel's history, the offerings and sacrifices of Numbers 28—29

172

could be made at the Jerusalem Temple as long as it existed. When it was destroyed by the Babylonians in 587 B.C.E. and again by the Romans in 70 C.E., the Jewish community continued to observe these rhythms of time through the offering and sacrifice of thanksgiving, prayer, and worship centered in the Jewish synagogue. Morning and evening prayer, sabbath worship, and the observance of festivals continued as a way of ordering time and participating with God in the work of creation begun in Genesis 1.

Christian practices of prayer and worship have deep roots in this Jewish tradition and understanding of the rhythm of holy time. Christian traditions of morning and evening prayer, Sunday worship, the structure of the church or liturgical year (Advent, Lent, etc.), the special festivals such as Christmas and Easter all reflect the understanding of time as a means of participating and sustaining God's ordering work in the midst of the threatening chaos of the world. Marking these transitions of time with the offering of prayer and worship enables the community to be in tune with God's order and will for creation. The ordered structure of time provides regular opportunities for refocusing priorities, rededicating commitments, and reentering the biblical story of God and God's people as a means of finding meaning and order in the midst of the chaos of life.

In the context of the book of Numbers, the list in Numbers 28—29 of sacrifices and offerings as the means of maintaining order in time is analogous to the structure of the Israelite camp in Numbers 2—4 that sought to maintain order in space. The camp and its spatial structure, which was centered on God's presence in its midst, enabled Israel to move from Egypt through the chaos of the wilderness. The new generation poised on the doorstep of Canaan is about to leave the wilderness. It is about to enter a land of fertility and agricultural seasons and a settled existence of rhythms and order. The structured order of time and appointed offerings will regularly remind the Israelites of their status as God's holy people and will help sustain the order of the community's social and religious life against the forces of chaos that will continue to threaten it. Moreover, the large quantities of animals and grain and wine in the offerings described in Numbers 28—29 presuppose a prosperous agricultural life in a fertile land. Thus, the laws for the offerings offer hope and confidence to the new generation that they are about to enter a land of abundance, peace, order, and stability. God's holy presence will be in Israel's midst, and God's holy rhythms of time will order Israel's life.

Men, Women, and the Fulfillment of Vows (Numbers 30)

The preceding chapters in Numbers had established a regularized schedule and disciplined system of sacrifices and offerings given to God. A summary statement at the end of Numbers 29 mentions another option—that of giving "votive offerings and your freewill offerings," which are more spontaneous expressions of thanksgiving, devotion, or petition to God (29:39). Numbers 30 takes up a particular dimension of voluntary or freewill offerings in the form of voluntary vows or pledges made to God by men and women. Through such vows or pledges, people promised either to abstain from certain activities (as in the Nazirite vow in Numbers 6) or to dedicate some sacrifice or other offering to God or God's service. Such promises were linked to certain conditions that the petitioner would ask God to fulfill. An example may be found in Numbers 21:2 where the Israelites ask God for military victory over the Canaanites in exchange for dedicating all the booty to God by destroying it: "Then Israel made a vow to the LORD and said, 'If you will indeed give this people into our hands, then we will utterly destroy their towns.'" Other conditions or requests from God in exchange for the vow include Jacob's safe return home to his father's house (Gen. 28:20–22), the judge Jephthah's military victory over the Ammonites (Judg. 11:30–31), or the birth of a son to Hannah (I Sam. 1:11).

The bulk of chapter 30 treats situations in which a woman's vow may or may not be made void by the objection of a father or a husband. The general principle is stated at the beginning of the chapter: vows made to God by men are not to be broken. "He shall not break his word; he shall do according to all that proceeds out of his mouth" (30:2). The rest of the chapter delineates when husbands and fathers may or may not be responsible for vows made by women. In the cases of women making vows, the immediate objection by a father or husband to the vow nullifies the vow without penalty (30:5, 8, 12). If a woman's husband does not immediately protest his wife's vow and only later objects, however, then the husband is responsible for fulfilling the vow and for any penalty involved (30:15). The sequence of the chapter moves through various possible scenarios: the man's own vows (30:2), a woman's vow made in her father's house (30:3–5), a woman's vow made in her father's house but then transferred to her husband's responsibility (30:6–8), a woman's vow that becomes her own responsibility when divorced or widowed (30:9), a woman's vow under the responsibility of her husband (30:10–15).

In the patriarchal society of ancient Israel, women were often economically dependent on men. In certain circumstances, the ultimate responsibility for fulfilling vows made by a woman could rest upon her father or her husband. The laws in Numbers 30 thus protect the husband or father from the requirements to honor a woman's vow in special cases. But the laws also protect women and the integrity of their vows to some extent by requiring a clear and immediate response by a father or husband if the vow is to be nullified. Otherwise, the vow is in force and the man bears the responsibility and any guilt resulting from the vow not being fulfilled.

The central concern of these laws is that all obligations and pledges made to God be fulfilled. The laws in chapter 30 delineate who is ultimately responsible for any vow that is spoken. An unfulfilled vow threatened the holiness of the community, and thus it was important that the community be clear about which vows were valid and who was responsible for fulfilling them. The portrait of family and marriage relationships in these laws in which a father or husband has veto power over a woman's religious decisions with no reciprocal right on the part of the woman obviously reflects a different and ancient social situation that is not analogous to many families or marriages today. Reciprocity, joint decision making, and the sharing of responsibilities would be considered a more viable model of family and marriage life for our contemporary context. As in the case of the legal dispute of the five women in Numbers 27, we may need to distinguish the deeper principle at work in these laws from the particular customs through which they were expressed in ancient Israel. In this case, the overriding concern is that humans be faithful in the obligations that they take upon themselves in service to God. The laws allow the freedom to make such vows, but the vows and pledges are to be taken seriously as real commitments to God. If God is faithful in satisfying the conditions of the vow, then humans should also be diligent in fulfilling their side of the obligation. It is the mutual responsibilities of God and humans, not men and women, that is the core concern of these provisions about vows and pledges to God. The combination of the discipline of observing appointed times for offerings in chapter 28—29 and the more spontaneous making of vows in the context of dire need or petition in chapter 30 reflects the full rhythm of life before God. The life of prayer, of stewardship and offerings, of care for the poor, and of worship requires disciplined regularity as well as room for more spontaneous and unplanned expressions of our relationship to God.

Numbers 31

War against the Midianites:
Judgment for Past Sin,
Foretaste of a Future Conquest

In the last episode in the life of the old wilderness generation in Numbers 25, Israel had been seduced by Moabites and Midianites into the worship of a false god named Baal Peor and into sexual relations with foreign women, including one Midianite woman named Cozbi (Num. 25:1–6). The three consonants of Cozbi's name in Hebrew, *kzb,* form the verb "to lie, deceive." At the end of chapter 25, God alludes to this deception when God instructs Moses: "Harass the Midianites, and defeat them; for they have harassed you by the trickery with which they deceived you in the affair of Peor, and in the affair of Cozbi" (25: 17–18). Numbers 31 recounts the second generation's obedient response to these instructions concerning the Midianites. The new generation's first military action becomes Moses' last act of military leadership as God commands Moses in Numbers 31:2: "Avenge the Israelites on the Midianites; afterward you shall be gathered to your people."

The Israelites send out one thousand soldiers from each of the twelve tribes to fight the five Midianite kings (31:3–8). The priest Phinehas joins the Israelite warriors bearing the sacred vessels of the sanctuary and the trumpets for battle, both signs that this is a holy war campaign (Num. 10:1–10; Deut. 20:2–4). The high priest Eleazar, Phinehas's father, does not go out in battle lest he become contaminated by contact with dead bodies in the battlefield. Such contamination is strictly forbidden for the high priest (Lev. 21:11). The actual battle is summarized in two verses: Israel kills all Midianite males, the five kings of Midian, and Balaam the prophet as God's punishment for having lured the Israelites into apostasy in Numbers 25. The prophet Balaam had been portrayed in Numbers 22—24 as a faithful spokesperson for God who spoke genuine words of blessing on Israel. But Balaam is accused in 31:15–16 of encouraging the women of Midian to entice the Israelites into the false worship of Baal Peor, and thus he is listed among those killed in the raid against Midian. Balaam is both a true prophet (Numbers 22—24) and an instigator of apostasy (31:15–

176

16) at the same time. Likewise, Midianites can be both welcomed and trusted guides to the promised land as was Hobab the Midianite (10: 29–32) as well as deceitful and misleading guides into the worship of alien gods as in the case of Baal Peor (25:16–18). The boundary between Israel and the "other" is always two-sided, negotiable, and not absolute as God's people seek to define themselves as a distinct community while also remaining open to those outside the community.

The battle report in Numbers 31:8 may be based in part on the account of the conquest of five Midianite kings and the killing of Balaam the prophet in Josh. 13:21–22. Judges 6—8 also recounts another Israelite victory against the Midianites led by the judge Gideon. Whatever the historical background of the story, Israel's war against Midian in Numbers 31 focuses less on the battle itself and much more on the issues that arise in the aftermath of the battle. The bulk of the chapter deals with the purification of soldiers and booty from the impurity of war and the allotment of the spoils of the battle to the priests, Levites, commanders, soldiers, and all the Israelites.

The Israelite soldiers kill all the Midianite adult males, but they "took the women of Midian and their little ones captive; and they took all their cattle, their flocks, and all their goods as booty" (31:10). As the soldiers march back to the Israelite camp with their captives and booty, they are met by Moses, Eleazar, and all the leaders of the congregation. Instead of receiving a rousing cheer of gratitude for their success, however, the commanders of the army are met by the anger of Moses. We are conditioned as readers of Numbers to assume that Moses' anger is a sign that the people have rebelled or acted unfaithfully and that the judgment of God is imminent. That was true for the rebellions of the first generation, and so we pause in suspense, wondering whether the new generation is about to slide down the same slippery slope of disobedience and revolt.

But what have the Israelite soldiers done wrong in their overwhelming victory over the Midianites? Why is Moses angry? The holy war regulations laid out most fully in Deuteronomy 20 seem to form a part of the background of Numbers 31. Some holy war texts in the Old Testament assume that everything and everyone in an enemy town is to be destroyed (e.g., Josh. 6:20–21). But the holy war instructions from Deuteronomy 20 seem to be those operative in the minds of the Israelite commanders in Numbers 31. Deuteronomy dictates that in a holy war battle, Israel must kill all adult males. "You may, however, take as your booty the women, the children, livestock, and everything else in the town, all its spoil" (Deut. 20:14). The Israelite commanders have apparently obeyed these general holy war regulations. But Moses

177

is angry because the war against Midian is a special case of holy war. The women of Midian had seduced the earlier generation into sexual relations and apostasy guided by the counsel of Balaam the prophet. Thus, a compromise is reached and a special arrangement is made: Israel must kill all the Midianite women who have had sexual relations with a man and all the Midianite male children. But "all the young girls who have not known a man by sleeping with him, keep alive for yourselves" (31:18). The Midianite adult males were warriors and thus clearly enemies. The Midianite male children are apparently viewed as potential warriors and thus enemies who need to be killed. Midianite women who had slept with Midianite men were tainted with the impurity and otherness of the enemy, and the incident at Baal Peor in Numbers 25 was evidence of their status as enemies of Israel and Israel's God. All of these Midianites were thus put under the holy war ban or destruction. But in the symbolic world of purity and impurity in Numbers, the young Midianite females who had not had sexual relations with a Midianite man were not enemies and could become part of Israel's community (Niditch, pp. 46–51). Some Midianites like Hobab and the young virgin girls were welcome; other Midianites were enemies and thus not welcome.

The entire notion of holy war, the act of killing and especially the killing of women and children, and the notions of purity and impurity that animate this text will seem alien and reprehensible to many people in our modern world. Other texts in the Old Testament put forth a very different vision for God's people, that of peace rather than war among nations (e.g., Isa. 2:2–4). It is important to see that the holy war is portrayed as only a temporary measure in the Bible, confined to the time of the conquest of Canaan. No later texts in the prophets or elsewhere ever urge Israel to take up a holy war again. The holy war as an act of violence does not provide a continuing paradigm for the actions of God's people. In fact, the goal of the holy war against Canaan, to eliminate all the inhabitants so that they could not tempt Israel to follow their gods, was never achieved (Judg. 2:1–5). The holy war of violence was a strategy that failed in its attempt to define a clear boundary between the Israelites and the "other." Israel continued to struggle throughout its history to discern when to welcome and when to resist the culture and people of other nations. Israel continued to wage battles against the enemies of God's will, but it became more and more a battle of words, persuasion, obedience, and education through devotion to God's word of Scripture (Josh. 1:7–9; cf. Olson, *Deuteronomy and the Death of Moses,* pp. 162–64).

178

The remainder of Numbers 31 likewise raises its own limitations and reservations about the ethics of violence in the attack on Midian. The soldiers have been rendered unclean by killing people or touching corpses and must go through a ritual of separation and cleansing (31: 19). The booty must be shared widely with the community and a proportion dedicated to the priests and to God (31:28–31). The soldiers give a special offering to God "to make atonement . . . before the LORD" for their guilt in participating in the war and in the shedding of blood (31:50). The war is holy, but the killing defiles and incurs guilt.

Two other features stand out in this account of the war against the Midianites. First of all, the Israelites capture a fantastic amount of booty, a sign of God's faithfulness to this new generation and a foretaste of the conquest of Canaan that is yet to come. The Israelites capture 675,000 sheep, 72,000 oxen, 61,000 donkeys, 32,000 young women, and 16,750 shekels of gold seized just by the commanders and more by the other soldiers (31:32–35, 52). The abundance is shared proportionally with all the people, the priests, the Levites, and the service of the sanctuary. This distribution of resources mirrors the distribution of the land and its bounty among the various tribes of Israel, which will be one of the central themes of the following chapters, Numbers 32—35. The second feature of note in Numbers 31 is that no Israelite soldier dies in the battle against the Midianites. The officers report to Moses, "Your servants have counted the warriors who are under our command, and not one of us is missing" (31:49). In contrast to the first generation whose members all died in the wilderness, there are no deaths recounted in the second generation throughout Numbers 26—36. This note in chapter 31 simply underscores the life and hope that this second generation represents as it stands ready to enter the land of Canaan.

In general, the story of the battle with the Midianites portrays the faithfulness of the new generation of Israelites to God's commands. The battle victory and the distribution of the abundant booty are signs that the new generation is obeying the laws given to the old wilderness generation earlier in Numbers. The priest Phinehas blows the trumpets to sound the alarm for the holy war as prescribed in Numbers 10:1–10 (31:6). The ritual of the water made with the red cow ashes in Numbers 19 is used to purify the soldiers contaminated by corpses and to purify the booty as it is brought into the camp (31:19–24). Numbers 18 had provided instructions for the material support of priests and Levites; that same concern for the support of the clergy is expressed in the share of the booty given to the priests and Levites in 31:25–47. Numbers 7 had recorded the old generation's support of the sanctuary through the gifts given by each of the twelve tribes; the new generation obediently continues that support in the special gifts offered by the commanders to the sanctuary (31:48–54). The portrait of the new generation emerges as a community devoted to God and God's commands. But as we noted above, the obedience is not overidealized. Moses' anger signals trouble, but the dispute is arbitrated and an acceptable compromise is reached.

Chapter 31 functions not only as a fulfillment of commands given to the old generation. The victory against the Midianites also in a sense reverses or redeems two earlier incidents in Numbers in the experience of the old wilderness generation: the spy story in chapters 13—14 and the apostasy of Baal Peor in chapter 25. The earlier generation had once stood where the new generation stands, poised on the threshold of Canaan. But the old generation had failed to trust and obey God's wishes that Israel move forward in its conquest of the land, and the result was death in the wilderness. In chapter 31, the new generation trusts that God will give them victory, and the result is a tremendous victory wherein not one Israelite dies (31:49). The first military victory of the new generation in chapter 31 reverses the catastrophe of the old generation's first military defeat in chapters 13—14.

In the second incident in Numbers 25, the Midianites and Moabites had seduced Israel into worshiping a false god and had thereby conquered them through deception. The old generation of Israelites were dead and punished. Numbers 31 reversed the scenario. This time Israel conquered Midian. The old generation of Midianites died, and only the "little ones" lived on through the young Midianite women. The whole new generation of Israelites were alive and blessed. Many aspects of this holy war text may be troublesome to a contemporary reader. But understood within the symbolic world of the ancient writers of Numbers, the story of the war against the Midianites is a kind of dress rehearsal that builds confidence and hope in anticipation of the actual conquest of Canaan that lay ahead.

Numbers 32—33

A Crisis Averted, a Journey Remembered:
Warning and Encouragement
from a Generation Past

In Numbers 32, a potential crisis erupts that threatens the whole enterprise of entering Canaan. Two of the Israelite tribes do not want to settle inside the borders of Canaan; they are lured by the lush pasture land on the east side of the Jordan River and wish to settle there. This was land captured from King Sihon and King Og in Num. 21:21–35. Moses is angered by their request, just as he was angered by the troops returning with their booty in Numbers 31. His anger is a danger signal that the new generation may repeat the failure of faith as in the spy story of Numbers 13—14 and incur God's judgment. However, Moses and the two tribes negotiate and reach a compromise, and the crisis is averted.

Numbers 33 is a summary of all the places Israel stopped to camp in its journey through the wilderness from Egypt to their present location in the plains of Moab. This summary of Israel's itinerary of travel contains notes of warning and encouragement to the new generation who have come so far and have reached their final destination, the promised land of Canaan.

A Crisis Averted: Reuben and Gad's Request to Settle outside the Promised Land (Numbers 32)

"Now the Reubenites and the Gadites owned a very great number of cattle" (32:1). This opening parenthetical note explains the request by Reuben and Gad to settle in the Transjordan region. The rich grasslands east of the Jordan River, they argue, "is a land for cattle; and your servants have cattle" (32:4). Moses and the other leaders listen to their argument and their final words, "Let this land be given to your servants for a possession; do not make us cross the Jordan" (31:5). These final words trigger in Moses a memory of a similar request he had heard once before when the old generation of Israelites had been at the border of the promised land. In chapters 13—14, Israel had sent spies into

181

the land, and they returned with discouraging news about the dangers of the land of Canaan and the awesome might of its inhabitants. Frightened, the Israelites decided not to cross the border and enter the land. The result was God's angry judgment that the entire old generation of Israelites would be condemned to die in forty years of wilderness wandering; only the new generation would have the opportunity to enter the promised land.

The request, "do not make us cross the Jordan," stirs up memories of old Israel's rebellion. As memory bearer and interpreter of that older tradition, Moses brings the light of the past to bear on this new but analogous situation. Moses is fearful that if Reuben and Gad do not cross over into Canaan with the other ten tribes, the whole Israelite camp will become discouraged and refuse to move forward into the land. Reuben and Gad are in danger of acting like the spies in Numbers 13—14 who discouraged the rest of the Israelites from invading Canaan (32:13). Moses warns Reuben and Gad that they are in danger of stepping into the shoes of their parents:

> And now you, a brood of sinners, have risen in place of your fathers, to increase the LORD's fierce anger against Israel! If you turn away from following him, he will again abandon them in the wilderness; and you will destroy all this people." (32:14–15)

The lesson of the past becomes a paradigm that interprets the potential rebellion of the new generation located again on the edge of the promised land. Although the experience of the new generation thus far has been positive and hopeful, their ultimate destiny remains an open question. The old generation had experienced a positive and hopeful beginning in Numbers 1—10, but the rebellions unexpectedly appeared in Numbers 11 and finally ended in the death of the old generation in the desert. The same could happen to the new generation, whose beginning has also been positive. The new generation continues to live under the threat of God's judgment.

But something is different about this new generation. The final word in this story is not judgment but promise and encouragement. Rather than rebel against Moses and the old tradition, Reuben and Gad take Moses' words to heart and propose a compromise. They will build sheepfolds for their flocks and towns as protection "for our little ones" in the Transjordan in anticipation of settling there permanently. The old generation had also worried about the safety of "our wives and our little ones" in the spy story, but they had used them as an excuse for refusing to go in and conquer the land (14:3). In the new generation, Reuben and Gad will leave their wives and children and livestock in the Transjordan. But the warriors of Reuben and Gad agree to cross the Jordan River and join the rest of the Israelite tribes in the conquest of Canaan itself. Only after the conquest is complete will the men of Reuben and Gad return to the territory on the east side of the Jordan River to settle. Moses accepts their proposal as a reasonable compromise, and the crisis is resolved (32:16–27). Moses charges Joshua and Eleazar, the leaders of the new generation, to enforce the negotiated agreement. Reuben and Gad pledge to keep their commitment to "cross over armed before the LORD into the land of Canaan" in return for receiving the grasslands of the Transjordan as their inheritance (32:28–32).

Moses then formally grants the territory captured from King Sihon and King Og (Num. 21:21–35) and its various cities to Reuben, Gad, and to the half-tribe of Manasseh (32:33). The mention of the half-tribe of Manasseh comes as a surprise since they have not been mentioned before in the narrative. Their addition may be the product of some later editing of the story in an attempt to reflect some historical and literary associations of a part of Manasseh with the Transjordan area (cf. Josh. 13:29–32). The other half of the Manasseh tribe will settle inside the borders of Canaan (Josh. 17:1–13). Reuben and Gad rebuild cities already captured from Kings Og and Sihon. The partial tribe of Manasseh goes on its own conquest mission and captures the area of Gilead from the Amorites and renames their villages (32:34–42). This conquest and the division of the territory among the tribes of Reuben, Gad, and the half-tribe of Manasseh become dress rehearsals for the larger conquest of the land of Canaan itself.

The narrative of chapter 32 functions as an important link in the larger structure of Numbers. The story forms a literary bridge from the new generation of Israelites back to the central theme of the book as defined in the spy story of chapters 13—14, the death of the old wilderness generation and the birth of the new generation of hope on the edge of the promised land. Moses focuses both the promises and the warning of the tradition of the old generation upon the experience of the new generation of God's people. The final fate of this second generation remains unknown at this point. Everything has proceeded well up to this point, just as it had for the old generation through the first ten chapters of Numbers. But the successful resolution of the potential crisis brings the narrative to a conclusion on a positive and hopeful note. The new generation continues to be characterized as faithful but 183 also creative adherents to God and the traditions of the past. The give and take of compromise and negotiation in a spirit of genuine reverence for the Mosaic traditions of the past allow the new generation to move forward in its journey toward the promised land.

A Journey Remembered:
The Travel Itinerary of the Old Generation
(Numbers 33)

In the preceding chapter, Moses had used the incident of the spies and Israel's rebellion at the place called Kadesh-barnea in Numbers 13—14 as a teaching lesson for the new generation. Numbers 33 expands this mention of Kadesh-barnea and provides a listing of all the sites where Israel camped in its travels from Egypt to the plains of Moab at the boundary of the promised land. The source of the wilderness itinerary is purported to be a written record from Moses himself: "Moses wrote down their starting points, stage by stage, by command of the LORD; and these are their stages according to their starting places" (33:2). Many of the names of the campsites are unique to this list and not found anywhere else in the Bible (33:13, 19–29). Most of the actual locations of the sites in the wilderness are unknown today. The list of places may have some relationship with itineraries used by travelers or pilgrims in ancient times, but the precise background of the itinerary is difficult to reconstruct.

However, several of the place names in the list have appeared earlier in the books of Exodus and Numbers. In general, the campsites listed in 33:6–15 from Succoth to the wilderness of Sinai correspond to Israel's travels recorded in Exodus 13:17—19:1. The itinerary in 33:16–49 from the wilderness of Sinai to the plains of Moab is a summary of Israel's movements in Numbers 10:11—22:1. Some of the campsites listed include brief synopses of incidents that occurred at that place which seem to function as words of warning or hope for the new generation. For example, the exodus out of Egypt is recalled:

> The Israelites went out boldly in the sight of all the Egyptians, while the Egyptians were burying all their firstborn, whom the LORD had struck down among them. The LORD executed judgments even against their gods. (33:3–4)

These words seem designed to inspire confidence in the new generation as they prepare to meet the forces of Canaan whose inhabitants had been described as semi-divine beings, the so-called Nephilim (Num. 13:32–33). God's victory over the mighty empire of Egypt and even the gods of Egypt bodes well as the new Israelites ready themselves to face the Canaanites. Remembrance of the victory over the Canaanite king Arad would seem to have the same function in this context (33:40).

Other events in the wilderness journeys of the old generation may be remembered more as warnings to the new generation. God's judgment on the worship of foreign gods (33:4; cf. chap. 25) and the death of Aaron for his sin (33:38–39; cf. Num. 20:22–29) may well remind Israel that God's judgment continues as a real possibility for those who fail to trust in God and obey God's will. The list of place names in the wilderness concludes with a general word of instruction and encouragement from God to Moses and the people. These final instructions suggest that the list of wilderness campsites and the reminders of the past are intended to guide and shape Israel's actions as they enter the promised land. God commands Israel to drive out all the inhabitants of Canaan and "destroy all their cast images, and demolish all their high places" where they worship their false gods (33:50–53). After driving out the Canaanites, Israel should apportion the land among the twelve tribes by giving a larger inheritance of land to larger tribes and a smaller inheritance to smaller tribes. But the precise location of each tribe's territory will be decided by lot (33:54).

Chapter 33 ends with a warning. If Israel does not drive out all the Canaanites or other nations from the land, then those inhabitants of the land shall remain "as barbs in your eyes and thorns in your sides" to tempt and trouble Israel. The ideal envisioned here is a land devoid of Canaanites and completely clear of all foreigners and any foreign gods. But that ideal promised land is never achieved in the biblical history. When Joshua later leads Israel in the conquest of Canaan, Israel is compelled by circumstances to allow the family of the Canaanite prostitute Rahab and the people of Gibeon to remain in Canaan (Joshua 2; 6:22–25; 9). Moreover, the tribes of Israel were not able to conquer all of the land of Canaan, and so some of the original inhabitants remained to live among the Israelites (Judg. 1:1—2:5; 2:11—3:6). The situation at the end of Israel's conquest of Canaan is summarized in Judges 3:5–6:

> So the Israelites lived among the Canaanites, the Hittites, the Amorites, the Perizzites, the Hivites, and the Jebusites; and they took their daughters as wives for themselves, and their own daughters they gave to their sons; and they worshiped their gods.

Israel never achieved the ideal of a promised land without any temptations, any other nations, or any other gods. The situation in Judges 3 with the marrying of other peoples and worshiping other gods reminds the reader of Numbers of the apostasy of Baal Peor in chapter 25 during the final days of the old generation. Even after Israel's conquest and entry into Canaan, Israel remained in a sense on the edge of the promised land. The goal of a pure and undefiled Canaan remained an elusive goal, a future hope, an end not yet fully realized. That future hope remained unfulfilled throughout the time of Israel's judges, the monarchy, the exile to Babylon, and the return in the postexilic period. Israel constantly struggled with the worship of foreign gods and the benefits as well as the dangers of relationships with people of other nations and religions. Thus, every succeeding generation of God's people could continue to return to the story of the wilderness in the book of Numbers and claim it as a tradition of continuing relevance for a people who had not yet entered fully into the land of promise. God's people will always find themselves at some stage of the wilderness journey, straining forward in hope but never fully at home in the promised land.

Numbers 34—36
Law as Promise: The Division of Land, Levitical and Refuge Cities, and the Daughters of Zelophehad Revisited

These last chapters in Numbers bring the book to a close with a series of laws and instructions that assume that the conquest of Canaan is near at hand. These laws shine the spotlight of Numbers ever more brightly ahead to the promised land with a uniformly positive tone and sense of expectation.

Boundaries of Canaan and Tribal Supervisors for Dividing the Land (Numbers 34)

A precise description of the outside boundary of the promised land of Canaan begins this chapter. The boundary of Canaan begins in the south at the southern tip of the Dead Sea, curves south and west to Kadesh-barnea and the Wilderness of Zin, and then west to the Wadi (or Brook) of Egypt and on to "the Sea" (namely, the Mediterranean Sea) (34:2–5). The "Great Sea" or Mediterranean Sea forms the western border of the promised land (34:6). The northern boundary extends from the Mediterranean Sea out past Lebo-hamath into territory that includes parts of present-day Syria and Lebanon (34:7–9). The eastern boundary of the promised land extends from the northern border down past the eastern slope of the "Sea of Chinnereth" (later known as the Sea of Galilee or Gennesaret) and then follows along the Jordan River down to the Dead Sea (34:10–12).

The delineation of the land's borders in Numbers 34 follows very closely the description of the area covered by the spies in chapters 13—14. The southern boundary is the Wilderness of Zin (13:21; cf. 34:3), and the northern boundary reaches to Lebo-hamath (13:21; cf. 34:8). The Jordan River forms the eastern boundary of Canaan in the spy story, and "the Sea" (the Mediterranean) forms the western border as in the boundary description in Numbers 34 (13:29; cf. 34:6, 12). These precise correspondences between the extent of the promised land in the spy story of Numbers 13—14 and the boundary description of Numbers 34 communicates reassurance to the new generation that the original promise of the land to the old wilderness generation has been extended in its entirety to the new generation.

The outline of Canaan's boundaries in chapter 34 is similar to other biblical descriptions of Canaan's borders in Josh. 15:1–14 and Ezek. 47:15–18 and 48:1–2. It also corresponds to the delineation of the land as stretching from "Lebo-hamath to the Wadi of Egypt" in I Kings 8:65. In contrast, another traditional designation of the northernmost and southernmost points of the land is the lesser area designated by the phrase, "from Dan to Beersheba" (e.g., Judg. 20:1; I Sam. 3:20; I Kings 4:25; cf. Budd, p. 365). This would include an area significantly smaller than that promised in Numbers 34, an indication that the promise in chapter 34 far exceeded the historical fulfillment in most periods of Israel's history. Israel's territory was the largest during the united monarchy of David and Solomon, but even then it did not include some of the Philistine territory on the western border along the coast of the Mediterranean Sea. Thus, the portrait of the land is an idealized one that always outdistanced its historical realization. Yet the land was a very real and material promise from God; it was not simply a vague or otherworldly hope.

The land inside the boundaries outlined in Numbers 34 is to be divided among the nine-and-a-half tribes of Israel. This excludes Reuben, Gad, and the half-tribe of Manasseh, since they have already received their land in the Transjordan region east of the Jordan River (34:13–15). This raises the question about the status of the Transjordan and the two-and-a-half tribes who will live there. Is that region part of the promised land? Or are the tribes living there in a kind of "exile"

187

outside the land? Jacob Milgrom points out that there was no divine command to capture the Transjordan, no use of lots to decide its distribution, and no mention of the Transjordan in the boundary description of the land in Numbers 34:1–14. Thus, Milgrom contends that the Transjordan was not considered by the writers of Numbers to be part of the promised land. This is in contrast to the tradition of Deuteronomy 2:24. In Deuteronomy, Milgrom argues, God does command the conquest of the Transjordan and so it is considered part of the promised land (Milgrom, pp. 501–02).

In my judgment, the status of the Transjordan area in Numbers is not so clearly outside the promised land. It is true that it is not included in the boundaries of chapter 34, and that it is not apportioned by lot. But in the conquest of the Transjordan area ruled by the kings Sihon and Og, there is this note about the conquest of King Og in typical holy war language:

> The LORD said to Moses, "Do not be afraid of him; for I have given him into your hand, with all his people, and all his land. You shall do to him as you did to King Sihon of the Amorites who ruled in Heshbon." (Num. 21:34)

God does indeed seem to command the conquest of this territory, and the request by Reuben, Gad, and the half-tribe of Manasseh to settle the land in Numbers 32 is negotiated with Moses as acceptable. The Transjordan is a place of fuzzy borders, an in-between land not fully part of the promised land, yet settled by Israelite tribes. It represents a place of negotiation, compromise, fluid boundaries, a place between exile and home. Such a place is characteristic of this entire section concerning the new generation in Numbers 26—36; they are a generation for whom some boundaries are less than absolute, some laws are in need of negotiation, some traditions require creative interpretation and compromise.

Numbers 34 concludes with a list of ten tribal leaders who are commissioned to supervise the future division of the land among the nine-and-a-half remaining tribes (34:16–29). Three such lists of the leaders of Israel's tribes appear in Numbers: the list of twelve census supervisors in Numbers 1, the list of twelve spies in Numbers 13, and the list of those who will divide the promised land in Numbers 34. Each of these lists marks significant turning points in the book: the organization and inauguration of the march toward the promised land (Numbers 1), the decisive rebellion of the wilderness generation (those who were numbered in the first census) that led to their death in the desert (Numbers 13—14), and the future allocation of the promised land to the members of the new generation who were counted in the second census (Numbers 34). These lists help to bind the beginning, middle, and end of the book together, signaling key turning points in the narrative.

Levitical Cities, Cities of Refuge, and Borderline Cases in the Shedding of Blood (Numbers 35)

The theme of the distribution of the land among the tribes continues from chapter 34 into chapter 35, where provisions for cities and pastureland for the tribe of Levi are made. In Numbers 1—3 and chapter 26, the census of the twelve tribes was followed in each case by a census of the Levites. Similarly, the distribution of the land to the twelve tribes in Numbers 32 and 34 is followed by instructions for living space for the Levites. The twelve tribes will provide forty-eight towns in which the Levites may live; the larger tribes will contribute more cities than the smaller tribes (35:1–8). The Levites, who guard the holiness of God and the sanctuary, will be distributed throughout the land of Israel. The proffered towns are necessary since the Levites do not have any tribal land of their own: "there was no allotment given to them among the Israelites" (Num. 26:62; cf. Num. 18:24). The Levitical cities are thus not the permanent possession of the Levites but rather a place for them to live and pasture their flocks.

The actual history of the Levites in the social and religious life of ancient Israel is a much-debated issue among scholars. For example, the provision for land for the Levites is much different in Ezek. 48:13–14, where a single plot of land is given to the tribe of Levi (Budd, pp. 370–76). Apart from the question of Levites in the history of Israel, we may ask about the role of the Levites within the narrative world of the book of Numbers. Like the Transjordanian tribes, the Levites in the book of Numbers are a liminal group within Israel. They cross boundaries, and they do not fit neatly into any one category. They are clergy but not full priests like the sons of Aaron. They are a tribe but not one of the twelve tribes. They live in designated cities with surrounding pasture, and yet they have no allotted tribal land. The social and economic structure that Numbers envisions for the Levites mirrors their function as a buffer zone or boundary around the holy sanctuary. They mark the boundary between the presence of God at the center of the community and Israel's twelve tribes around the outside. The Levites both protect the boundary and cross the boundary between the divine

189

and human, between God's holy love and the people's sinful rebellion. The scattered presence of the Levites throughout the land of Israel suggests that the presence and holiness of God will likewise be distributed over the entire land. There will eventually be a special intensity of God's presence in the temple in Jerusalem (I Kings 8—9), but the presence of God eludes capture in any fixed structure or place. God is greater than any house in which God's presence dwells, and the scattering of the Levites is a sign of God's wide presence throughout Israel.

Six of the forty-eight Levitical cities are designated as cities of refuge (34:6). These special cities are designed to provide shelter for "a slayer who kills a person without intent" (34:11). The holiness of God's promised land could be threatened by the shedding of human blood, one of the most serious defilements in Israel's understanding of God's requirements of purity. Murder and its defilement of the land could be expiated only through shedding the blood of the one who did the killing (35:33–34). Thus, a close relative had an obligation to act as an "avenger" of his relative's blood by slaying the murderer in order to expiate the impurity caused by the murder. But the cities of refuge are a compromise provision for sheltering those who kill another person unintentionally. The unintentional killer was safe as long as that person remained within the designated city of refuge (35:9–15).

This legislation's primary concern is to preserve the holiness and purity of the land while also recognizing certain gradations and negotiations necessary when setting boundaries between premeditated murder and unintentional killing. The city of refuge is a compromise which protects the unintentional killer while also requiring that person to be in a kind of "exile" within the land, unable to return to home and family. This exile lasts until the high priest within the city of refuge dies. The priest's death functions as a substitute expiation for the blood shed by any unintentional killers living within the city (35:25).

The city of refuge is properly associated with the cities of the Levites, who are charged with guarding the holiness of God in Israel's midst. The Levites are associated with issues of crossing and negotiating boundaries. This case involves boundaries between purity and impurity of the land. But the levitical cities of refuge also wrestle with the boundary between murder and manslaughter in the borderline cases of unintentional killing.

The provision for cities of refuge quite naturally leads into a set of guidelines for determining when a killing may be deemed intentional murder or unintentional killing (35:16–34). Echoes of Numbers 15 and its distinction between the serious guilt of highhanded sins and the

190

lesser guilt of unintentional sins are in the background. Killing a person with a weapon or in an act of hatred is deemed murder, which requires the death penalty (35:16–21). Accidental killing without hatred or intent to harm constitutes unintentional killing, but such cases must be adjudicated by "the congregation." If found to be guilty only of accidental slaying, the killer may seek sanctuary in a city of refuge until the high priest of that city dies (35:22–29). The imposition of the death penalty in a murder case requires not one but at least two witnesses for a conviction (35:30). Finally, no monetary payment of a ransom can be substituted for the death of the murderer himself or for the requirement that the unintentional killer remain in the city of refuge (35:31–34). As the new generation prepares to cross the boundary into Canaan, these provisions ensure the purity of God's holy land, which the new generation is about to receive.

The Daughters of Zelophehad Revisited: Maintaining the Fair Distribution of Tribal Lands (Numbers 36)

Chapter 36 once again picks up the case of the five daughters of Zelophehad that first appeared in Numbers 27. In this first narrative of the second generation, Mahlah, Noah, Hoglah, Milcah, and Tirzah had appeared before Moses to request that they inherit their dead father's estate, even though the custom had been that only male relatives inherited land. The women succeeded in their appeal by drawing on the deeper principle that the land originally assigned to a given tribe should remain within that tribe. The economic base of a given family group within Israel should not be eroded permanently through inheritance into another family group.

The last narrative in Numbers returns to the case of Zelophehad's daughters (chap. 36). Another question about land inheritance is raised, but this time the judgment is sought not by the women but by the heads of the tribe of Manasseh, the tribe to which Zelophehad and his daughters belong. They raise another question: May Zelophehad's daughters marry a husband who is a member of another tribe? Or must the women marry husbands only from within their own tribal group? The tribal leaders argue that if the women marry outside the tribe of Manasseh, then their tribe will permanently lose part of its landholdings. Even the fifty-year Jubilee redistribution will not bring the land back to the tribe, since it was not bought or sold but inherited. The Jubilee laws in Leviticus 25 apply only to land that is purchased, not inherited (36:1–4).

191

Moses agrees with the tribal leaders' concerns. He commands "according to the word of the LORD" that the five women in Zelophehad's family "may marry whom they think best," with one restriction. They must marry a man from a clan of their father's tribe, the tribe of Manasseh. They cannot marry outside that tribe "so that no inheritance shall be transferred from one tribe to another" (36:7). The overriding concern is once again that the ancestral inheritance of land stay within the tribe to which God originally gave it (36:9). The five daughters of Zelophehad comply with the judgment and marry only husbands from their own tribe (36:10–12). Thus, the book of Numbers and the story of the second generation of Israelites draws to a close on a positive, hopeful and forward-looking note.

The two accounts of the daughters of Zelophehad in Numbers 27 and Numbers 36 form a literary frame that holds together the texts related to the new generation. Most of the material inside this literary frame relates in some way to the future settlement of Israel in the land of Canaan. Thus, the two narratives about the five women and land inheritance serve as positive confirmation that God's promise of the land will soon be granted to this new generation. Moreover, the compromise achieved in this clash of traditions and new circumstances affirms the flexibility of the tradition and the need for reinterpretation in the face of new questions and experiences faced by succeeding generations of God's people. This adaptability opens the door to a new interpretation from another tradition within Israel in the form of the book of Deuteronomy. Presented as Moses' last words to the new generation of Israelites, Deuteronomy follows the book of Numbers as the fifth book of the Pentateuch and provides a somewhat different but complementary vision of the past, present, and future of God's people.

Concluding Reflections on Numbers 26—36: What Is Different about the New Generation of God's People?

The distinctive character of the new generation of Israelites has begun to emerge more clearly as we have worked through these concluding chapters of Numbers. The old generation had been fiercely, almost mechanically, obedient in the opening chapters of Numbers 1—10. Even then, subtle undertones of danger and death lurked beneath what appeared to be an ideal surface of obedience. But the first instances of rebellion in Numbers 11 launched the old generation of Israelites into a downward spiral of revolt and disobedience from which they seemed unable to recover. The rebellions continued to the very end of that generation with the last and most idolatrous rebellion being the matter of Baal Peor in Numbers 25. The old generation had resisted authority through self-serving rebellions. Envious of one another, leaders juggled for position. The people made unreasonable demands. They refused to trust God's power and will to accomplish what God had promised. They believed more in their own power or in the power of their enemies than in the power of God. The nature of the conflicts of the old generation was often more like the collision of two uncompromising and absolutist positions than reasoned negotiation by differing voices with a spirit of reverence, mutual respect, and creativity.

The new generation is portrayed as having a different character. They respect the authority of Moses and their leaders, but they are also willing to be bold in asking for reasonable compromise or reconsideration of old customs based on deeper values and convictions embedded within the tradition. The new generation honors the tradition of the old generation. But they seek to be faithful to that tradition through a process of dialogue, compromise, and negotiation, whereby new circumstances and factors may be accommodated in a spirit of obedience and creativity. The tradition is not a dead letter but a living spirit. Persuasive arguments are made. Conflicting voices are adjudicated. Compromises are negotiated. God's direct presence is less in the foreground and seems mediated more through the tradition and memories of the past. The sense is that the tradition of the past generation functions somewhat like the protective buffer zone of the priests and Levites surrounding the tabernacle and God's presence in the middle of the camp (Numbers 2—4). Like the priests, the interpreted traditions and memories of the past not only protect the people from God's direct holiness. The verbal traditions and memories of the past also become the positive mediating vehicles of God's power, God's judgment, and, most of all for the new generation, the vehicles of God's promise and hope. The legacy of the book of Numbers is not in the end one of death and judgment. Numbers ultimately leaves an inheritance of life and hope for all future generations who read and study this ancient narrative of Israel's journey in the wilderness and who find themselves captured and shaped by its story.

BIBLIOGRAPHY

For Further Study

ASHLEY, TIMOTHY R. *The Book of Numbers.* NEW INTERNATIONAL COMMENTARY ON THE OLD TESTAMENT. Grand Rapids: Eerdmans, 1993.

BUDD, PHILIP J. *Numbers.* WORD BIBLICAL COMMENTARY 5. Waco, Tex.: Word, 1984.

CALVIN, JOHN. *Commentaries on the Four Last Books of Moses Arranged in the Form of a Harmony, Third Volume.* Trans. Charles William Bingham. Grand Rapids: Baker, 1989.

DOUGLAS, MARY. *In the Wilderness: The Doctrine of Defilement in the Book of Numbers.* Sheffield: Sheffield Academic Press, 1993.

GORMAN, FRANK H., JR. *The Ideology of Ritual: Space, Time and Status in the Priestly Theology.* JSOT SUPPLEMENTS 91. Sheffield: Sheffield Academic Press, 1990.

LEVINE, BARUCH. *Numbers 1—20: A New Translation with Introduction and Commentary.* ANCHOR BIBLE. New York: Doubleday, 1993.

MILGROM, JACOB. *Numbers.* JPS TORAH COMMENTARY (Philadelphia: Jewish Publication Society of America, 1990).

MILLER, PATRICK D., JR. "The Blessing of God." *Interpretation* 29:250–51 (1975).

NELSON, RICHARD D. *Raising Up a Faithful Priest: Community and Priesthood in Biblical Theology.* Louisville: Westminster/John Knox, 1993.

SAKENFELD, KATHARINE DOOB. *Journeying with God: A Commentary on the Book of Numbers.* Grand Rapids: Eerdmans, 1995.

Literature Cited

ALTER, ROBERT. *The Art of Biblical Narrative.* New York: Basic Books, 1981.

ATWAN, ROBERT, AND LAWRENCE WIEDER, eds. *Chapters into Verse: Poetry in English Inspired by the Bible, Volume One, Genesis to Malachi.* New York: Oxford University Press, 1993.

BACH, ALICE. "Good to the Last Drop: Viewing the Sotah (Numbers 5:11–31) as the Glass Half Empty and Wondering How to View It Half Full." In *The New Literary Criticism and the Hebrew Bible,* ed. J. Cheryl Exum and David J. A. Clines, eds., pp. 26–54. Valley Forge, Pa.: Trinity Press International, 1993.

BUDD, PHILIP J. *Numbers.* WORD BIBLICAL COMMENTARY 5. Waco, Tex.: Word, 1984.

COATS, GEORGE. *Rebellion in the Wilderness.* Nashville: Abingdon, 1968.

DOUGLAS, MARY. *In the Wilderness: The Doctrine of Defilement in the Book of Numbers.* Sheffield: Sheffield Academic Press, 1993.

EBERLE, GARY. *The Geography of Nowhere: Finding Oneself in the Postmodern World.* Kansas City, Mo.: Sheed & Ward, 1995.

FELDER, CAIN HOPE. *Troubling Biblical Waters: Race, Class and Family.* Maryknoll, N.Y.: Orbis Books, 1989.

FISCH, S. "The Book of Numbers," in A. Cohen, ed., *The Soncino Chumash: The Five Books of Moses with Haphtaroth.* Hindhead, Surrey: Soncino, 1947.

FISHBANE, MICHAEL. "Accusations of Adultery: A Study of Law and Scribal Practice in Numbers 5:11–31," *Hebrew Union College Annual* 45:25–45 (1974).

————. "Forms and Reformulation of the Biblical Priestly Blessing." *Journal of the American Oriental Society* 103:115–21 (1983).

FREDERICKSEN, PAULA. "Did Jesus Oppose the Purity Laws?" *Bible Review* 11:18–25, 42–47 (1995).

GORMAN, FRANK H., JR. *The Ideology of Ritual: Space, Time and Status in the Priestly Theology.* JSOT SUPPLEMENTS 91. Sheffield: Sheffield Academic Press, 1990.

GRAY, GEORGE BUCHANAN. *Numbers.* INTERNATIONAL CRITICAL COMMENTARY. Edinburgh: T. & T. Clark, 1903.

GREGORY OF NYSSA. *The Life of Moses.* Trans. Abraham Malherbe and Everett Ferguson. New York: Paulist, 1978.

JEFFREY, DAVID LYLE, ed. *A Dictionary of Biblical Tradition in English Literature.* Grand Rapids: Eerdmans, 1992.

JOINES, KAREN RANDOLPH. *Serpent Symbolism in the Old Testament: A Linguistic, Archaeological, and Literary Study.* Haddonfield, N.J.: Haddonfield House, 1974.

KSELMAN, J. S. "A Note on Num. XII 6–8." *Vetus Testamentum* 26: 500–505 (1976).

LEE, SANG. "Pilgrimage and Home in the Wilderness of Marginality: Symbols and Context in Asian American Theology," *Princeton Seminary Bulletin* 16:49–64 (1995).

LEVENSON, JON. *The Death and Resurrection of the Beloved Son: The Transformation of Child Sacrifice in Judaism and Christianity.* New Haven, Conn.: Yale University Press, 1993.

LEVINE, BARUCH. *Numbers 1—20: A New Translation with Intro-*

duction and Commentary. ANCHOR BIBLE. New York: Doubleday, 1993.

MAUSER, ULRICH. *Christ in the Wilderness: The Wilderness Theme in the Second Gospel and Its Basis in the Biblical Tradition.* Naperville: Alec R. Allenson, 1963.

MILGROM, JACOB. *Numbers.* JPS TORAH COMMENTARY. Philadelphia: Jewish Publication Society of America, 1990.

MILLER, PATRICK D., JR. "The Blessing of God." *Interpretation* 29:250–51 (1975).

NELSON, RICHARD D. *Raising Up a Faithful Priest: Community and Priesthood in Biblical Theology.* Louisville, Ky.: Westminster/John Knox, 1993.

NIDITCH, SUSAN. "War, Women and Defilement in Numbers 31." *Semeia* 61:39–57 (1993).

NOTH, MARTIN. *Numbers, A Commentary.* OLD TESTAMENT LIBRARY. Philadelphia: Westminster, 1968.

OLSON, DENNIS T. *The Death of the Old and the Birth of the New: The Framework of the Book of Numbers and the Pentateuch.* BROWN JUDAIC STUDIES 71. Chico, Calif.: Scholars Press, 1985.

———. *Deuteronomy and the Death of Moses: A Theological Reading.* OVERTURES TO BIBLICAL THEOLOGY. Minneapolis: Augsburg Fortress, 1994.

ORIGEN. *Origen.* CLASSICS OF WESTERN SPIRITUALITY. Trans. Roland A. Greer. New York: Paulist, 1979.

RASHI. *Commentaries on the Pentateuch.* Trans. Chaim Pearl. New York: W. W. Norton, 1970.

SAKENFELD, KATHERINE DOOB. "In the Wilderness, Awaiting the Promised Land: The Daughters of Zelophehad and Feminist Interpretation." *Princeton Seminary Bulletin* 9:179–96 (1988).

———. *Journeying with God: A Commentary on the Book of Numbers.* Grand Rapids: Eerdmans, 1995.

———. "The Problem of Divine Forgiveness in Numbers 14." *Catholic Biblical Quarterly* 37:317–30 (1975).

SCHART, AARON. *Mose und Israel im Konflikt: Eine Redaktionsgeschichtliche Studie zu den Wüstenerzählungen.* Gottingen: Vandenhoeck & Ruprecht, 1990.

DE VAULX, JULES. *Les Nombres.* Paris: J. Gabalda, 1972.

WEEMS, RENITA. *Just a Sister Away: A Womanist Vision of Women's Relationships in the Bible.* San Diego: LuraMedia, 1988.

WILLIAMS, DELORES. *Sisters in the Wilderness: The Challenge of Womanist God-Talk.* Maryknoll, N.Y.: Orbis, 1993.